Rethinking
PROTESTANTISM
in Latin America

Felicitas

March 1995

Rethinking
PROTESTANTISM
in Latin America

Edited by

Virginia Garrard-Burnett
David Stoll

TEMPLE UNIVERSITY PRESS

Philadelphia

Temple University Press, Philadelphia 19122
Copyright © 1993 by Temple University. All rights reserved
Published 1993
Printed in the United States of America

Library of Congress Cataloging-in-Publication Data
Rethinking Protestantism in Latin America / edited by Virginia Garrard-Burnett,
David Stoll.
    p.   cm.
Includes bibliographical references and index.
ISBN 1-56639-102-4 (alk. paper). — ISBN 1-56639-103-2 (pbk. : alk. paper)
1. Protestant churches—Latin America—History—20th century.
2. Protestants—Latin America—History—20th century.   3. Latin America—
Church history.   I. Garrard-Burnett, Virginia, 1957–   .   II. Stoll, David,
1952–   .
BX4832.5.R48   1993
280'.4'09809045—dc20   93-6582

CONTENTS

INTRODUCTION
Rethinking Protestantism in Latin America

David Stoll

O NE OF THE more surprising phenomena of recent years is the success of born-again Protestantism in Latin America. Perhaps its success is not so surprising if we think of Latin America as a Catholic continent trapped in an increasingly Protestant world.[1] Still, it was not expected by any but the truest believers. Evangelical Protestantism seemed so anomalous and so escapist. Its doctrines and passions seemed so peripheral to the issues that really mattered—land reform and popular organization, national debts and stabilization programs, the power of the military and drug traffickers, human rights and elections. But Pope John Paul II raises the subject with increasing urgency on his trips to this most Catholic part of the world. He warns Catholics to close ranks against an "invasion of the sects," and no wonder. His visits no longer draw the multitudes they used to, perhaps not even as large as the crowds at the Protestant rallies competing with his. At the quincentennial of the European colonization of the Americas, as the Catholic Church celebrated five hundred years of missionization, the majority of active churchgoers were becoming evangelicals.[2]

Only recently have scholars paid much attention to born-again religion in Latin America. In the 1970s and 1980s, the main topics of interest were liberation theology and the Catholic Church. The first was presumed to be revitalizing the second and, even more important, mobilizing the popular classes

1

for a wave of social change. As for research on evangelicals, it often went unpublished, and conferences on the Latin American church included the subject only as an afterthought.[3] Two circumstances are forcing scholars to attend to evangelicals. One is the Catholic hierarchy's repression of its progressive wing, together with growing evidence that liberation theology does not express popular aspirations as effectively as it was presumed to.[4] The other reason scholars are attending to evangelicals is, of course, their rapid growth.

Ten percent or more of the Latin American population identifies itself as *evangélico*, with the percentage substantially higher in Brazil, Chile, and most of Central America. It is true that a majority of Latin Americans still call themselves Catholics, but of these relatively few participate in church life. Because a much higher percentage of evangelicals do, they have become the movers and shakers on the religious scene. In the 1980s, evangelical strategists grew so bold as to project growth rates and predict when their converts would become the majority of the population. Such a prognostication, as this volume will make clear, cannot be taken very literally. But if the growth of the last several decades continues, Latin Americans claiming to be *evangélicos* could still become a quarter to a third of the population early in the twenty-first century.

Because of the parenting role played by North American missions, Latin American Protestantism is usually understood in terms of the North American genealogy of the mainline or "historical" denominations, followed by a sometimes confusing succession of fundamentalists, evangelicals, and Pentecostals. First we hear about the fundamentalist revolt of the early 1900s, against modernist views of the Bible in the mainline denominations. As the fundamentalists lost these battles, they withdrew from established churches to organize their own independent congregations, Bible institutes, and missions, a number of which directed their activities to Latin America. Following bitter doctrinal quarrels between fundamentalists, in the 1940s the more moderate groups renamed themselves "evangelicals," to express their wish to rise above sectarianism and get on with the task of evangelizing the world.[5]

In Latin America, this pedigree is translated into various "waves" of missionary activity that are held to have shaped the contemporary evangelical movement. Immigrant churches from Europe (such as the German Lutherans of Brazil) and mainline denominations from the United States made up the first two waves, in the nineteenth and early twentieth centuries. While both created enduring churches, neither converted large numbers of people. Strangely, neither did the third wave, the fundamentalist "faith missions," despite their manifest zeal and determination to evangelize beyond their predecessors. More successful is a fourth wave of evangelists, the Pentecostals, who until recently have been considered outcasts in the North American pedigree. This is because of their claim to receive special gifts from the Holy Spirit—speaking in tongues, faith healing, and prophecy—that non-Pentecostal fundamentalists and evangelicals eschew. Even though the majority of missionaries have come from non-Pentecostal backgrounds, more Latin Americans have been attracted to Pentecostal churches than to any other kind: two-thirds to three-quarters of all Protestants. Pentecostal churches have so outgrown others that perhaps, Donald Dayton suggests, evangelicals should be regarded as a subset of Pentecostals rather than the other way around.[6]

Regardless of denominational affiliations, Latin American Protestants most often refer to themselves as *evangélicos*; hence "evangelical" is often used as an umbrella term. But mission pedigrees have to be recognized for what they are. They beg the question of what was there before the missionaries came. According to Jean-Pierre Bastian, the first Protestant churches in Brazil, Cuba, and Mexico in the 1850s grew out of Liberal lodges rebaptizing themselves in the name of the new religion.[7] In the Guatemalan town where I did fieldwork in the 1980s, local men took credit for founding the churches over which they presided; but to find a larger body with which to affiliate, some had to go to the capital to find a *misión*.

Not only can "Protestant" organization exist on the landscape before Protestantism, so can "Protestant" standards of behavior, which evangelical churches only make more visible and assertive. When David Dixon probed conversion stories in Santiago, Chile, evangelicals reported changing their lives of sin to lives of righteousness before they started going to church. Evidently there is a "Protestant" ideal of self-discipline available within popular culture, an alternative that becomes more attractive as economic crisis forces Latin Americans to tighten their household economies. Dixon goes on to suggest that evangelical churches may serve not so much as sources of moral innovation than as points of congregation for like-minded individuals.[8] At the very least, evangelical churches need to be viewed in terms of local predispositions and initiatives as well as of "planting" a mission.

Why Protestantism Instead of Liberation Theology?

To date, the main question about evangelical growth in Latin America has been, Why? Why are so many Latin Americans abandoning the established church? In pastoral letters, Catholic bishops blame North American evangelists and their generous budgets. It is true that missionaries continue to have an impact, but most churches now are led by Latin Americans. This has forced the Catholic hierarchy to recognize its own pastoral failings. Most often cited is the perennial shortage of personnel, especially ordained priests. But heated debates over clerical prerogatives show that the dilemmas go deeper than that. At issue is the Catholic structure of authority—the oldest bureaucracy in the world, dating to the Roman empire—and whether it can respond to far-reaching changes in what Latin Americans want from church life.

For two decades, progressive Catholics thought they were successfully reforming their church, and simultaneously responding to the needs of the Latin American poor, with liberation theology. At a time when the Catholic Church seemed out of touch with the masses, pastoral agents would reconnect it with its popular roots through their "option for the poor." Meanwhile, ecclesial base communities would encourage participation and make church life more democratic by training lay leaders. Empowered by the pedagogical technique of "consciousness-raising," a newly popular church would work for the Kingdom of God here on earth. The vision was a bold one, of a still-hegemonic established church leading a defense of community against the combined forces of military dictatorships and world capitalism.

What has to be asked is whether liberation theology responded to the needs of ordinary Latin Americans. Perhaps the key issue is the traditional role of Roman Catholicism as a mystifier of social inequality and the implications of demystifying that function. In practice, liberation theology usually meant spurning the Catholic Church's mystique as an intermediary with higher spiritual and political powers. Unfortunately, what might seem a welcome advance in social consciousness could strip the church of its ability to manage social conflict, in ways that were disturbing to the poor as well as the wealthy. While activists deployed Catholic authority for new objectives, sometimes very effectively, in the process they alienated Catholics from the lower as well as the upper classes, who continued to expect traditional forms of patronage. Another implication of rejecting the church's historical function as an intermediary between social classes was to expose Catholics to reprisals from the state.

Worse, if the Catholic Church simply attended to its traditional constituency, it would fail to address new spiritual arenas in which evangelicals seemed to have competitive advantages. In societies whose economies are being globalized, whose traditional social structures have heaved apart, where people must fend for themselves in hostile new environments, how can a single, centralized religious hierarchy satisfy a newly individuated population whose members need to chart their own courses? For those same individuals, afflicted by new forms of personal insecurity, how can sprawling, territorially based Catholic parishes satisfy the desire for closer-knit congregational experiences? How can a religious system organized around sacraments satisfy the hunger for personal transformation? In each of these respects, the decentralized structures of Latin American Protestants, their multiple leaders competing for followers through charisma, and their emphasis on conversion proved to be distinct advantages.

Perhaps inevitably, the Catholic hierarchy turned against efforts to democratize church authority. Owing to the steady replacement of sympathetic bishops with conservatives appointed by Rome, progressives who regarded themselves as the future of the Catholic Church are now clearly an oppositional network, mainly at the middle and lower levels of the pastoral hierarchy. It is also clear that the popular constituency for liberation theology was overestimated, owing to the hopes and fears it aroused.[9] Many of the people reporting on liberation theology were activists who started their research through contacts in the Catholic pastoral structure, worked down to model projects at the grass roots, then presumed their findings to be more representative or influential than was the case. In a forthcoming book, *Looking for God in Brazil* (1993), our contributor John Burdick explains the lesson to be learned. Instead of focusing on a single institution like the Catholic Church and its representatives, or "message carriers," researchers must look at the social clusters receiving the message. We have to ask how ordinary people choose between the religious discourses available to them, bend these to their own purposes, and wend their way in and out of particular groups.

Distrust of ideological imports from the United States is widespread in Latin America, and so is the wish to protect local traditions from capitalism. Hence, many intellectuals find themselves in agreement with Catholic bishops on at least one point: Evangelicals are captive to a foreign ideology and alienated from national culture.[10] A less reductive, yet compatible, explanation for evangelical growth is what Daniel Levine calls the "crisis/ solace" model, which presents born-again religion as a form of escapism.[11] The classic work is Christian Lalive d'Epinay's *Haven of the Masses* (1969), a study of Chilean Pentecostals. According to Lalive, Pentecostals re-create the traditional society of the hacienda by replacing the figure of the *patrón* with that of their pastor. Imbued with the power and glory of the Holy Spirit, the pastor re-creates a tributary structure of authority—that is, one in which members render tribute to a patronal figure—in the guise of a church.

When Lalive studied Chilean Pentecostals in the 1960s, their pastors rejected participation in trade unions and other reform movements. The believers seemed engaged in a "social strike" that expressed their protest against the Chilean social order but failed to direct it constructively against their oppressors.[12] Liberation theologians and the Latin American left have found such an interpretation congenial to their own critique of evangelicals—for being too sectarian, for becoming absorbed in spirituality or personal advancement, and for turning their backs on class peers.

Generally, researchers from North America and Protestant Europe have shown only limited interest in the crisis/solace model. Instead, they tend to explain the new religion as a creative response to capitalist development and its uprooting of traditional society. The resulting "crisis/adaptation" model, in Daniel Levine's terms, is exemplified by Emilio Willems's study of Protestants in Chile and Brazil, *Followers of the New Faith* (1967). This school of thought emphasizes the ability of evangelicals to transcend social dislocation by establishing new forms of community, learning new forms of discipline, and stabilizing their family situations, with the result that at least some climb higher in the class structure.[13]

Rethinking Who Latin American Protestants Are

Explaining why so many Latin Americans join Protestant churches is not the object of this collection. Nor will we dwell upon the mission apparatuses, the North American religious right, and the North American political connections that I explored at length in *Is Latin America Turning Protestant?* Instead, our contributors—a historian, two sociologists, five anthropologists, and a team of four political scientists—address two main issues: How are evangelicals responding to social crisis in Latin

America, and how are they affecting the societies around them?

Dealing with such questions requires, first of all, rethinking who Latin American evangelicals are, especially in terms of gender. Pointing out the central position of women in Latin American Protestantism is Elizabeth Brusco, author of a groundbreaking (1986) dissertation on the evangelical reformation of machismo. Because scholars tend to focus on leaders and most evangelical structures are run by men, women can easily appear to be of secondary importance. Yet the majority of evangelicals are women, church life is especially responsive to their needs, and they play a critical role in the diffusion of Protestantism. Even though male pastors and evangelists attract most of the attention, their main function is reinforcing converts who originally came to church because they were recruited person-to-person by family members and neighbors who are predominantly female. Based on research with Colombian evangelicals, Brusco argues that born-again religion helps Latin American women resocialize their men away from the destructive patterns of machismo, in ways that may be far more effective than secular feminism. Evangelicals have succeeded in this difficult endeavor, Brusco suggests, precisely because they maintain the pretense of male control.

Lesley Gill and Linda Green describe how indigenous women use evangelical social organization as a survival vehicle. Understanding how they do so requires a deeper appreciation of the shifts and overlaps in how Latin Americans identify themselves religiously, a neglected issue that both authors explore under the heading of "religious mobility." Identifying oneself in terms of religion is, as Gill points out, a process that takes place over an entire lifetime. The typical reversals and ambiguities require a crucial distinction, introduced in this volume by Green, between "conversion" and "affiliation." If conversion implies a significant transformation, affiliation (or adherence) is the fact of how one identifies oneself. It can be quite tentative, and it encompasses a wider range of participants. Despite the teleological thinking surrounding the term "conversion," a missionary premise that has often been accepted unconsciously by scholars, it would be a mistake to assume that most people who attend evangelical churches are converts and that becoming an evangelical is a one-way, irreversible process.

Evangelical leaders usually downplay ambiguities in the loyalties of their followers, to avoid disrupting the dichotomies that maintain church boundaries. This is especially true of the Catholic/Protestant contrast that most observers take for granted, including the church growth experts who calculate the expansion of the evangelical movement. Generally speaking, evangelicals acknowledge the ambiguities of religious identification only in terms of "backsliding," which places the onus on individual moral failure. However, the tactics responsible for the rapid growth of the evangelical movement are also responsible for a rapid increase in the number of "post-Protestants." For several decades, evangelical strategists have tried to make their churches as open as possible to newcomers.[14] But the more people who join evangelical churches, the more people become available for "backsliding." In a 1989 survey of Costa Ricans, nearly as many said they used to be evangelicals as currently identified themselves as such.[15] Evangelicals have long boasted of their ability to convert Catholics, but we have yet to hear much about evangelicals who go back to being Catholics.

Classifying the population into Protestants and Catholics is not meaningless, but Green and Gill show that it is equally important to see how Latin Americans juggle such identities. With a majority of the population not active in church structures, there is a huge potential for straddling ecclesiastical categories. One increasingly visible phenomenon disrupting the Catholic-Protestant distinction is the Catholic charismatic movement. It comes out of a Pentecostal revival that, unlike earlier outbreaks of the Holy Spirit, spread into ecumenical Protestant denominations and the Catholic Church. Like their Pentecostal mentors, Catholic charismatics seek special gifts (*charisma* in Greek) from the Holy Spirit. Because the charismatics worship as Pentecostals do, emotionally and loudly, skeptical Catholics view the movement as a one-way street into Protestant churches. Many charismatics have indeed made the journey, typically after colliding with unsympathetic Catholic clergy.

Yet the charismatic renewal may also be "capturing" disillusioned evangelicals. And Catholic charismatics have taken over at least one influential Protestant organization, the Guatemalan branch of the Full Gospel Businessmen's Fellowship.[16] According to charismatics, they are the Catholic Church's best chance to hold onto parishioners attracted to the evangelical experience of personal transformation. The most prominent charismatics are from the upper classes and belong to tight-knit "covenant" communities with ties to the North American religious right. But judging from unpublished field research by Jacob Bernstein, the movement is growing rapidly among the poor, where charismatics have practically taken over certain rural parishes and account for a growing majority of the movement in Costa Rica, Nicaragua, and Guatemala.[17] To date, charismatics have shown little interest in social issues and political activism, so they are usually pictured as being at loggerheads with Catholic progressives. Judging from my acquaintance with Mayan charismatics in Guatemala, the class position of poorer, parish-based followers could change this.

Interpreting Pentecostalism

The transitions between all these manifestations—Pentecostal churches, charismatic fellowships, folk Catholicism, and Afro-American spiritism—suggest what Rowan Ireland has called "a common folk religion cutting across religious boundaries." [18] According to Jean-Pierre Bastian, "The heterodox religious effervescence that we are witnessing in Latin America is none other than a renewal of the 'popular religion,' of rural Catholicism without priests." [19] Questioning whether even "Protestantism" is an appropriate term for the phenomenon, Bastian refers to it in the plural, as *"protestantismos."* He denies the parallels that others have claimed between the Protestant Reformation in Europe and the evangelical boom in Latin America. Instead, according to Bastian, there is little continuity between the "historical" Protestants of the mainline denominations—Presbyterians, Methodists, Baptists, Lutherans—and Latin American Pentecostals.

The first Latin American Protestants, Bastian argues, were

associated with radical liberal minorities who questioned the region's corporatist social order. Pentecostals, in contrast, come out of a popular, Catholic, and shamanistic religious culture that, instead of rejecting corporatism, reinforces it. This has implications for the social contribution to be made, according to Bastian. So while historical Protestantism was "a religion of literacy and education characterized as civil and rational"—hence a vehicle for "liberal democratic values"—Pentecostalism represents "religions of oral tradition, illiteracy and effervescence" that reinforce "caudillist models of religious and social control." Consequently, sectarian Protestantism in Latin America has "no relation whatsoever to religious reform and . . . even less to do with political and social reform."[20]

It is true that the ecumenical incarnation of historical Protestantism, influenced recently by liberation theology, has fared poorly against more conservative evangelicals, and possibly these defeats have influenced Bastian's argument. Indeed, he denies that any contemporary religious movement has the potential to promote reform, even liberation theology, which he dismisses (following Jean Meyer[21]) as another manifestation of intransigent Catholicism setting itself against secularization and modernity. What Bastian does emphasize is the autonomy displayed by Pentecostals, what some North American scholars would call "resistance," and he firmly rejects conspiracy theories, which reduce them to a North American plot. But he denies that their congregational life is constructing any alternative to the status quo.

A low church man from Britain disputes the latter point. David Martin, a sociologist of religion known for his work on secularization, sees powerful continuities between the Protestant experiences in Europe, the United States, and Latin America. Just as Puritanism and Methodism were associated with democratizing trends in Britain and the United States, Martin argues that Latin American Pentecostalism is a "third wave" of Protestant revivalism that could have broadly similar implications. Not ony is this the latest stage of a centuries-old struggle between Anglo Protestantism and Hispanic Catholicism, it is also a struggle for modernity against the Catholic spiritual monopolies that, according to Martin, have discouraged the kind of pluralism necessary for a democratic society. This is where the seemingly divisive sectarianism of congregational religious life has performed a historical duty, Martin argues, by opening up social space for new forms of association, authority, and dissent.

Depending on your point of view, this may sound like a hopeful sign for the future or the latest neocolonial thinking. But both Martin and Bastian address the question of whether Protestantism, specifically Pentecostalism, could transform entire national societies. Martin's argument recalls the long-standing Protestant dream of reforming Latin America along Anglo-American lines— that is, with a broader distribution of rewards and more respect for civil liberties.[22] Unfortunately such hopes may underestimate Latin America's disadvantageous position in the world market and the devastating pressures on its resource base, not to mention the brutal exigencies of international debt that continue to pauperize the majority of Latin Americans. But Martin's argument does have the virtue of breaking with common assumptions used to evaluate the impact of Protestantism, particularly those associated with liberation theology.

One such assumption is that the conservative politics of North American missionaries and national leaders is a reliable guide to how evangelicals actually behave.[23] That is, it has been presumed that evangelicals will be bulwarks against the left. With this presumption in mind, two of this volume's chapters present new evidence that not as much separates Latin American evangelicals from their class peers as is often assumed. For El Salvador, Kenneth Coleman, Edwin Eloy Aguilar, José Miguel Sandoval, and Timothy Steigenga obtained fascinating data on religious affiliation and political attitudes from the surveys carried out by Ignacio Martín-Baró, one of the six Jesuit priests murdered by the Salvadoran army in 1989. In Brazil, specifically the group of industrial suburbs of Rio de Janeiro known as Duque de Caxias, John Burdick observed lower-class Pentecostals taking an active part in local neighborhood, labor union, and political party structures that evangelicals are usually thought to shun.

Brazil looms so large in our subject, representing almost 40 percent of the Latin American population and possibly half its evangelicals, that we made a special effort to recruit Brazilianists who could use their field experience to project wider trends. Hence Paul Freston's account of the major Protestant denominations and their political trajectories during Brazil's democratic opening, an analysis that is unprecedented in distinguishing the various tendencies in a movement usually subject to glib generalization. As the movement becomes larger and penetrates higher in the class structure, Pentecostals are being forced to respond to the debt crisis in new ways. Even as Freston explains how Brazilian Pentecostals have arrived at their conservative reputation, he suggests why their leadership is not as conservative as it might appear. The opportunism and desperation he describes point to a varied political performance that could include increasing involvement with populist movements and the left.

Brazilian Protestantism is situated in the wider field of Brazilian religious options by Rowan Ireland. By sketching the lives of two *crentes* (believers) in a town near Recife, in the Northeast, Ireland suggests how evangelicals can draw on their repertoire of doctrine, myth, and practice to construct (or, alternatively, struggle against) various "political economies" that compete for the loyalty of Brazilians. These include traditional patronage networks, the bureaucratic-authoritarian state, populism, and the communitarian structures of liberation theology; hence "the religious construction of politics." Ireland's evocative work, published at greater length in his book *Kingdoms Come*, suggests how, if we can understand the religious foundations of competing political styles in Latin American life, religious trends can help us understand political ones.

In 1990–91 alone, twenty-two evangelical congressmen took office in Guatemala along with Jorge Serrano Elías, that country's first Protestant to be elected president; seventeen evangelical congressmen did the same in Peru along with President Alberto Fujimori, a Catholic whose vote was mobilized largely by evangelical churches; and thirty-three evangelicals were elected to the congress of Brazil.[24] But as Latin America's "return to democracy" disappoints expectations, especially for economic recovery, there is little sign that evangelical politicians will avoid being tarred with the same brush as the rest of the political class.

What remains is the distinction made by Donald Dayton between direct social action, the impact of which seems slight at present, and the possible longer-range social impact of Protestantism.[25] It is far easier to see how Protestantism has led to upward mobility for particular individuals, families, and social groups than how it will change relations of authority and the distribution of rewards in society as a whole. But various questions remain. Is Latin American Pentecostalism a step on the road to demystifying, secularizing, and rationalizing Latin American society, as predicted by David Martin, or is it inevitably thaumaturgical—that is, magical and mystifying—as argued by Jean-Pierre Bastian? And what are the implications for patterns of authority? Is Latin American Protestantism basically caudillistic, or do its tendencies to fragmentation give it more democratic implications?

Evangelical groups have often been criticized in Latin America for separating their members from the larger society. Presumably there is something bad about this. Yet numerous local studies suggest that evangelical congregations have at least become a way for significant minorities of Latin Americans to reform themselves, their relations to each other, and perhaps their relations to the larger society.[26] Hence David Martin refers to these groups as a "free social space" or "protective social capsule," like a cocoon, for generating new kinds of social relations.[27] Through the door of religious conversion, individuals and families join small, tight-knit groups that reinforce new patterns of behavior, encourage the transmission of these patterns to future generations, and generate new kinds of social cohesion which empower members (or perpetuate relations of domination, depending on your point of view). Like conversionist religion in general, evangelical Protestantism can therefore be regarded as a way for believers to alter their cultural inheritance. It is a popular new orientation to being Latin American that could, conceivably, open up the sadly diminished panoramas of the 1990s.

NOTES

1. Enrique González Pedrero, quoted in Jean-Pierre Bastian, "Les protestantismes latino-américains: Un objet à interroger et à construire," *Social Compass* 39 (3) (1992): 346. Translation by Kharana Olivier.
2. This is an observation most often made of the countries with the greatest percentage of Protestant population: Brazil, Chile, and Central America. Hard figures are lacking, but evangelical chapels can be observed outdrawing Catholic churches in many localities, as corroborated by Catholic sources such as the June 29, 1989, special issue of *Latinamerica Press*, a newsletter published in Lima.
3. The present volume is the first English-language collection of social research on the subject since 1980, its only predecessor being Stephen D. Glazier, ed., *Perspectives on Pentecostalism: Case Studies from the Caribbean and Latin America* (Washington, D.C.: University Press of America, 1980). Unpublished Ph.D. dissertations include Donald Edward Curry, "Lusiada: An Anthropological Study of the Growth of Protestantism in Brazil" (Columbia University, 1968); Wilson H. Endruveit, "Pentecostalism in Brazil" (Northwestern University, 1975); Ronald Glen Frase, "A Sociological Analysis of the Development of Brazilian Protestantism" (Princeton Theological Seminary, 1975); Bernhard John Gellner, "Colta Entrepreneurship in Ecuador" (University of Wisconsin, 1982); Mark L. Grover, "Mormonism in Brazil: Religion and Dependency in Latin America" (Indiana University, 1985); Judith Chambliss Hoffnagel, "The Believers: Pentecostalism in a Brazilian City" (Indiana University, 1978); David Knowlton, "Searching Minds and Questing Hearts: Protestantism and Social Context in Bolivia" (University of Texas, Austin, 1988); Kent Maynard, "Christianity and Religion: Evangelical Identity and Sociocultural Organization in Urban Ecuador" (Indiana University, 1977); and John Anthony Page, "Brasil para Cristo: The Cultural Construction of Pentecostal Networks in Brazil" (New York University, 1984).

Published dissertation research includes Sheldon Annis, *God and Production in a Guatemalan Town* (Austin: University of Texas Press, 1987); Elizabeth Brusco, *The Reformation of Machismo* (Austin: University of Texas Press, forthcoming 1994); John Burdick, *Looking for God in Brazil* (Berkeley: University of California Press, 1993); and Cornelia Butler Flora, *Protestantism in Colombia: Baptism by Fire and Spirit* (London: Associated University Presses, 1976). Other Ph.D. dissertations that, because of new interest in Protestantism, are being revised for publication, include Virginia Garrard-Burnett, "A History of Protestantism in Guatemala" (Tulane University, 1986); Timothy Edward Evans, "Religious Conversion in Quezaltenango, Guatemala" (University of Pittsburgh, 1990); and Cecilia Loreto Mariz, "Religion and Coping with Poverty in Brazil" (Boston University, 1989).

4. For evaluations of the impact of liberation theology, see Phillip Berryman, *Liberation Theology* (Philadelphia: Temple University Press, 1987), and his "Churches in Conflict" (book MS, 1991); Roland Robertson, "Liberation Theology, Latin America, and Third World Underdevelopment," and W. E. Hewitt, "Myths and Realities of Liberation Theology: The Case of Basic Christian Communities in Brazil," in Richard L. Rubenstein and John K. Roth, eds., *The Politics of Latin American Liberation Theology* (Washington, D.C.: Washington Institute Press, 1988), pp. 117–55; Penny Lernoux, *People of God: The Struggle for World Catholicism* (New York: Viking, 1989); Daniel H. Levine, "Protestants and Catholics in Latin America: A Family Portrait," paper prepared for the Fundamentalism Project, University of Chicago, 1991; Rowan Ireland, *Kingdoms Come: Religion and Politics in Brazil* (Pittsburg: University of Pittsburgh Press, 1992); Edward L. Cleary and Hannah Stewart-Gambino, eds., *Conflict and Competition: The Latin American Church in a Changing Environment* (Boulder, Colo.: Lynne Rienner, 1992); and Burdick, *Looking for God in Brazil.*

5. "Fundamentalist" and "evangelical" should not be regarded as mutually exclusive categories. Instead, the terms often refer to two different faces of the same interpretive community, that is, the wish to defend the fundamentals (or sectarian principles) of the faith versus the wish to expand its boundaries or evangelize, after the Greek root for spreading the good news. Hence, when a self-defined fundamentalist appeals to new constituencies, s/he behaves like an evangelical. When an evangelical is placed on the defensive, s/he may behave like a fundamentalist. Christians who refer to themselves as fundamentalists, evangelicals, Pentecostals, or simply "believers" continue to have strong traditional beliefs in God, the afterlife, sin, and redemption, including the need for personal transformation through Jesus Christ, often experienced in terms of being "born again." They believe that salvation can be achieved only through Jesus Christ, that the Bible is inerrant, and that the most important duty of a Christian is to spread the faith.

6. Donald W. Dayton, "The Holy Spirit and Christian Expansion in the Twentieth Century," *Missiology* 16 (4) (1988): 401.

7. Jean-Pierre Bastian, "Les protestantismes latino-américains," *Social Compass* 39 (3) (1992): 330.

8. David E. Dixon, "Popular Culture, Popular Identity and the Rise of Latin American Protestantism: Voices from Santiago Poblacional," unpublished paper in author's collection, 1992.

9. In 1987, Phillip Berryman (*Liberation Theology*, p. 72) estimated that there were "several times as many active Protestants and evangelicals as there are members of Catholic base communities."

10. See Rafael Mondragón, *De indios y cristianos en Guatemala* (México, D.F.: COPEC/CECOPE, 1983); María Albán Estrada and Juan Pablo Muñoz, *Con Dios todo se puede: La invasión de las sectas al Ecuador* (Quito: Editorial Planeta, 1987); and Alfredo Silletta, *Las sectas invaden la Argentina* (Buenos Aires: Editorial Contrapunto, 1987).

11. Levine, "Protestants and Catholics in Latin America."

12. Christian Lalive d'Epinay, *Haven of the Masses* (London: Lutterworth Press, 1969), pp. 118, 122.

13. See, for example, Curry, "Lusiada"; Flora, *Protestantism in Colombia*; David L. Clawson, "Religion and Change in a Mexican Village" (Ph.D. diss., University of Florida, 1979); Gellner, "Colta Entrepreneurship"; Annis, *God and Production*; Knowlton, "Searching Minds"; and Mariz, "Religion and Coping with Poverty."

14. A church-planting guide from the Assemblies of God, the largest Protestant denomination in Latin America, advises evangelists against erecting a church building until the new congregants insist on one. The idea is to avoid setting up walls and boundaries that could discourage further converts. David E. Godwin, *Church Planting Methods* (De Soto, Tex.: Lifeshare Communications, 1984), pp. 37, 119.

15. The survey was designed by church growth researcher Jean Kessler. See his "A Summary of the Costa Rican Evangelical Crisis: August, 1989," unpublished paper (Pasadena, Calif.: IDEA/Church Growth Studies Program, 1989, p. 5). Costa Ricans who identified themselves as Catholics were asked, "Have you been an evangelical at any previous time in your life?" In a representative sample of 1,276 adults, 8.9 percent said they were evangelicals, another 1.6 percent said they were Mormons or Jehovah's Witnesses, and another 8 percent said they had been evangelicals at some previous time in their lives. This suggests a desertion factor of 47 percent. Two-thirds of the evangelical defectors went back to identifying themselves as Catholics, while another third said they had no religious affiliation. Given how recent the evangelical

boom is and how rapidly the category of ex-evangelicals is growing, the ultimate dropout rate could go significantly higher. But Kessler's survey also suggests that the experience of being an evangelical could spread far beyond the percentage of the population that presently attends or claims to attend a church.

16. Because of the recruiting strategies of the Full Gospel Business-men's Fellowship, including quasi-ecumenical relations with the Catho-lic Church despite the founder's background in the Assemblies of God, Catholic leadership of the Guatemalan chapter is probably compatible with the Houston-based organization's aims. But Catholic leadership of the Guatemalan chapter has motivated defections by Guatemalan evangelicals who are unwilling to accept it. David Stoll, " 'Jesus Is Lord of Guatemala': The Prospects for Evangelical Reform in a Death Squad State," in Emmanuel Sivan and Gabriel Almond, eds., *Accounting for Fundamentalism* (Chicago: University of Chicago Press, forthcoming).

17. Untitled draft paper submitted to this volume. For an earlier report on Catholic charismatics, see T. J. Chordas, "Catholic Pentecostal-ism," in Stephen Glazier, ed., *Perspectives on Pentecostalism: Case Studies from the Caribbean and Latin America* (Washington, D.C.: University Press of America, 1980).

18. Ireland, *Kingdoms Come*, p. 239.

19. Bastian, "Les protestantismes latino-américains," p. 329. Trans-lation by Kharana Olivier.

20. Ibid., pp. 332, 344.

21. Jean Meyer, *Historia de los cristianos en América Latina, siglos XIX y XX* (México, D. F.: Vuelta, 1989).

22. For recent expressions of this thinking in print media, see David Martin and David Lee, "After Catholicism: The New Protestants and the Rise of Capitalism in Latin America," *National Review*, September 29, 1989, pp. 30–35; Tim Stafford, "The Hidden Fire," *Christianity Today*, May 14, 1990, pp. 23–26; "Spreading the Faith: The Protestant Explo-sion in Latin America," *Insight* (supp., *Washington Times*), July 16, 1990, pp.8–17; John Marcom, Jr., "The Fire Down South," *Forbes*, October 15, 1990, pp. 55–56, 64, 66, 71; Thomas Kamm, "Evangelicals, Stressing 'Cures' for Masses' Misery, Make Inroads in Roman Catholic Latin America," *Wall Street Journal*, October 16, 1991, p. A12.

23. This is most evident in mass media treatments that reach a far larger audience than does scholarship. "Onward, Christian Soldiers," a video by Gaston Ancelovici and Jaime Barrios (First Run/Icarus, 1989), summarizes the left's conventional wisdom about evangelicals in the

1980s. Some of the first investigators to challenge stereotypes of theologically conservative Pentecostals as politically right-wing were Flora, *Protestantism in Colombia*; Jean-Pierre Bastian, *Breve historia del protestantismo en América Latina* (México, D.F.: Casa Unida de Publicaciones, 1986); Carlos Garma Navarro, "Liderazgo protestante en una lucha campesina en México," *América indígena* 44 (1) (1984):127–41; and Joanne Rappaport, "Las misiones protestantes y la resistencia indígena en el sur de Colombia," *América indígena* 44 (1) (1984):111–26.

24. *Lausanne Letter* no. 6 (December 1991). See also "Evangelicals and Politics in Latin America," *Transformation* 9 (3) (1992), a special issue.

25. Donald W. Dayton, "Pentecostal/Charismatic Renewal and Social Change: A Western Perspective," *Transformation* 5 (4) (1988):7–13.

26. A partial list would include Emilio Willems, *Followers of the New Faith* (Nashville, Tenn.: Vanderbilt University Press, 1967); Curry, "Lusiada"; Flora, *Protestantism in Colombia*; Douglas Brintnall, *Revolt Against the Dead: The Modernization of a Mayan Community in the Highlands of Guatemala* (New York: Gordon and Breach, 1979); Clawson, "Religion and Change; Page, "Brasil para Cristo"; Carlos Garma Navarro, *Protestantismo en una comunidad totonaca de Puebla* (México, D. F.: Instituto Nacional Indigenista, 1987); Rappaport, "Las misiones protestantes"; Brusco, "The Household Basis of Evangelical Religion"; Annis, *God and Production*; Mariz, "Religion and Coping"; Stoll, " 'Jesus Is Lord of Guatemala' "; and Burdick, "Rethinking the Study of Social Movements," in Sonia Alvares and Arturo Escobar, eds., *New Social Movements in Latin America* (forthcoming).

27. David Martin, *Tongues of Fire: The Explosion of Protestantism in Latin America* (Oxford: Basil Blackwell, 1990), pp. 268, 279, 284.

1 Struggling Against the Devil: Pentecostalism and Social Movements in Urban Brazil

John Burdick

I N CONTRAST TO Catholic base communities, which have long been depicted as important contributors to the struggle for social justice throughout Latin America, Pentecostalism has usually been portrayed as an inherently conservative force that teaches submission to authority, erodes collective identity, and undercuts justifications for social action. This view has been particularly pronounced in the literature on Brazil.[1] In this view, *crentes* ("believers," as Brazilian Pentecostals call themselves) become involved in electoral politics only to defend freedom of religion and the existing class order,[2] and their occasional appearances in social movements are little more than temporary "ruptures" from their usual acceptance of the status quo.[3]

Brazilian scholars who take this position have traditionally based their view on readings of Pentecostal literature and interviews with pastors. Fortunately, the growing number of researchers who have lived among ordinary Pentecostals have begun to complicate the conventional picture.[4] They point out that the self-valorization brought about by Pentecostal conversion often paves the way for a strong sense of natural rights and citizenship.[5] Regina Novaes has argued that the Pentecostals who participated in a rural union in the Brazilian Northeast tended "to have greater conviction about their rights" than did others.[6]

Still, despite their potentially strong sense of citizenship, there is no denying that Pentecostals generally give social movements a wide berth. To penetrate this apparent paradox, we must move away from trying to identify what is "essential" to Pentecostal politics. Instead, we should try to clarify the various linkages between Pentecostal identity and a range of political tendencies, then investigate the conditions under which any given tendency prevails. The advantage to this conjunctural perspective is that it allows us to avoid regarding Pentecostals as inevitably "unmobilizable" while clarifying why they so often remain unmobilized.

This discussion is based on a year and a half of anthropological fieldwork in several small towns in Duque de Caxias, a municipality of about a million people located an hour to the north of Rio de Janeiro. The towns range from tiny settlements of a few hundred people to major centers of fifteen to twenty thousand. The men in these towns work either in one of the many metallurgical, chemical, food processing, or electronics plants in the region's industrial center, or in civil construction. Most of the women are engaged in work at home, domestic service, or factory work. The majority of households earn less than three minimum salaries a month, or about $120.00, which means that, on average, the per capita monthly income in the region is about $20.00. People live in brick and clay-tiled houses with both running water from wells and electricity, but have very rudimentary sewage systems, only sporadic garbage pickup, roads that turn to impassable mud during the rains, and very unreliable bus service. Chronic gastrointestinal diseases are rampant, especially among children.

Pentecostals in the towns of Duque de Caxias illustrate the larger political paradox of Pentecostalism throughout the country.[7] On the one hand, the Pentecostal services and prayer meetings I observed contained precious little "mixing of religion and politics." Here, the highest value is placed on spiritual salvation. Indeed, it is not surprising that many Pentecostals attribute their conversions to the politicization of the Catholic Church. One young man, who had been raised in a Catholic family, stated that when "the Church got mixed up with politics, that was mixing things too much. We know so little of the Word of God, why waste time with politics? The Church is concerned about spiritual life, not material things."[8]

On the other hand, there can be no doubt that the religious logic of pentecostalism includes a number of tensions, contradictions, and sources of empowerment that facilitate rather than hinder participation in social movements. In some cases, these may even nurture the development of a highly critical social consciousness. In order to explore such tensions and contradictions, let us examine more closely whether, when, and how pentecostals come to participate in collective action for social change.

Crentes *in Neighborhood Associations*

At first glance, anyone concerned about the political consequences of Pentecostal identity would take little solace in the level of Pentecostal participation in many of Duque de Caxias's neighborhood organizations. In a fairly representative town of about eight thousand people (which I shall call São Jorge), of the many dozens of men who participated during the 1980s as directors of the neighborhood association, only two have belonged to the Assembly of God. Furthermore, in a 1988 election for directorate members, only a dozen Pentecostals cast votes, compared with the three hundred votes cast by non-Pentecostals. How to account for such apparent alienation?

If one poses this question to a non-Pentecostal, he or she will offer a favorite explanation: Pentecostals care little for material improvement. "Pentecostals," one association director told me, "don't care about sewage or streets. They feel they can walk in the mud." The explanation continues: *Crentes* think they need only pray to get what they want; they therefore have little use for collective efforts. "They think if they stay at home and ask God," said another director, "it will just fall from the sky."

Accounts such as these are not entirely wrong. Pentecostals do cite Jesus' statement "My Kingdom is not of this world." They also are quick to rationalize a good deal of their material deprivation as God's way of bringing His chosen closer to Him. Yet the assumption that Pentecostals are indifferent to the material world is off the mark. *Crentes* denounce the world for its corruption; they do not denounce the world entirely. Most Pentecostals, after all, studiously avoid the dogmatic world renunciation of the relatively few moonstruck converts who attract such a disproportionate amount of attention; I often heard Pentecostals call such people "fanáticos." Rather than such world-renouncing mysticism, most *crentes* seek the Christian life envisaged by the Apostle Paul, one implicated in such worldly relations as marriage, family, work, neighborhood, and the maintenance of physical health. From this point of view, whatever permits these to be nurtured and maintained is good; whatever threatens them is bad.

Crentes express this worldview by pointing to their commitment to living "correctly" and "decently" in the here and now; it is especially important to them, for example, to strive for "improvement" and "cleanliness." The Pentecostal can thus be heard as often as anyone else decrying bad drinking water, dangerous buses and roads, unstable tenure of house plots, and the lack of electricity. As one Pentecostal presbyter explained,

> We have salvation, but salvation is in heaven. We are here on earth. Jesus will come, but He's not here yet. Look, this road here was bad: Wasn't it better to asphalt it? Didn't that benefit people? If you don't improve things, they worsen. When I arrive at home after work, I have to take my bath: I've improved! I'm not going to lie down in a bed all dirty. God loves improvement, and everything that improves is clean.

Even those observers who acknowledge Pentecostals' appreciation of material benefits sometimes claim that *crentes* believe the only way to obtain them is through prayer. This may characterize the attitudes of some Pentecostals (as it does some non-*crentes*), yet most Pentecostals I spoke with embraced the conventional dictum that God helps those who help themselves. The following statement by a deacon illustrates the logic.

> Let's suppose there is an empty glass here, and I say, "Let's pray for water to fill it up." That won't happen! We have to go over there and fill it. So they have to go to CEDAE [the water authority] and

ask and talk. They need to pray for strength to walk and speak. You
have to form those groups and go to the mayor and ask for things.
To make a meal, you can't ask God; you have to build your own
house. Is He going to pave your street? No, you have to go to the
mayor. Look at Nemias [Nehemiah], he was a servant of the king
in Jerusalem. He went to demand from the king, and prayed, he
didn't just fold his arms.

If we take such views seriously, it becomes difficult to maintain that *crentes* remain uninvolved in neighborhood associations
simply out of indifference or an overweening reliance on prayer.
While these may be contributing factors, we must also consider
the fact that Pentecostals usually feel socially marginalized from
the groups that tend to dominate neighborhood associations.

This marginalization has several dimensions. First, *crentes*
rarely see their coreligionists in positions of leadership in neighborhood associations. The associations of most towns in Duque
de Caxias are run by closely knit cliques of local notables—
often the lay leadership of the Catholic Church and local merchants—who promise to deliver votes to local politicians in
exchange for infrastructural improvements. In São Jorge, for example, the association has rotated posts among such notables
for over twenty years, with decision making monopolized by factions that crystallize in the street and bars.[9] The result is politics
by back-room faction, requiring skill in saying things one does
not mean and making promises one does not intend to keep.

It should thus not surprise us that non-Pentecostal leaders
hesitate to ask Pentecostals to run on slates with them: they
clearly wish to avoid constraints on practices they deem essential
to local male-dominated politics—including smoking, drinking,
swearing, and swapping of tales of adultery. Such activities are
not acceptable for practicing *crentes*; Pentecostals are forbidden
to frequent the bars where much factional caucusing takes place.
When a Pentecostal attends association meetings, he therefore
quickly becomes frustrated. One of the two *crentes* elected to the
directorate told me,

> Sometimes you have a good plan, but you get lost. There at the
> table, they don't call on you, they don't respect your opinion, they

won't even listen. The *crente* isn't shrewd, he doesn't know how
to get support, go out drinking, give favors, lie. He can't! He's not
around, hanging out on the street and in the bars, getting people
on his side.

This man was a presbyter in his church. His annoyance points
to another problem: as proud members of a church with its own
hierarchy, Pentecostal deacons and presbyters balk at subject-
ing themselves to people who do not respect their opinion. The
presbyter said bitterly that the current directors had asked him
to run for office with them, but once he had brought in Pentecostal votes, they ceased consulting him about anything. "They
wouldn't even tell me when the association was meeting!"

Non-Pentecostals' lack of solicitude for *crentes* is further mani-
fested in their insensitivity to Pentecostal religious schedules.
Whenever the directors set dates for town meetings, they care-
fully consider the possibility of conflicting with Catholic wed-
dings, but never Pentecostal ones. Moreover, elections for new
directorates always take place in the *sala* (hall) of the Catholic
Church. "I won't attend there because they will treat me differently," one Pentecostal explained. "They are Catholic, I am
crente."

That the obstacles to Pentecostal participation in local neighborhood associations are mainly social and practical, not doctrinal, is suggested by the fact that in several associations, Pentecostals have become actively involved, to the point of outnumbering
progressive Catholics. *Crentes* have a better chance of becoming
involved in associations in places with newer, more heterogeneous populations, where the association has not been dominated by a Catholic clique.

Consider Sarapuí, a sprawling town of about fifteen thousand
inhabitants located on the outskirts of Duque de Caxias. In this
town, Pentecostals stepped into a virtual organizational vacuum.
In the early 1970s no association existed there. In the late 1970s,
a middle-aged Pentecostal named Dalila, who had lived in town
for nearly fifteen years, found herself and her neighbors threatened with eviction: "They sent us a paper saying we had only
ninety days to get out. We were worried, it was a Wednesday,

we were in prayer. Then God said to me, 'I will show you that here at home there will be a person behind the Word.' "

Emboldened by this voice, Dalila sought the assistance of a lawyer; witnessing her initiative, neighbors heeded her call when she convened a meeting in her house. There the lawyer explained that "We had a better chance if we were organized into an association. My husband became president . . . we had lots of *crentes* there in the association, because we founded it." In the association, Dalila had to meet on equal terms with people of all religions, including the Afro-Brazilian religion known as *umbanda*. But the Bible inspired her: "When Jesus walked upon the earth, He sat down and ate with sinners," she explained. "He cured the sick. He worked and helped all without exception. He said, 'I have not come for the healthy, but for the sick.' " Dalila never wavered from the conviction that she was doing God's will. "We have two struggles in life: material and spiritual," she declared. "In anything material, when things are good, God is acting." The struggle dragged on for four years. "And I was always talking to the people, saying 'don't lose heart, because nothing is going to happen.' God was always speaking to me, you know? 'Do not fear,' He would say, always inspiring me."

In 1978, the state government finally ruled in favor of the association, a victory that solidified Dalila's own commitment. She then persuaded the pastor to release her from church services to attend the conferences of the regional confederation of neighborhood associations. She and her husband inspired dozens of their coreligionists, as well as non-*crente* neighbors, to participate in the organization. "The people around here believe a lot in us, they support us. They trust us." Such expressions of trust are common whenever Pentecostals take on roles of political leadership. Non-Pentecostal smallholders who support a local Pentecostal as the leader of their peasant union, for example, spoke of his honesty.[10] Elsewhere, non-*crentes* voted for Pentecostal candidates for assemblyman on the ground that "they won't rob and steal."

While Pentecostals in Sarapuí stepped into an organizational vacuum, in Pilar, a larger and more heterogeneous town than either São Jorge or Sarapuí, the *crentes* encountered not a lack of preexisting organization (the place had had an association for almost ten years) but a crisis of Catholic leadership. This crisis, which illustrates some of the rigidities of the Catholic Church's relation to social movements, opened a window through which Pentecostal leaders stepped, bringing coreligionists in their train.

Pilar was home to a progressive Franciscan priest named Orlando, who in 1983 persuaded his protégés to run for the local association's directorate. After winning, the Catholics gained improvements for the geographic center of town (where they happened to live) rather than for the area at the town's margins, largely inhabited by *crentes*, who live near their churches. Consequently, during the Catholics' tenure, Pentecostals did a slow burn. Then scandal struck: Orlando had an affair with a married woman and was forced to abandon the Church. Recalled one Catholic: "Many people lost heart when he left and stopped participating in the association."

Soon after, the Catholic hierarchy's paternalism—a tendency to abandon any movement it cannot dominate or engineer— reared its head.[11] A non-practicing Catholic won the presidency of the association, no doubt partly as a result of general disillusionment with the Church after Orlando's scandal. No longer in control of the association, the progressive bishop promptly expelled its members from the Church-owned building where they met, forcing them to convene at the public school, which happened to be located near the residential concentration of *crentes*. Many Pentecostals jumped at this opportunity to redress the inequity of past directorates, seeing the arrival of meetings in their neighborhood as a way to gain access to the improvements from which they had been excluded. They began attending meetings in large numbers. During this crucial period, water pipes were installed throughout the town, the first major improvement to affect the *crentes'* area. Though this benefit had been in the works before the arrival of the Pentecostals, for many people it seemed hardly coincidental. The *crentes*, some began to say, get results for the whole town, not just one part of it. When the pastor of the Assembly of God threw his weight behind a bloc of his congregants running for the new directorate in 1985, they had little difficulty getting elected. "In many Pentecostal churches," the pastor told me, "they think it's a sin to work in things. But not here; I teach differently. I let the neighborhood association use this *sala*, and I give them a word of support. And we are setting up a medical consultation room upstairs. We are preparing a little school."

The Catholic leaders in Pilar, demoralized by the collapse of church support, eventually resigned. By 1988 Pentecostals were still so active in the association that its two remaining Catholic leaders freely admitted, "We now rely more on the people of the Assembly of God than on the Catholics." Despite the Catholic Church's progressive position, say these leaders, Catholics "just stay there in meetings, the guy doesn't apply it in practice, he just stays there in the church."[12]

Crentes *in Labor Struggles*

If under some circumstances *crentes* throw themselves into neighborhood improvement, they seem harder-pressed to translate experience of the more direct contradictions of capital into collective action. Local labor organizers point to Pentecostals as the major culprits in undermining union strength. They often remark on the low levels of involvement among Pentecostal industrial workers in newer, more combative labor organizations.[13] Among Rio's municipal transport workers, for example, Pentecostals are said to "keep their distance" from the union; in Rio's metalworkers' union (which in 1988 elected a militant directorate[14]), an organizer told me, "We invited the *crentes* and the pastors, but they say that we fight too much. A master craftsman who is a *crente* said that Christians cannot fight. He didn't like that we spoke badly of the current president [of the union]."

As with their account of Pentecostals' noninvolvement in neighborhood associations, non-Pentecostal critics commonly attribute such passivity to lack of material ambition. "*Crentes* are not excited by material things," explained a metalworkers' organizer. "They don't want to get ahead, they don't have that drive [*pique*]. They don't think they need to go on strike, because they think they've got it made in heaven."

There may be some truth to this. Religious ideology may influence the conduct of Pentecostals engaged in industrial labor, especially among operatives not engaged in precision work. In factories, for example, I heard that Pentecostal operatives sometimes leave machines running while going off to pray, sing, or read the Bible. Though such tales undoubtedly involve a dose of malice, I did meet several *crentes* who had been fired more than once for "loafing." At any rate, Pentecostals seem better equipped spiritually to deal with unstable employment than Catholics are. They say they do not worry about losing their jobs, for unemployment is a Jobian trial. "God is working His will," a Pentecostal told me after being fired. "He didn't want me to stay there. He has another plan for me." *Crentes* point to Isaiah's prophecy that in the final days man shall receive his salary "in a bag with a hole in it," which they say accounts for the high inflation rate and the low minimum wage in Brazil.

Yet the opinions of Pentecostal industrial workers on wages and unemployment are contradictory, contradictions that have been missed because of Brazilian scholars' overreliance on the statements of pastors.[15] Major differences separate the views of working-class Pentecostals from those of salaried pastors. "The employer is the worker's brother before God," insisted pastor Alcyr, who receives five minimum salaries and owns a car, "and Jesus said, 'Do not hurt your brother.' But strikes hurt them!" What of Christ's denunciations of wealth? "You can be as rich as you want," he argued, "but if you are humble of spirit, you are a servant of God." The pastor even tried to downplay the thrust of Christ's "eye of a needle" pronouncement by saying, "Jesus was talking about those who were greedy and valued money above Him. Sometimes a person isn't even rich, but has an ambition for money, he'll kill for money." Such apologetics ring hollow for working-class *crentes*. One explained,

> Most pastors earn a salary, so they don't need to strike. They earn two or three salaries, with a pension. They don't need to enter the

fray, they stay cozy in their churches. So of course they don't think it's necessary to go there. But whoever earns only enough for his daily bread is obliged to go! It is biblical that we must work by the sweat of our brow. The *crente* doesn't go there to create fights or anarchy; he goes to offer his help.

It is as much of an error to attribute Pentecostals' avoidance of labor struggles to indifference to wages as it is to argue that *crentes* "like walking in mud" in their towns. Brazil's inflationary economy forces the working class, whether Pentecostal or non-Pentecostal, to be all too aware of the wage-price squeeze. Like other workers, Pentecostals need no lectures to grasp that unless wages keep up with the cost of rice and beans, misery quickly results.

The crucial point is that while Pentecostals accept poverty, they do not accept immiseration. If *crentes* see poverty as nurturing virtue, beggary signifies disobedience to God, as implied in the psalm, "I have never seen a servant of God beg for bread." Pentecostals hesitate to turn to each other for financial help, lest their obedience to God be placed in doubt. "God said that by the sweat of your brow you would make bread," said one, "so He wanted you to make bread." Another argued, "God doesn't want things to become super-bad. He wants them to be a way that we can tolerate. God does not like misery!"

If God does not approve of misery, neither does He look favorably upon the life-style of rich bosses. The sacralization of poverty carries with it a compelling denial of legitimacy of the rich and powerful. The less well-off members of Pentecostal congregations have no illusions as to why they see so few persons of wealth in their church. "You never see merchants in our church," remarked one, "because they think 'we have our money!' Money is everything for them, and the church isn't going to give them any money. It is harder for a rich man to be saved, because he thinks he has everything. Our everything is God. We need work and all, but the rich man already has that." *Crentes* do not hesitate to denounce rich Pentecostals as hypocrites. "They are wasting their time," said one. "When they really convert, they won't want

that wealth and vanity anymore! They give it all up. Job lost all
of his wealth, and all the prophets in the Bible are poor. The rich
cannot save themselves."

This denial of legitimacy, combined with the Pentecostals'
awareness that misery is due at least in part to the wage-price
squeeze, opens the way for an interpretation of economic deprivation as resulting not from workers' own sins but from the
sins of employers and the government. "There is misery because
the employer has no love for his employee," one Pentecostal declared. "He treats him like an animal, an object, he doesn't care if
he lives or dies." Many working *crentes* point out that employers,
by firing them, make it impossible to fulfill the biblical injunction to work by the sweat of their brow and not burden their
neighbors. "The Bible said we must work," another Pentecostal
argued, "that by the sweat of our brow shall we live. But when
the employer fires you, you become a burden, you have to get
INPS,[16] that is a burden on your neighbor."

At the same time, working-class Pentecostals understand that
only organized pressure will induce employers to raise wages to
keep pace with inflation. "Without strikes," said one, "there is
no raise in salary, so there have to be strikes. They won't give
it to you any other way." Biblical prophecies do not obviate the
need for workers' action: "You have to live," one Pentecostal
worker said, "you have to survive. That saying about receiving
salary in a sack with holes, that's true, but that doesn't mean you
have to accept misery! No! We must survive, stay healthy, so we
can preach the Word." One deacon simply sidestepped Isaiah's
prophecy altogether, justifying strikes by the divine injunction
to help oneself. "Without strikes," he declared, "you can't get
anything. And we can't just sit back with our arms folded while
others are struggling there in battle! God told us to help ourselves. So we have to bring our strength together, because in
unity there's strength. Without unity how can we win?"

Given these attitudes, why do *crentes* so often avoid union
militancy? The first part of an answer may be gleaned from the
fact that many Pentecostals explain their apathy about organizing in the same nonreligious terms used by non-*crentes*: Hard

experience proves that employers still hold the cards and use strikes to get rid of troublemaking or unprofitable workers. One Pentecostal disavowed any theological rationale for his skittishness about strikes. "My opinion on this has nothing to do with me being *crente*," he insisted. "I always felt this way, even before I converted. I'm against the strike because when it doesn't work out, it's the little guy who always has to pay, he's the one who suffers!"

From this point of view, Pentecostals' lack of participation may partly be a matter of perception. I have not come across any statistical analysis that compares rates of participation of *crentes* with non-Pentecostals, but to the extent that most workers, irrespective of religion, do not participate in labor activism of any kind, it is quite possible that Pentecostal participation may not differ dramatically from that of non-*crentes*. In terms of the percentage of any given work force, Pentecostals are always less numerous than peripheral and practicing Catholics, and hence make up only a small percentage of unmobilized workers. Because of their dress and demeanor, however, *crentes* stand out. By remaining outside union drinking and politicking networks, Pentecostals provide organizers a convenient scapegoat to account for the weakness of organizing drives.

When Pentecostals *do* participate, however, their conduct provides backbone to work stoppages and other actions. In some factories, Pentecostals represent up to a tenth of the work force. "*Crentes* are very firm in a strike," explained one non-Pentecostal organizer. "They give credibility to the movement." A Pentecostal confirmed this. "We won't scab, we won't vacillate. When they want our support, we say, 'OK, but without any violence.' " Indeed, because of their tactical importance, organizers often rely on Pentecostals' support as a way of building legitimacy for the action, both among the workers and in negotiating with employers. "*Crentes* are very firm, honest," explained one organizer. "Their example counts a lot." During a strike of metalworkers in one plant, the strike committee nominated a Pentecostal to approach the employer. Those with him clearly remember the effect this had on the climate of negotiations. "He spoke calmly," one recalled. "He said, 'Look, we're not able to tolerate these wages.' He was right, because the salary was low. That gave the workers a real boost, and the manager got the rug pulled out from under his feet."

For all this, there is no denying that working-class Pentecostals always impose a condition for supporting union militancy. To be legitimate, a strike must not have any *baderna*—confusion, violence, disorder. Thus, in 1988, local *crentes* tended to support the municipal teachers' strike in Rio because of its overall non-violence, but were horrified by the picket-line confrontations that same year in the retail workers' strikes. To the extent that the government and business have been willing to use police to break strikes, many of the most visible Brazilian labor conflicts in recent memory have involved *baderna*, and the resulting climate of tension and polarization makes for quickly flaring tempers on picket lines and the shop floor. Yet *crentes'* sense of what is required for survival continues to intervene. I met numerous Pentecostals who approved of passive resistance. Under some circumstances, they were willing to accept nonviolent civil disobedience. Said one retired man,

> It's a legitimate weapon of the worker. Look, they were going to take away our pension; and there was a whole bunch of people who went to Brasília to invade the office of INPS. I couldn't go because it's so far. We achieved an 80 percent increase in INPS through an invasion of the INPS office there in Brasília. I saw that on TV. That was right. The *crente* can't throw stones; he can strike and support his brothers, though.

Crentes *in Radical Party Politics*

Discussions of the relations between Pentecostals and political parties generally agree with José Francisco Gomes[17] that *crentes* voted for governmental or conservative parties (especially in 1982), guided primarily by self-interest or religious group or local interests, rather than by class interest or ideology.[18] At the same time, these writers acknowledge the sizable presence of Pentecostals in the Workers' Party.[19] What can this presence mean?

According to estimates from different sources, roughly one-tenth of the thirty-five hundred members of the Duque de Caxias branch of the Worker's Party (PT) are *crentes* of the Assembly of God. Three-quarters of them have been members for nearly ten years. Working-class Pentecostals began to enter the party during its founding period between 1979 and 1982, for the same reasons non-Pentecostals did. The PT was new on the political scene, and hence free from the taint of corruption and unfulfilled promise.[20] Many of the original Pentecostals in the party were, like Dalila, whom we met earlier, active in neighborhood associations, an experience that persuaded them of the importance of electing trustworthy politicians. Through her work in the neighborhood association, Dalila met regional leaders who offered advice and support. Their honesty impressed her, so when they campaigned for the PT ticket in 1982, she entered the party. "They were very good," she reported, "very honest. They wanted to help the poor people, not just get their vote."

Dalila and other *crentes* found support from Liborio, the president of the regional convention of Assemblies of God. As a town councilman, Liborio decided to abandon his party label in 1982 and take advantage of the vote-getting appeal of the new party's still unblemished record. The PT's directors welcomed the pastor as their standard-bearer, judging that the party could use an established politician to attract Pentecostal votes. Not only did Liborio do this, he also drew and reinforced a core of Pentecostal party activists who otherwise might have stayed away.

Though the PT's reputation for confrontation frightened many Pentecostals, by the late 1980s a softer-spoken Catholic leadership and improved linkages to neighborhood movements had drawn numerous Pentecostals into the party. As an increasing number of the region's union directorates became affiliated with the militant labor central (CUT) and began winning improvements in the workplace, the PT's legitimacy also increased. A member of the Assembly of God and leader of the civil construction union has personally recruited numerous other *crentes* into the PT.

Yet in light of Romans 13 (the Apostle Paul's injunction to

obey worldly authority), how could Pentecostals accept the PT's anti-governmental stance? By appealing to the prophetic tradition of the Old Testament. When I asked whether the military in Brazil had been placed in power by God, one replied,

> Yes, placed by God, but then they got corrupt. There is a lot of money there. Man is very drawn to things of the flesh. They want to fill their pockets. When they turn into "maharajahs" [corrupt high officials], God starts to distance Himself from them, He doesn't give them any more grace. They're like Judas. Sarney fell into the corruption of his ministers. "Woe unto you who afflicts my people with unjust laws."

Dalila, meanwhile, quoted Isaiah 10 to the same effect: "Woe unto them who decree unjust laws, and unto scribes who write perversity." She was reinterpreting Pauline obedience as a way for God to protect the weak from the powerful: "God tells us to respect them, so they won't attack us. If an authority comes along and the police come, how is it going to be? With a lawyer by your side it's better, because if we just do it on our own, disasters will occur."

The theoretical and ideological clarity of the *crentes'* political vision may be doubted; its combativeness cannot. To place their peculiar sense of militancy in greater relief, let us compare it with the surprisingly conciliatory stance of leaders from the Catholic base communities in Duque de Caxias. Although Catholics comprise a large majority of the local branch of the PT, those Pentecostals who have become involved as leaders appear firmer and more ideological than they. A non-Pentecostal director of the PT observed:

> Once they are in the party, the evangelicals are really very combative. The people of the Catholic Church have a very vague vision; but not the evangelicals. They have a vision of transformation of society. The evangelicals are able to develop a clear socialist class vision; but the Catholics cannot. That much is very clear.

A brief excursion into the ideological world of *igrejeiros* (CEB —Christian-base community—militants who participate in the directorate of the local PT) should help us unravel the paradox.

For all their claims to have a "prophetic voice," militant Catholics still have a visceral preference for conciliation over confrontation. This is partly the result of the Church's social etiquette: accustomed to consensus and reliance on the authority of the priest, Catholics often seem disoriented when faced with political debate. "We have a lot of trouble with confrontation," said a Catholic militant. "Many leave the movement because of that: 'That's not good, because God is calm,' they say." Catholics also face problems stemming from the conviction that anger is un-Christian. When I asked Maira, a Catholic leader of the PT, whether one might feel angry at a landlord evicting a tenant, she replied,

> We shouldn't feel angry. You must feel compassion for the ones who lost their land, and try to help them. Pity the land grabber. You must forgive him, he is a child of God. [Then how can one struggle against the landlord?] You don't struggle against him; you struggle for the poor man. One must not be angry against the exploiters; one must simply show them the truth. We can argue, appeal to their conscience, without aggression. . . . The Bible doesn't permit you to keep anger in your heart. The *patrão*, the boss, he must understand, he must change his ways.

The demanding (if paternalist) ideal that one should struggle out of compassion is compelled by the Catholic stress on universal brotherhood. "Whatever party someone is," one *igrejeiro* explained, "they are my brother; they, too, call God 'father.' I don't care if he is from party A or B." Hardly a stance to endear one to the PT faithful. Indeed, Maira acknowledged, "If you are in the Church, you speak a lot about brotherhood, love, peace, caring, forgiveness, those things. But when you arrive there in the political party, things are the exact opposite of all that. We are made fun of."

In light of these attitudes, it is not surprising that progressive Catholics concentrated through the 1970s and 1980s on local infrastructural issues. The neighborhood association places people in a relation with the state in which their primary source of power is reliance on the electoral process and law rather than confrontation and extralegal pressure. The Church has been famous for championing the rights of the landless to legal title; but this priority is also rooted in an ideal of small property ownership and strict legality.[21]

As for the labor movement in this region, it has remained a secondary concern for militant Catholics, who tend to be as uncomfortable with direct action, picket lines, slowdowns, low productivity, and strikes as the average *crente*. The Catholics in the PT directorate have, for example, provided only reluctant support for general strikes. They usually vote against them and, once obliged to participate, balk at picketing or, as one non-*igre-jeiro* put it,

> refuse to yell at the scabs. . . . Look, we prioritize the union movement, but the *igrejeiros* prioritize the associations. It is not by filling in a pothole, getting electricity, that you're going to transform society. There are very few comrades in the unions who are linked to the Church. The church people want to conciliate with the bourgeoisie. We feel we have to safeguard the . . . independence of our class.

These political attitudes have led to rifts in the Duque de Caxias PT. In the 1980s, the party directorate had several Catholic militants as members, but their political style grated on the nerves of non-CEB militants. When marchers were surrounded by police at a demonstration, the ranking Catholic party member gave the order to retreat. "We left the square," he explained, "so as not to create a conflict with the police, so that no one would leave there injured. . . . We're the ones, in the church, who always try to soften any potentially conflictual situation." Non-*igrejeiros*, meanwhile, tell this story with some bitterness. Recounted one,

> They wanted to leave, but that wasn't the moment for leaving. We had a right to be there, and we should have advanced, together, to demonstrate that right. . . . They are too soft, all they think about is God, God, God. They say "brother." They think you can change the world through love. But some things aren't that way.

While the Catholic is taught to think in conciliatory terms, the Pentecostal sees the world as a battleground in which the

Devil plays a constant role. *Crentes* are thus able to claim with relative ease that many of the rich are in league with the Devil.[22] The Pentecostal in politics speaks of the politician or captain of industry as a "tool of the Devil" while, as we have seen, the Catholic emphasizes that "we are both children of God." "There are employers," one Pentecostal affirmed, "who sell their souls to the Devil for money. Most of the rich people, the merchants around here, they seek out the Devil to make compacts, there in *macumba* [witchcraft], to make money."

Dalila explained,

> The enemy only wants to see us thrown to one side. He doesn't want to see anyone doing well. He's only satisfied with destruction. When we don't have any electricity, no drainage, that's the work of the Devil, because God is light. From the moment we are concerned with improving, I believe we are struggling against the Devil.

According to a Pentecostal in the civil construction workers' union, "Ninety percent of wealth is contributed by the Devil . . . in fraud. All action against society is made by him. Whenever someone sins against God and the nation, that comes from the Devil, fraud, robbery."

The association of the middle class and businesspeople with the Afro-Brazilian spiritist religions has widespread notoriety among the working class. It dovetails with Pentecostals' images of the wealthy as entering into pacts with the Devil. As one Pentecostal in the PT declared, "The great capitalists serve the Devil, they come from *Candomblé*, spiritism, Buddhism, magic."

Perhaps the clearest evocation of this connection came from Murao, the Pentecostal construction workers' leader who is also currently on the board of directors of the PT in Caxias. Though Murao's political stances are clearly heterodox, they are rooted in basic premises of Pentecostal theology. "When I struggle against capitalism," he told me, "I feel that I am struggling against the Devil. I struggle against the capitalist because he is the Devil's partner. I struggle so as not to give in to the Devil. Capitalists don't believe or trust in God. The rich man doesn't need to distribute things; he just has pride."

Murao's reference to "struggle" brings us to the very heart of Pentecostalism as a religion of overcoming adversity. "With *crentes*," he explained, "the struggle against evil is a very large, a very great struggle. The Apostle Paul said, 'Struggle ferociously against the spirit of the Devil.' So our daily life is a struggle." No fatalism or quietism here. Murao continued:

> You achieve some victory only through struggle. Life is a struggle. Our struggle must be tireless, because God is going to judge us. The Bible says, "Do not accept this world." And another part says, "Do not be quiet, because your rest is not here!" So why should we be quiet in front of a situation that enslaves us?

It is possible that Murao's heterodoxy will begin finding adherents among his coreligionists.[23] He is, after all, well situated institutionally in the PT, his union, and his church. If the objective conditions of the Brazilian working class continue to decline at the current rate, Murao may be able to tap into the widespread, deep-seated *crente* rejection of immiseration. Perhaps he will even be able to persuade some Pentecostals that socialism is a precondition for spiritual liberation. For Murao, true liberation means living in a world in which one is free to discover Christ; and this means living in a socialist world. He prophesied,

> Through changes in society, man will be able to improve himself religiously. Improvement comes only through a transformation, whether material or spiritual. Because if you don't have a transformation in your material life, you can't get one in the other. The system doesn't let man liberate himself from things. The corrupt system doesn't let people become *crentes*.

The idea that in Brazil's deepening crisis, Murao's Pentecostal socialist vision might actually catch on is not too farfetched. Though Brazilian Catholics may go only so far politically before breaking with the Church, Pentecostals have no specific political line for their members to toe. *Crentes* are thus freer than progressive Catholics to develop their own thinking. Unrestrained by the official political position of a church, the Pentecostal can maintain religious identity even while becoming radical. If the miraculous signs of salvation that Jesus foretold would "accompany those

who believe," they might include the ability to remake the world.
We have not yet heard the *crentes'* last word.

NOTES

1. Jether Pereira Ramalho, "Algumas notas sobre duas perspecti-
vas de pastoral popular," *Cadernos do ISER* 6 (1977): 31–39; Rubem
Alves, *Protestantismo e repressão* (São Paulo: Ática, 1980); Pedro Ribeiro
de Oliveira, "Comunidade e massa: Desafio da pastoral popular," *Revista eclesiástica brasileira* 44 (1984); Francisco Rolim, "Afinal, o que es-
taria levando as pessoas ao pentecostalismo?" paper delivered at ISER
seminar on religious diversity, ANPOCS, 1987; Judith Hoffnagel, "The
Believers: Pentecostalism in a Brazilian City" (Ph.D. diss., Indiana University, 1978); Beatriz de Souza, "Protestantismo no Brasil," in Cândido
Camargo, ed., *Católicos, protestantes, espíritas* (Petrópolis; Vozes, 1973),
134–54; Gary N. Howe, "Representações religiosas e capitalismo: Uma
'leitura' estrutualista do pentecostalismo no Brasil," *Cadernos do ISER* 6
(1977): 39–48. The writings of Christian Lalive d'Epinay have been influential. He makes this argument sweepingly for all of Latin America in
"Religião, espiritualidade, e sociedade," *Cadernos do ISER* 6 (1977): 5–10,
and in his *The Haven of the Masses* (London: Lutterworth Press, 1969).
For earlier assessments of pentecostalism, see Emilio Willems, *Followers
of the New Faith* (Nashville, Tenn.: Vanderbilt University Press, 1967); and
William Read, *Fermento religioso nas massas do Brasil* (Campinas: Livraria
Crista Unida, 1967). For the changing political backdrop of the study of
Pentecostalism, see Rubem César Fernandes, "O debate entre sociólo-
gos," in " 'Religiões populares': Uma visão parcial da literatura recente,"
Boletim informativo e bibliográfico de ciências sociais 18 (1984): 13–14, and
"Conservador ou progressista: Uma questão de conjuntura," *Religião e
sociedade* 9 (1983).

2. Sandra Stoll, "Púlpito e palanque: Religião e política nas eleições
de 1982 num município da grande São Paulo" (Ph.D. diss., Universidade
Estadual de Campinas, 1986).

3. Cecilia Mariz, "Religion and Coping with Poverty in Brazil" (Ph.D.
diss., Boston University, 1989), 188–89; David Stoll, *Is Latin America
Turning Protestant?* (Berkeley: University of California Press, 1990).

4. Oneide Bobsin, "Produção religiosa e significado social do pentecostalismo a partir de sua prática e representação" (Ph.D. diss., Pontífica
Universidade Católica de São Paulo, 1984); José Francisco Gomes, "Reli-

gião e política: Os pentecostais no Recife" (master's thesis, Universidade Federal de Pernambuco, 1985). Comparable work in Ecuador includes that of Blanca Muratorio. The gap between pastors' and followers' views has been more readily acknowledged in the literature on Pentecostalism in Central America.

5. For a clear exposition of this argument, see especially Rolim's effort to reassess his earlier, more pessimistic position in light of recent research and political developments in Brazil, *Pentecostais no Brasil* (Petrópolis: Vozes, 1985).

6. Regina Novaes, *Os escolhidos de Deus* (Rio de Janeiro: Marco Zero, 1985), 131.

7. For the sake of clarity and consistency, I have limited my analysis to members of the Assembly of God, the largest and most influential Pentecostal church in Brazil. In *Os deuses do povo* (São Paulo: Brasiliense, 1980) Carlos Brandão has argued for a further distinction in the Pentecostal arena between institutionalizing churches, such as the Assembly of God, and smaller, looser groups, such as the House of Blessing, that crystallize around faith healers. The latter, Brandão suggests, tend to encourage greater world rejection than the former. While the distinction is valid, it is important to remain alert to three issues: (1) there is great variation in world rejection as the official orthodoxy of Pentecostal churches, from the most "institutional" to the most "charismatic"; (2) there is much variation in intensity (or "fanaticism") within particular churches; and (3) there is a good deal of mobility between churches.

8. In 1983 the youth group began to publish a newsletter, invite outside speakers to lecture on political topics, and elect its members to the neighborhood association's directorate. The unexpected result was to trigger a mass exodus of young people. "They weren't remembering God," said one young man, "just talking about *ganância* [greed], about money. A youth group should participate in the Church, in the songs, the Mass . . . should help old people and children, should read and reflect on the Bible. They shouldn't worry about getting mailboxes."

9. The neighborhood association has a small following in São Jorge. The style of the leadership is to present petitions to personal contacts in the mayor's office rather than to confront the office with collective demands backed by the threat of withholding votes. The most frequently reelected directors are those with personal links to the prefecture. While such links create access, they also turn the association into a buffer. For example, the neighborhood association promised to deliver a junior high school to São Jorge. So eager was the association to take credit for

the improvement, rather than identify itself as a conduit for pressures coming from town, that when the government reneged on its promise, locals were angrier at the association than at the government.

10. See interview with Chico Silva, *crente* leader of the Núcleo Agricola Fluminense, rural union of Duque de Caxias; also see works on Julião, the *crente* leader of the Peasant Leagues in the 1950s.

11. Critiques of the paternalism at work even in the liberationist wing of the Catholic Church include José Comblin, "Os leigos," *Comunicações do ISER* 26 (July 1987): 26–37; Carlos Brandão, "A partilha da vida," in *Condições . . . Goiás: As pessoas e as famílias* (Goiás: Goiania, 1988); Eduardo Hoornaert, "Os três fatores da nova hegemonia dentro da igreja católica no Brasil," *Revista eclesiástica brasileira* 26 (1986): 371–84; Rowan Ireland, "The Prophecy That Failed," *Listening: Journal of Religion and Culture* 16 (1981): 253–64; Lygia Dabul, "Missão de conscientização: Agentes e camponeses em experiências comunitárias," in Nidia Esterci, ed., *Cooperativismo e coletivização no campo* (Rio de Janeiro: Marco Zero, 1987), 99–136; José Ivo Follman, "O 'ser católico': Diferentes identidades religiosas," *Comunicações do ISER* 26 (1987): 17–25; Affonso Gregory, *CEBs: Utopia ou realidade?* (Petrópolis: Vozes, 1973); Claudio Perani, "Pastoral popular: Serviço ou poder?" *Cadernos do Centro de estudos e ação social* 82 (November/December 1982): 7–19.

12. The presence of *crentes* in the directorate of a neighborhood association does not come without contradictions. In another town, where the federal government named a Kardecist center as an official distribution point for milk, a municipal truck arrived with a hundred liters. When the center tried to deliver the milk to the neighborhood association, the latter's *crente* president refused to accept it, saying it had been tainted by the Devil.

13. In the state-controlled clientelist unions, few workers of any religion participate. In these, there is room only for the *pelegos*, the "saddles" ridden by the managers. On the tensions between clientelist and independent unionism in Brazil, see Celso Frederico, *Consciência operária no Brasil* (São Paulo: Ática, 1979).

14. It was dominated by the Central Única dos Trabalhadores (CUT). This is Brazil's largest national federation of combative unions, standing in contrast with the Central Geral dos Trabalhadores (CGT), associated with *pelego* unions. The CGT supported Fernando Collor de Melo in the last elections and the CUT supported Inácio da Silva (Lula).

15. Hoffnagel, "The Believers"; Souza, "Protestantismo no Brasil"; Ramalho, "Algumas notas"; Alves, *Protestantismo e repressão*; Ribeiro de

Oliveiia, "Comunidade e massa"; Rolim, *Pentecostais no Brasil*; Howe, "Representações religiosas e capitalismo"; Willems, *Followers of the New Faith*; Délcio Monteiro de Lima, *Os demônios descem do norte* (Rio de Janeiro: Francisco Alves, 1986).

16. Instituto Nacional de Previdencia Social, Brazil's federal office of social security.

17. Gomes, "Religião e política," 256.

18. See also Sandra Stoll, "Embú, eleições da 1982," *Comunicações do ISER* 3 (1982), and "Púlpito e palanque," 313–314; Bobsin, "Produção religiosa"; Regina Novaes, "Os crentes e os eleições," *Comunicações do ISER* 3 (1982); G. L. Kliewer, "Assembléia de Deus e eleições num município do interior de Matto Grosso," *Comunicações do ISER* 3 (1982).

19. See, for example, Stoll, "Púlpito e palanque"; Rolim, *Pentecostais no Brasil*, 246; and Mariza de Carvalho Soares, "É permitido distribuir 'santinho' na porta da igreja?" *Comunicações do ISER* 4 (1983): 57; and Paul Freston's article in this volume. A related, still unanalyzed phenomenon was the Assembly of God's official support for Leonel Brizola, a social democrat, against Collor de Melo, a conservative, in the 1989 presidential elections.

20. In this regard, *crentes* were no different from non-*crentes* in their contempt for politicians. See Teresa Pires do Rio Caldeira, *A política dos outros* (São Paulo: Brasiliense, 1984); Alba Zaluar, *A máquina e a revolta* (São Paulo: Brasiliense, 1985). For a history of the foundation of the Worker's Party in the late 1970s and early 1980s, see Isabel Ribeiro de Oliveira, *Trabalho e política: As origens do partido dos trabalhadores* (Petrópolis: Vozes, 1988).

21. See Lygia Dabul et al., *Unidade e prática da fé* (Rio de Janeiro: CEDI, 1987); for analyses of the tensions between cooperativism and small-ownership ideals in the church, see Nidia Esterci, ed., *Cooperativismo e coletivização no campo: Questões sobre a prática da igreja popular* (Rio de Janeiro: Marco Zero, 1984).

22. Michael Taussig has found that the Devil plays an important role in how sugar workers in Colombia diagnose social differentiation. See Taussig's *The Devil and Commodity Fetishism in South America* (Chapel Hill: University of North Carolina Press, 1980). Certainly the Devil, or some refraction of him, is invoked with great frequency throughout the world to account for clearly visible differences in fortune. In Christianity, however, he loses any vestige of moral ambiguity and takes on an absolute quality. The problem then becomes what to do about the Devil: resign oneself to his wiles or take arms in a millennial battle against him?

23. As Roger Lancaster argues occurred among a segment of evangelicals in revolutionary Nicaragua. See Lancaster's *Thanks to God and the Revolution* (New York: Columbia University Press, 1988), 100–26. It may be significant that in studies of the February 1990 electorate (see especially the analyses "Electoral Democracy under International Pressure: The Report of the Latin American Studies Association Commission to Observe the 1990 Nicaraguan Election," LASA, Pittsburgh, Pa., March 15, 1990) the evangelicals *were not* singled out as a distinctive voting bloc.

2

The Crentes of Campo Alegre and the Religious Construction of Brazilian Politics

Rowan Ireland

The Town

CAMPO ALEGRE, my name for a town of twelve thousand on the perimeter of greater Recife, seems an unlikely locus for Brazilian history in the making. For most observers of Brazilian politics and culture, it would seem doubly outrageous to claim that Pentecostal *crentes* in Campo Alegre were debating models of Brazilian political economy, let alone deepening democracy. The prevailing stereotype of Pentecostal *crentes* is that they are apolitical conservatives who leave the injustices of the world to the Lord's care, privatizing public issues and giving implicit support to authoritarian political projects. And the *crentes* of Campo Alegre? What could come out of a peripheral suburb in the peripheral Northeast?[1]

Putting aside stereotypes and such rhetorical questions, I will argue that the *crentes* of Campo Alegre are indeed makers of Brazilian political history, and that their contribution is not altogether what we might expect.

Campo Alegre, like hundreds of towns on the outskirts of the great, exploding cities of Brazil, has always been something of a backwater, its changing demography and the shifting economic fortunes of its inhabitants a product of history made elsewhere. There was a time when the economics of the Northeastern sugar industry gave it a certain socioeconomic coherence, and for its tiny landowning and commercial elite, a degree of prosperity. From the 1890s until the 1940s Campo Alegre was an entrepôt for one of the weaker clusters of plantations in the state of Pernambuco. Roads and railways developed by the state government passed this cluster by, though it was only twenty-five kilometers up the coast from the state capital, Recife. So with a quay on an ocean channel opposite an island with no well-protected harbor of its own, Campo Alegre became the port for a peak number of ten sugar mills on the island. It was also the trading center for up to five more mainland mills that were close to the sea but without easy access to the state capital by road or rail.

During that time, for what now seems to some old-timers a golden age, a Catholic religious brotherhood provided an institutional focus for town life. Dominated first by landowners, then by men of commerce, the governing board was the visible, recognizable elite controlling the amenities of civilization. Above all, a decent Christian burial attended by the berobed brothers was guaranteed and, in case of indigence, paid for by the brotherhood. The benefits of the one true religion were received in the brotherhood chapel, and the board attended to the upkeep of the chapel, paid the visiting priest, and organized the celebration of the great feast days, including the feast of São Gonçalo, the town's patron saint. The brotherhood provided meager charity to the indigent, and its board controlled access to an increasingly scarce resource that might allow the recipient to rise above indigence: patrimonial land.

By midcentury, the local sugar industry was dying, urban transport networks made Recife much more accessible, and Campo Alegre's institutional focus on brotherhood patronage relationships, though still sought by many Campo Alegrenses, was increasingly difficult to maintain. Not only had the elites become more diverse and less locked into Campo Alegre, but the town's population was newer and the range of relationships with the central institution of the town was much more varied than in previous decades. The inner coherence and the outer boundaries of the town were becoming less well defined. By the 1970s, there was no one institution, and certainly not the brotherhood of old, that could integrate the urban diversity that Campo Alegre had become.

The dismantling of a previous coherence (not necessarily a harmonious one) left Campo Alegre a social mélange, a conglomerate of residents divided according to their "different modes of integrating past and present, the local and the cosmopolitan."[2] Although the town's social and economic coherence was being dismantled, the brotherhood and patron-client ties were not obliterated. Instead, alongside them grew up a variety of new ways of being a Campo Alegrense, each juxtaposed and in untidy interaction with the others. Side by side with patronage ties still anchored in the Catholic brotherhood were networks linking many residents to Recife, to urban employment and urban politics of the populist or bureaucratic-authoritarian kinds.[3] Into an increasingly urban world came refugees from a disappearing rural world, bearing the myths and political instincts of the world of rural patronage that Brazilians call *coronelismo*. There were even representatives of a movement for communitarian, participatory democracy that Brazilians call *basismo* and scholars discuss under the heading of liberation theology.

Communitarian politics in Campo Alegre grew out of attempts by the parish priest to engage his parishioners in struggles for justice and peace, drawing on the precepts, strategies, and mythology of liberation theology. But that linkage of religion and politics reflected only one of the affinities between the jostling political orientations and the religions that, by the 1970s, competed in a flourishing market. The priest, as he attempted to build a number of "base communities" among dispossessed farmers and exploited fishermen, had to compete and negotiate not only with various streams of popular Catholicism but also with members of various Afro-Brazilian groups and with *crentes* of the Assembly of God.

Some of his parishioners, though telling themselves and census takers they were Catholics, were clients of Afro-Brazilian spiritist mediums whom they consulted regularly to enlist the power of the spirits for help and protection in daily life. The more powerful mediums gained prestige as they established reciprocal exchanges with local populist politicians. These included financial and other forms of support from the politicians for lavish cult festivals, in return for electoral support and valued advice from the mediums.[4] To the priest, this sort of flourishing spiritism was doubly regrettable. Not only did it encourage "alienated religion" among nominal Catholics but it provided a religious base for patron-client politics of the populist kind—the antithesis of his ideal for a more communitarian Campo Alegre.

In my twelve years of intermittent fieldwork from 1977 to 1989, the priest, agents of the military regime, populist politicians, landowners, and businessmen had to work in and through the religious market to find support and legitimacy for their projects. As I did, they found religiously motivated Campo Alegrenses proclaiming their paradigms for the future and constructing the Brazil that their Lord or their spirits enjoined them to construct.

This constructing of the local and even the national society according to religious paradigms can be seen in the negotiations and conflicts surrounding the annual fiesta of the patron saint. In the 1970s and 1980s the priest, anxious to bring the fiesta under the control of the base communities and other community groups he was fostering, did battle against politicians, local businessmen, and state tourist authorities who wished to promote the fiesta as a commercial attraction. But he also had to do battle with Catholics trying to restore the fiesta to what it was in the golden age of the brotherhood. They had no patience with a priest rejecting the individual and state patronage necessary to make a good fiesta. They would have nothing of his attempt to use the fiesta to rally dispossessed farmers and champion their cause against the landowner and the government authorities supporting him.

The *crentes*, some Baptists but most members of the Assembly of God, were also part of the making of the fiesta—by their absence. Like a growing number of Campo Alegrenses, they did not wish to restore the Catholic traditions of a dismantled town, nor did they want to join the new base communities of the priest, nor were they willing to wheel and deal in local politics. In their absence from the fiesta, *crentes* showed their part in Campo Alegre's dismantling into a social mélange. But *crentes* are underrated if seen only in their undermining of an order constructed by other groups. Focusing on individual *crentes* and their group life shows them, even in their differences with one another, to be active constructors of an emergent Campo Alegre and to have a distinctive voice in the Babel of Brazilian political history in the making.

Some Crentes

Severino, son of an itinerant farm worker, is now in his fifties and has been a municipal street cleaner for more than twenty years. Giving up the struggle to support his growing family on marginal land, he came to Campo Alegre in the mid-1960s for secure if low-paid employment. He had become a *crente* long before, as part of a youthful struggle to acquire literacy. Against the will of his father, he learned to read and write in night school, then started attending the religious services his teacher held following the lessons. Conversion was, as he tells it, "reading, reading, reading, and thinking, thinking, thinking." And the thinking has continued. Though never escaping the poverty of his birth family, his literate Pentecostalism confirmed his declaration of independence from his father's moral world, the world of rural bossism, or *coronelismo*. He makes the point again and again in his stories about becoming literate and finding "the correct and sure path." The unlettered poor person is forced into a miserable life over which he or she has no control—a life in which material welfare has no relation to personal effort; assertions of rights may be counted as offenses; death or madness is the only escape. Learning provides the tools for survival, for some control over destiny, and for the acquisition of doctrine that, against all odds, sustains confidence in law-abiding, self-controlled action.

Because he is so intelligently reflective about his life and his beliefs, Severino allows us to chart a terrain of *crente* views of the world and the emerging politics of *crentes*. Some themes in my long interviews with him in 1977, 1982, and 1989 confirm certain stereotypes about Brazilian Pentecostals. Severino emerges as something of a Holiness enthusiast, for example. He warmly and vividly evokes baptism in the Spirit and the accompanying sense of possession by divinity. He celebrates the immediacy and transcending emotion of possession:

> It's not something that you can pick up; that seeing, you might imitate. Nobody can imitate it, nobody can stop it happening. There you are in a meeting in the church and the Holy Spirit comes and makes you move in such a manner that you appear drunk, that you have a demon, that you're mad. But it's none of those things. It's because when the Spirit of God enters into a man, that man is so deeply moved and so stirred that he becomes like a child and loses comprehension. And though poor people doubt that a man who eats meat and manioc flour can receive the Spirit of God, through Him we are all shown that we can. God was a man, Christ was a man on Earth, and God made that promise to man: that an animal may not receive the Spirit of God but a man may.

Together with his enthusiasm for the Holiness experience, Severino displays the trustful spontaneity of this kind of faith:

> And if we pray to God in the spirit of truth, God is completely with man and will help him conquer in every struggle of day-to-day life, of life itself. And so it often ends up like this. The time of fiesta comes around. One hasn't bought sandals for the children. No one has any clothes. There's nothing. I'm not going to lament the fact that in the state capital there's Sr. Araújo [the owner of a chain of drapery stores] with so many shops while I lack even a small piece of cloth. There's this and that person with an inheritance of so many shops while I've got nothing. Am I going to lament that? No, not at all. I am going to trust that God is the *dono* [owner or giver] of everything. We see something very close to us, right close up, in every corner of the world. Have you ever seen a sparrow with two sets of clothes? No—they've only got one set, all the birds: the parrot, the canary, the *ché-ché*, the rooster . . . God takes care of him every day.

However, Severino shows us that there can be a Puritan side to the Pentecostal versions of the self and the world. Living the faith requires asceticism: "In this life, there's the part of the flesh and the part of the spirit. Many times, when it comes to a conflict, for the spiritual part to be satisfied, the flesh must be denied. You know that the *crente* leads a *vida privada* [a life of self-denial]. He has to deny himself everything. At every moment of temptation he has to *dar a chave* [turn the key on himself] so as to contain desire." The Puritan's moral eye is turned not only on the self but also on politicians, governments, and businessmen. They, too, in Severino's view, are called upon to know God's laws and live by them; and in his relentless judgment, they almost always fail to heed and obey.

The mix of Puritan and Holiness elements is the key to understanding Severino's religious vision. He is never simply one or the other—the Holiness enthusiast, turning away from the world, is drawn back to work on it as the judging, calculating Puritan. Unlike Max Weber's Puritan, however, he is not driven by anxiety about the ultimate goal of salvation, nor is he propelled, taut, wound-up, single-minded in lifelong pursuit of material achievement and success for his soul's sake. Rather, he has the Holiness believer's certainty of salvation, believing that the terms of his spiritual exchange with God are perfectly clear. His only anxiety, in fear of eternal punishment, is that he might not remain impeccably faithful, until the end of his life, to the true doctrine and the true, revealed path. But there is nothing of the Holiness enthusiast's lack of interest in ethical issues.

On the contrary, Severino's religious vision and its attendant anxieties lead to a distinctive profile of ethical concerns. Rejecting important elements of the famous work ethic, he nonetheless has well-considered, and indeed well-practiced, ethics relating to work. He rejects, very explicitly, any equation of wealth with moral stature, and he denies any empirical correlation between hard labor and wealth. Work, to be meritorious, must, like every other area of life, conform to exacting moral laws. God-pleasing work requires that the worker should have defined his responsibilities, publicly conformed to them, and fulfilled them to the letter, even when bosses or colleagues fail to reciprocate. Given the general failure to acknowledge responsibilities and the radical corruption that arises from competitive greed, Severino seems to expect the rich and powerful to be engaged in work that is not pleasing to God. Indeed, without exception, the successful lawyers, military men, police, landowners, politicians, priests, pastors, and businessmen of Severino's stories are engaged in what he judges to be immoral work. They are all bit players in his story of stories, the continuing Fall of the Holiness apocalyptic vision. In that story, the little man, the moral worker, loses land and livelihood to those who are out for a quick profit, and "no one takes care of anyone else" until "Christ comes again."

Judging the world and assessing his responsibilities in it according to his puritan ethics, Severino's practice has also been shaped by the Holiness vision of continuing Fall until the Lord comes. Hence his complex politics. His keen perceptions and moral judgments, often identical to the priest's, seem to draw him to the edge of political radicalism. Reflecting on his own experience and the actions of Campo Alegre's largest landowner, he comments on the destruction of local small-scale production:

> It's disappearing. But people need manioc flour, yams, sweet potatoes, and no one knows who is going to plant these things. Because the rich man wants what? Sugarcane. Or he wants to get the poor off the land to carve it up into expensive lots. It's investment that he's interested in: investment of money to produce interest for himself. And what's the little man, who wants to plant and look after himself while living in town, going to do? Nobody knows. The little man has nothing to eat and nothing to sell now. When he loses his plot, how can he consume? If we had access to the land here where people have just been expelled, we'd produce enough for our own families and to sell to those who work in the aluminum factory. But, as it is, we don't have enough to maintain ourselves or produce for others. So everything comes through CEASA [the central produce market of Recife]. And, more and more, what's sold there comes from down south. We don't have an economy. Everyone gets a cut on the way: so we have to pay for transport, taxes, bank interest. And the people have no possibility of resisting.

That last phrase suggests part of the explanation for Severino's critical social analysis failing to translate into radical political action. He knows from experience that the local and national powers have the will and the capacity to defeat the little man.

When his neighbors ask his advice on how to cope with expulsion from the land, he urges them *não fazer questão* (not to make an issue) with the landowner. He backs his advice with supporting evidence: The landowner is ruthless, prepared to use ex-prisoner *pistoleiros* to shoot protestors; he has the local judiciary and the police in his pocket; and the people have only hoes and knives for defense. Then there are the arguments of God's law and God's history. As a contract-minded Puritan, Severino argues that the landowner has paid for his land and completed the legal formalities of transfer, so he has rights that cannot be negated by any injustices he might perpetrate. God might punish him, but no man has the right to take issue with his ownership and consequent right to dispose of the land as he wishes. Severino's Holiness version of history clinches the argument: "The world is of the powerful. If you have, you're worth something; if you don't have, you're worth nothing. That is the way the world has been since the Fall, and that is how it will be until Christ comes again." Righting the great injustices of the world is God's business, and He will achieve His justice at the end of time. In the meantime, the just man does not presume to act for God.

Yet Severino does act in some local matters, perhaps because of Puritan elements in his Pentecostal approach to the world. On a local level, Severino considers himself obliged to seek justice within the parameters of the law. He does so with the skill of a man with a duty to understand how the world works. His brother, who turned up during one of our interviews, encouraged him to tell the story of his protracted struggle to bring a local police chief to justice for shooting the son of a neighbor, with whom he was quarreling. At some danger to his own life, Severino gathered the facts of the case, lined up witnesses, and took the matter all the way to the headquarters of the Department of Public Security in the capital. In the end, the policeman was fired and forbidden to return to town—a most unusual outcome to such an affair. Severino is well known to his neighbors for the help and competent advice he provides in a crisis. When he sees a personal responsibility in the troubles of a neighbor, Severino acts fearlessly and effectively.

Severino's advice to his neighbors to lie low on the land question is consistent with his belief that the scope for such responsible action is narrowly circumscribed. God calls individuals to
achieve justice in their immediate neighborhood; He does not, in
Severino's view, call for collective action on wider public issues.
Shortly, I will suggest that the case of Manuel da Conceição, the
crente land-rights agitator, shows that these limits are not integral to Pentecostalism. But there is no denying that Pentecostal
politics in Brazil, at least as mapped through Severino, has no
place for mass mobilization for social justice. In many ways, his
tense syncretism of Puritan and Holiness religion produces a
conservative, even authoritarian politics. He believes that human
institutions are completely and incorrigibly fallen, a conviction
reinforced by his moral critique of contemporary institutions. So
it is no surprise that he scorns democracy as practiced in Brazil.
On the struggle for justice in Brazil's political arena, Severino
is epigrammatic: "Where others speak of democracy, I speak of
laxity." It is better to support a military president than a civilian
populist because a strong man is able to force the rich to give to
the poor the few rights they have. Whatever the prevailing political system, the *crente* must abide by the law and work within
the lawful institutions of property and the state, no matter how
personally corrupt the controllers of those institutions might be.
Only in the Kingdom to come, discontinuous in time and space
from the world of human action, will justice be done. In the
meantime, the just man can only prepare himself to be worthy of
that Kingdom, criticizing the powers that be and righting wrongs
in the neighborhood of personal stewardship.

It is worth noting three features of Severino's discourse and
practice. First, he is serious about identifying, discussing, and
occasionally taking considered action to right local wrongs. Second, his attention to local issues has involved him in the creation of what we might call moral community—a moral community apart from but curiously similar to the Catholic priests'
ideal of base communities. Third, Severino's skepticism of all
political ideologies and programs applies not just to democratic

populists but to military authoritarians as well. In the 1970s and 1980s he made his mark in Campo Alegre through verbal subversion of the military's claims to be producing a new and better Brazil. "God is a long way from these people," he said of the military dictatorship. Even when conceding their prowess in achieving order, he publicly disputed their claims of progress.

With these considerations in mind, I would argue that Severino points toward *crente* contributions to the development of communitarian democracy. But other *crentes* in Campo point to other possibilities. Among the *crentes* of Campo Alegre, Severino is a radical Protestant, one of a type I label the "sect *crente*." Although he constantly reads his Bible and talks through his faith, he nonetheless avoids the Assembly of God temple and its services. The pastor has become too much like a priest, Severino protests: No person or institution is to mediate between him and God, no more than any politician or party can represent his moral commitments in the political arena. Severino shares familiar Pentecostal doctrines with the Assembly of God in Campo Alegre: he was converted to the Assembly, and there are members of the Campo Alegre Assembly whom I classify with him as "sect *crentes*." But unlike them, many *crentes* of the Assembly emphasize the absolutes of the Fall and deemphasize both the subtle Puritan critique of the social order and the complex calculations about the requirements of salvation. Instead they seek in the Assembly a place apart, a haven from an utterly corrupt and irredeemable world. Venturing as little as possible from the unambiguous world of the temple, they leave politics to their church and its leaders, resulting in what we can typologize as the "church *crente*."

Valdo exemplifies the "church *crente*." He is a young, skilled factory worker, earning a low wage but able to provide adequate food, housing, and clothing for his family. Still, he and his extended family are not without problems in what they refer to as "the material life." Valdo is frequently ill. He was nearly killed in a factory accident and has never fully recovered. He did not receive compensation from the factory, though friends and relatives say he was entitled to it. He decided not to "make an issue" of the injury, stressing instead the blessing of his regular wage. He is more preoccupied with the problems of his extended family: his brother-in-law, chronically unemployed and with a pregnant wife, and his aging parents, facing expulsion from the farm they have worked all their lives.

Valdo considers these private troubles, certainly not to be discussed as public issues. Like many *crentes*, he frequently refers to life as a passing trial in which we are, above all, required to remain faithful to the terms of salvation won for us by Jesus Christ against the powers of darkness. Only within the limits of that vision—of Jesus offering and requiring, and Satan tempting and undoing—will Valdo refer to his troubles. Troubles take on importance only as trials in the cosmic struggle, with their meaning to be found in doctrine and biblical text.

To the evils of the everyday world Valdo contrasts the community of church life, finding in its discipline the only way to lead the life that God requires. For Valdo and his family (except for his father, a bitterly disillusioned brotherhood Catholic), that means deep involvement in the Assembly of God. To make an issue out of some personally experienced injustice (or, most senselessly, a political issue) is to breach the boundaries between church and world, entering Satan's territory.

Within Valdo's view of the world, his politics is a politics of rejection—of his father's old politics of brotherhood patronage, and of the blandishments of latter-day populist politicians. In interviews in the 1970s and 1980s, I could not persuade him to assess the military regime. However, he was very free in his criticism of participatory democracy. Valdo made it clear that he would approve of any government that cracked down on brothels, dance halls, and the sale of alcoholic beverages. Unlike Severino and the "sect *crentes*," Valdo's moral preoccupations lead him not out into his neighborhood to create moral community but back into the secure defenses of his church. The importance of this difference emerges more clearly when we look at Pentecostals assembled.

Crente *Collective Life*

A bus and several cars have brought *crentes* from Campo Alegre
to the central regional temple in a town between Campo Alegre
and Recife. They are to attend a special service, led by Pastor
Moisés of the central temple, that will celebrate the end of a
week of study in which pastors, evangelists, deacons, and senior
members of congregations from all over the region have taken
part. Officials of the church are seated together in a large ele-
vated area around the preacher's platform or tribune. They are
joined by about twenty dignitaries, including town councilors,
a couple of military officers, and the manager of a large new
factory. About a third of the congregation has some role in the
service. These include a choir of sixty from one town; a blue-
uniformed male band from another; and a female band from the
home church, each of whose thirty members is wearing a white
dress and jacket over a golden blouse.

Pastor Moisés calls on the pastors of each temple to give
testimony to the growth and achievements of the Assembly in
their area. Then he preaches, ranging his voice from whispered
assurances to shouts of exhortation and triumph. The "church
triumphant" theme dominates. Pastor Moisés takes off from a
hymn, sung by a special choir, about the Brazilian founding of
the Assembly in the city of Belém in 1919. He points to his very
aged mother, sitting with the dignitaries, as the link with that
beginning. And he recounts the story of the church's growth
in the region. Groans of anguish accompany his images of the
tribulations of the Assemblies—*crentes* dismissed from jobs because they admitted their faith; priests and politicians preventing
the establishment of temples. But then the times to be greeted
with alleluias—over twelve thousand members of the Assembly, baptized and with certificates; a regional Assembly school;
new temples in towns where the Catholics have had to close
their church—"Alleluia! Alleluia!" During the final exhortation,
a young woman and two children answer the call to surrender to
Christ, assuring the congregation of future triumph.

Not all the Sunday evening services in the Campo Alegre

temple are as dramatic, inspiring, or rewarding as this special regional service. Sometimes the routine program—initial hymns and welcomes, readings from the Bible, collective prayer, six to ten individual testimonies interspersed with hymns from the choirs, the final sermon and appeal for converts—seems to leave the congregation flat. But, on the evidence of responses of the moment and recollection days later, many of the services indeed move, motivate, and confirm. For regularly attending *crentes* like Valdo, the service legitimates that church world apart where the *crente* is filled with God's power and purpose. For him, the regional service was a demonstration of God leading his people to victory over "the forces of darkness and chaos." The church triumphant and the testimonies to God's miracles of salvation demonstrate the power of God.

Other *crentes* in Campo Alegre express unease with some of the features of the services that so impress Valdo. The size and formality of the temple bother them. Unlike Severino, they tolerate being preached at and endure the noise of bands. But they value two other *crente* rituals more highly than the Sunday service or the Sunday school classes. These are the closed-door prayer meeting and the house meeting. In the closed-door prayer meeting, the world is literally shut out: the windows of the temple are closed, the main door locked. Baptized *crentes* in good standing—fewer than for Sunday services—gather together to pray as the Spirit moves them. The meeting starts and finishes at an appointed time, and though, from the outside, the sounds of inspired prayer may appear the antithesis of the schooled harmonies of the Sunday service choirs, there is a framework of decorum achieved by the group, without pastoral direction. The platform at the front of the temple is empty; the faithful kneel, resting on the benches with their backs to the platform. As *crentes* who love these meetings point out, the Spirit chooses to speak most frequently and eloquently through the humblest members of the group as they prophesy. Leadership passes to whoever is most eloquent in the tongues of the Spirit.

The humblest may also lead in the house meeting or *congregação*. On most nights of the week in one or another of the neighborhoods of Campo Alegre, a small group of *crentes* gather in a private house to sing hymns, read passages of the Bible, and give testimony. In many ways the *congregação* meetings are like the Sunday services writ small, but they are also special as meetings of neighbors in a neighborhood house. Before the temple was built, this was how the *crentes* assembled, as it was when Severino and many others joined in a more rural world. As one recalled, here the ordinary *crente* can feel at home, confident that the Father is choosing to speak to the simple, "hiding these things from the learned and clever and revealing them to mere children" (Matthew 11:25).

In the *congregação,* and even more in the closed-door prayer meeting, teaching is inspirational rather than propositional: leadership passes from the institutionally designated pastor to inspired prophets of the moment. The spontaneity of the Spirit rather than ecclesiastical organization is manifest and glorified; signs of charisma distinguish a brother or a sister rather than his or her position in the formal structure. Severino distrusts the Assembly as a church, but he remembers the Assembly as sect with affection.

The Emergent Politics of
Campo Alegre Crentes

Two rather different Pentecostal versions of the world are beginning to emerge from this brief introduction to some *crentes* and their collective religious life in Campo Alegre. The church *crente* returns home from the Sunday service reminded of human weakness and the moral perils of everyday life in Satan's world. But the service has also offered consolation: It has demonstrated that though God tests, He also loves and saves and allows triumph over adversity to those who brave the tests and assemble regularly in the safety of the church. So the church *crente* resolves to accept the tests of sickness, or inadequate return from long hours of work, or loss of land—sure in the belief that God not only records the struggle of the faithful in the Book of Life but also allows victory over sin and suffering in the victories of the church. The organized church itself, then, provides the means for the poor *crente* to negotiate the structures of unequal wealth, power, and expertise without becoming tainted by the things of this world.

The church *crente* accepts the idea that social change for the benefit of the *crente* poor may come from the top down, through the elites with whom church leaders have worked to achieve the marvelous growth of the Assemblies. Although the ordinary church *crente* of Campo Alegre feels neither called upon nor competent to engage in legitimate politics, she or he will be confident that leading *crentes* are entering into alliances with legitimate power as they struggle to advance the church. And they do. Both Pastor Moisés and the pastor of Campo Alegre are active and influential in the PDS, the party that grew out of the pro-government ARENA Party under military rule. Indeed, Campo Alegre's pastor has joined the local elite, the network maintained by the landowner who, over the priest's ineffective protests, expelled ninety sharecropping families from his properties surrounding the town.

The sect *crente* exemplified by Severino is at the very least suspicious of such alliances. More generally, he or she lives a Pentecostal Christianity with very different political affinities. The sect *crente* acknowledges the dangers of the world and the need for a world apart just as much as the church *crente*. But that world apart is not equated with the organized church. In some ways, the sect *crente* is even more confident than the church *crente* of the miracles that God's power can achieve in individual believers. To the sectarian, a church that assumes a hierarchy of set human functions rather than a hierarchy of God's inspiration is just as liable to corruption as any other human organization. The *crente* may receive inspiration and power in the Assembly, especially in closed prayer or congregation meetings, but is ultimately alone with the problems sent to test him or her.

To the sect *crente*, responsibility must not be diluted by handing over the issue to a church or a parachurch body like a human rights office. Moreover, since churches are liable to corruption, they cannot negotiate on the individual *crente*'s behalf the problems that unjust political or economic structures present. When personal moral scrutiny reveals another's wrongdoing as the cause of one's own or one's neighbor's troubles, then action may or must be taken, whatever the status of the wrongdoer. Others who share both problem and motivation may be enlisted as allies. But action should not be taken for the sake of making an issue, to right what only God can right, or to jeopardize defenses against Satan.

Despite these provisos, the sect *crente* is clearly much further from compliant citizenship in bureaucratic-authoritarian Brazil than the church *crente*. Indeed, without an exalted church serving as a model for sanctifying structures of expertise or wealth or power, the sect *crente* is skeptical of all regimes. If the generals and their local agents can expect only a cool reception for their claims to legitimacy, populists and the bosses of *coronelismo* receive even harsher rejection. In fact, rare individual cases in Campo Alegre suggest that sect *crentes* share a common political dialect with Catholic communalists. Near the end of my stay in 1982 (too late to do further interviewing, unfortunately), I discovered that two Assembly of God *crentes* were the staunchest allies of the Catholic woman who had been trying to organize an invasion to regain the land taken over by the landowner. Just as she was departing from the prudential advice of her priest, they were defying the politics of their pastor.

The typing of Campo Alegre *crentes* in terms of sect or church has its failings like any typology. Among other shortcomings, it glosses over the continuous negotiation between different *crente* versions of the world, as well as with non-*crente* discourses in Campo Alegre. What is distinctive about *crentes* in the cultural mélange of Campo Alegre is clearly not one settled political ideology or style, nor a uniform religiosity, nor even a simple dialogue between two different religious and political tendencies. What is distinctive is a repertoire of myth, symbol, doctrine, and practice. The *crentes* of the Assembly of God are a cultural and political presence in Campo Alegre as they debate their repertoire within themselves, between themselves, and with non-*crente* neighbors.

The repertoire itself sets boundaries to the scope and radicalism of *crentes'* political action. It does not include myths and symbols that might rally the faithful as a collectivity for social transformation in the name of a this-worldly utopia. Even Severino's moral critique of injustice is a long way from the messianic enthusiasm for the cause of liberty of eighteenth-century New England clergy: there is no place for a city upon a hill, to be constructed and defended by God's faithful. Nor is there a basis upon which the battle for religious liberty, as celebrated by Pastor Moisés, might be extended into a struggle for a new social order along the lines of the priest's communitarian dreams.

Still, a politics of local resistance can emerge from the dialectic between *crente* repertoire and everyday experience. A fervent moralism, a conviction that God punishes the unjust in this world as well as in the next, and Old Testament images of a people struggling against injustice motivate some sect *crentes* to denounce and resist the unjust patron or the compromised bureaucrat. Among *crentes* who do not submerge their citizenship in the conservative opportunism of the Assemblies of God, Pentecostal images of God's power and the corruptibility of human institutions prompt rejection of the hegemonic claims of bureaucratic-authoritarian Brazil. The same images arm them against the blandishments of populist politicians and set limits to mobilization for any supralocal cause. The socially critical moralism of Pentecostalism and the religious enthusiasm that, among sect *crentes*, impels it into the political arena may be diverted and diffused by a local pastor, intent on the politics of church; but in Campo Alegre, at any rate, that diversion is not a foregone conclusion.

Conclusions

Crentes went their different ways on the hottest local issue of the 1970s and 1980s, the expulsion of ninety sharecropping families from lands around the town. Severino urged his neighbors not to make an issue. The pastor threw his support behind the landowner. A few members of the Assembly, defying their pastor and disregarding Severino, joined the group preparing the most radical resistance to the landowner. Each of these much-debated positions was defined and defended with ethics and images from the Pentecostal repertoire.

By engaging in their distinctive dialectic of myth, belief, and experience, *crentes* have affected the wider fortunes of the political economies that jostle for dominance in Campo Alegre as in other Brazilian towns. Most often, the dialectic has led toward the church *crente* tendency. When believers in Campo Alegre order their lives in terms of church, they enter into social formations that link the poor and relatively powerless to agents and actors of the ruling classes in an authoritarian, nonnegotiable mode. The increasing number of church *crentes* in Campo Alegre has threatened not only the popular Catholic dream of *coronelismo* but also the priest's utopia of Campo Alegre as a community of Catholic base communities. Through their pastors' alliances, church *crentes* have become a safe constituency for local and national bureaucratic-authoritarian projects.

On the other hand, those who ordered their lives as sect *crentes* tended to join citizens acting on local issues independently of local power brokers. Around Severino and a few others whom I consider sect *crentes* there were signs of those moral communities the priest strove to establish, but they were beyond his influence and control. The citizens in such communities were, like Severino himself, prudent and anything but political revolutionaries. Nevertheless, they mounted an influential critique of the *coronelismo* of the past and of bureaucratic-authoritarian pretensions for the future. Arguably, moral communities of the sort they were forming are essential to any deepening of Brazilian democracy.[5]

If this line of interpretation is correct, the opening claim that the *crentes* of Campo Alegre are involved in the religious construction of Brazilian politics becomes plausible. But my second claim at the outset of this article, that the contribution of *crentes* does not accord with stereotypes of Pentecostal politics, is less secure. Those of the church type have opted to confirm the stereotype, and numerically they are easily the predominant group among Campo Alegre's believers. The small minority of sect *crentes* has chosen differently within the repertoire, but none has emerged fighting the powers of this world quite like the legendary Manuel da Conceição.

The published autobiography of Manuel has tempted some of us to strong revisionist views about *crente* politics.[6] Starting with very local resistance to a landowner in rural Maranhão, in the 1970s Manuel became an agitator and political outlaw known throughout the Northeast of Brazil. In his own telling, every step in his increasing radicalism was informed by a *crente* version of the world very close to Severino's. Expelled by anxious officials of the Assemblies of God, he continued to protest his *crente* vision and commitment.

To date, Campo Alegre *crentes* have displayed a much milder radicalism. One can imagine Severino, like Manuel, engaged in a spiral of struggle such that his Holiness vision of continuing Fall is gradually overshadowed by the imperative Puritan quest for justice. This would be the imagination at work, informed by the cases of Manuel and of others brought to our attention by Regina Reyes Novaes,[7] not by the *crentes* of Campo Alegre. They take us only as far as the moral communities of neighbors that *crentes* have helped to build, moral communities that struggle to right small wrongs in anticipation of the Lord who alone achieves Justice. But that is already well beyond the stereotype of the conservative, otherworldly Pentecostal.

NOTES

1. These questions and others raised in this paper are addressed more fully in Rowan Ireland, *Kingdoms Come: Religion and Politics in Brazil* (Pittsburgh: University of Pittsburgh Press, 1991).

2. The notion of social mélange is borrowed from Clifford Geertz; the quotation is from his *The Social History of an Indonesian Town* (Cambridge, Mass.: MIT Press, 1965), p. 10.

3. The best account of Brazilian populism as political system and style is found in Michael L. Conniff, *Urban Politics in Brazil: The Rise of Populism, 1925–1945* (Pittsburgh: University of Pittsburgh Press, 1981). I use the term "populism" to refer to two things. First, urban-based

patron-client politics in which a political leader bestows state patronage through an organized network to those at the urban grass roots prepared to pledge him their vote. Second, I use it to refer to a political culture in which the heroes are great populist politicians of the past like Getúlio Vargas, and the stories of hope tell of the lowly job seeker landing a job or obtaining health care through an attentive politician or a benevolent institution in such a politician's keep.

Similarly, "bureaucratic-authoritarian politics" refers not only to the politics of Brazil's military dictatorship (1964–86) but also to a political culture in which the heroes are generals and civilian experts in high office who get things done for the people without the hoopla and corruption of democratic politics. The story of hope in this political culture is that in return for hard work and the acceptance of necessary disciplines, these heroes will make Brazil a better place for the poor.

4. In chapter 5 of *Kingdoms Come*, I show that there is another form of spiritism, unrecognized by the priest, that is much more compatible with his ideals. A similar contrast between two types of spiritism at the grass roots is found in Carlos Rodrigues Brandão, *Os deuses do povo* (São Paulo: Brasiliense, 1980). Diana Brown, *Umbanda: Religion and Politics in Brazil* (Ann Arbor, Mich.: UMI Research Press, 1986), discusses cases in which the role of *Umbanda* in urban patronage politics emerges very clearly.

5. I have argued along these lines in *Kingdoms Come*, ch. 8.

6. See Manuel da Conceição, *Essa terra é nossa: Depoimento sobre a vida e as lutas de camponeses no estado do Maranhão* (Petrópolis: Vozes, 1980). I am dissenting here from the interpretation of Francisco Cartaxo Rolim, one of the foremost scholars of Brazilian Pentecostals. Rolim sees Manuel as moving away from his Pentecostalism as he becomes more and more politically radical—F. C. Rolim, "Igrejas pentecostais," *Revista eclesiástica brasileira* 42 (1982): 29–59. I see him constantly moved and motivated by his faith.

7. Regina C. Reyes Novaes, "Os escolhidos: Doutrina religiosa e prática social" (Rio de Janeiro: Museu Nacional, 1979) (mimeograph).

3

Brother Votes for Brother: The New Politics of Protestantism in Brazil

Paul Freston

A New Heartland of Protestant Politics

SCENE 1: *A Pentecostal Meeting with a Difference*

Billboards announcing an "evangelical musical" in the Brazilian city of Campinas would not normally interest me. But it is election year, when nothing happens by chance. Further perusal confirms my suspicions: "Sponsors: Luna for federal deputy and Almino for governor." On the advertised date, the gymnasium is packed with members of the Assemblies of God. As I arrive, the candidate for governor follows the Pentecostal candidate for deputy to the podium. A typical speech by a non-Protestant chasing Protestant votes: he claims to be religious, lauds the work of "believers," and trips up on evangelical jargon. But not to worry; at his side is an elderly pastor who accompanies him with dramatic gestures that encourage the faithful to punctuate his speech with the traditional "Alleluias" and "Amens." As the candidate leaves, the elderly pastor preaches a short sermon and the music group begins to play. Strong rhythm, deafening volume, the young people clapping and swaying. What is all this? It is a Pentecostal political rally—unthinkable a few years back, and enough to make many a Pentecostal pioneer turn in his grave.

*I*T ALL STARTED with the 1986 elections for a Constituent Assembly to rewrite Brazil's constitution after twenty-one years of military rule. The thirty-three *evangélicos* (as all Protestants are usually called) elected took everyone by surprise, not only by their number but also by their denominational affiliation and political style. Journalists and social scientists began to make comparisons with the United States (and, in truth, the scandal that erupted in 1988 can be compared with that of the American television evangelists shortly before). But the real international significance was different. Brazil had become a pioneer: the first traditionally Catholic country in the world with a large Protestant electoral and parliamentary presence.[1] The breach that Protestants made in the Catholic religious monopoly in the nineteenth century had now become a threat to Catholic hegemony. Brazil does not have the largest percentage of Protestants in its population (a reasonable estimate is 13 percent, far smaller than in countries like Guatemala). But its total population is so huge that fully half of Latin America's forty million Protestants live there. Not a sufficient reason, but certainly sufficient temptation, to dream political dreams.

Soon, others were dreaming, too. In Peru, in 1990, the non-Protestant dark horse Alberto Fujimori drew the *evangélicos* into his campaign to such an extent that they were largely responsible for swinging the presidential election. On Fujimori's coattails, Protestants elected from among their own number the second vice president, four senators, and fifteen deputies. Months later, Jorge Serrano of Guatemala became the first active Protestant to be elected president of a Latin American nation. Stirrings elsewhere suggest that Brazil, Guatemala, and Peru are just the tip of the iceberg. The focus of militant Protestant politics is undergoing a momentous shift, from its previous centers in the English- and Dutch-speaking worlds to a new heartland in Latin America. This chapter will give an overview of the Brazilian case, concentrating on participation in electoral politics at the national level.

Protestants' comparative absence from Brazilian politics before 1986 had certainly not been due to a recent arrival on the scene. The first churches using the Portuguese language date from the 1850s. Congregational and Presbyterian missionaries were soon followed by Baptists and Methodists. Separation of church and state in 1890 facilitated Protestant insertion into national life. Brazil was almost the only Latin American country where Protestantism enjoyed some early success: in the 1910s, roughly 75 percent of the region's Protestants lived there. In that same decade the Pentecostals arrived. They differed theologically from the "historical" churches by their emphasis on the Holy Spirit, especially in speaking in tongues, and differed sociologically by their concentration among the poor.[2]

The history of Brazilian Pentecostalism can be divided into three waves: the 1910s, the 1950s and early 1960s, and the late 1970s and 1980s. Representing the first wave, the Christian Congregation (1910) still maintains a severely apolitical stance consistent with its rigid church/world dualism that goes so far as to reject all forms of mass media. The largest Pentecostal church, the Assemblies of God (1911), was brought by Swedish missionaries. The church now has about seven million members, an impressive geographical distribution (an important factor in its current predominance among Protestant congressmen), and a multifocal caudillo-style oligarchy. After long years of general apoliticism tempered by vote-trading with non-Pentecostal candidates, the time-honored slogan "believers don't mess with politics" was changed in 1986 to "brother votes for brother," with impressive results.

During the second wave, which began in the 1950s, Brazilian Pentecostalism fragmented. The first group founded by a Brazilian appeared in 1955 and, in tune with the nationalistic spirit of the age, was named Brazil for Christ. Its charismatic leader, Manoel de Mello, having outgrown his staid origins in the Assemblies of God and his brief link with the American faith healers of the National Evangelization Crusade, innovated by using the mass media and secular locales for religious rallies (stadiums, gymnasiums, cinemas), as well as adopting ecumenical affiliations and direct political involvement. In 1962, Brazil for Christ elected one of its leaders, a young former Methodist of middle-class origin, to the federal Congress. This initiative, repeated in 1966, remained unimitated by other Pentecostal groups until 1986. Even within Brazil for Christ the momentum was lost as Mello's personalistic leadership was replaced by a more bureaucratic hierarchy imbued with the traditional Pentecostal taboo on political participation.

Another major denomination in this second wave of Brazilian Pentecostalism is the Church of the Four-Square Gospel (1951), the denominational solidification of the National Evangelization Crusade. Of Californian provenance, its presidency remained in American hands until 1988, which was one factor in its apolitical posture. However, its impressive numerical growth by the 1980s, concentrated in the south-central states, contributed to a series of changes, including independence from American headquarters, the opening of a publishing house, and the 1986 decision to run its own candidates, chosen by the pastors in denominational primaries, in the election for the Constituent Assembly.

A third large church dating from this period is God Is Love (1962). Founded in São Paulo by Davi Miranda, a southerner with a minimal education but by no means of poverty-stricken origin, it has steadily accentuated its personalistic, miracle-working, and sectarian characteristics (officials said Miranda would not be able to give me an interview because he was "separated for the work of God"). Appealing to the very poor and offering an extremely rigid legalistic formula for redeemed life, God Is Love has steered clear of political involvement, to the point of denying support to Miranda's own sister, a member of Brazil for Christ, when she was a candidate for state deputy in 1990.

The third wave of Brazilian Pentecostalism began in the late 1970s and came to prominence in the 1980s. Its main representative is the Universal Church of the Kingdom of God, which probably has around eight hundred thousand adherents and a very uneven geographical distribution concentrated in Rio. This church is famous for its exorcisms and aggressive fund-raising, its packed rallies in the enormous Maracanã stadium in Rio and its purchase in 1989, for U.S. $45 million, of the fifth-largest television network in Brazil. It is an innovative updating of the range of Pentecostal theological, liturgical, ethical, and aesthetic possibilities, making it a fascinating counterpoint to the Assemblies of God and Brazil for Christ, the star attractions of the previous two waves.

If the emphasis of the Assemblies was on baptism in the Holy Spirit as certified by speaking in tongues, and that of Brazil for Christ was on healing, the Universal Church of the Kingdom of

God has stressed exorcism from demon possession, especially in relation to attendance at spiritist cults such as *umbanda*, as well as bondage to vices such as taking drugs. It also stresses rapid prosperity as the result of a real work of God in one's life. In contrast with the rather traditional ethic of the Assemblies, a long, disciplined haul to modest petty-bourgeois respectability, the Universal Church offers a moralized version of the yuppie gambling ethic, an overnight flight to rapid enrichment. It is significant that the Universal Church flourished in the 1980s, a time of unrelieved recession in Brazil, when the work ethic became less plausible than it had been when the economy was growing in the 1970s. It is also noteworthy that the Universal Church started and mushroomed in Rio de Janeiro, the economically decadent former capital where illegal gambling flourishes. If Brazil for Christ, spearhead of the second wave of Pentecostalism, was a São Paulo–based church founded by a poor migrant of low cultural level from the impoverished Northeast, the third wave consists of Rio-based churches founded by home-grown products of a slightly higher cultural level and whiter skin. Bishop Edir Macedo, the key figure in the Universal Church, is not in the same mold as Manoel de Mello or Davi Miranda of a generation before. His model of leadership is more entrepreneurial, and he is more capable of attracting young people of ability and ambition. Control is maintained by frequent transfers of pastors to prevent congregations from developing personal loyalties.

This is just one of the ways the Universal Church is attuned to urban Brazilian culture. It may be peripheral consumer capitalism's most definitive answer yet to the Methodism of the industrial revolution, diving straight into postmodern oral and sensory culture without passing through the Assemblies' attempt to work through the written word. Yet the secret of its success is perhaps that this bridge to modern Brazil is allied to remarkable continuity with traditional popular religiosity. This shows itself in many ways, but most significantly in its relative nonsectarianism. The very name of the Universal Church reflects the trend to worldwide economic integration, so distant from the nationalism of Brazil for Christ.[3] Unlike preceding Pentecostal groups, the Universal Church does not use a behavioral subculture and dress code as gatekeepers. As a result, one sees a range of social types at its services that would be unthinkable in the Assemblies of God. In keeping with a church rather than a sect model (in sociology of religion terms), the Universal Church works with the concept of layers. At the lowest level, it offers religious services in an undemanding way to a fluctuating clientele. One step up, there are members, but still without the legalistic expectations that characterize all other forms of Pentecostalism in Brazil. For "workers" (the numerous unpaid helpers who perform a variety of tasks at the services, from ushering people in to casting demons out) there are stiffer standards, though still left more implicit than in other churches. Finally, for paid pastors, expectations are conventionally strict.

The Universal Church of the Kingdom of God has been under considerable fire from the national media, initially for its exorcisms and fund-raising practices, later over the source of the money to purchase the television network. There are police investigations under way, ranging from tax evasion to involvement with Colombian drug dealers. The need for the church to defend itself is the reason given by all three of its federal deputies for their presence in Congress. The three were elected in 1990, together with state deputies in Rio, São Paulo, and Bahia, in a remarkable display of planning and esprit de corps. The churches in the state of Rio, for example, were divided up by computer, to guarantee the distribution of votes needed to elect two federal deputies. This they achieved comfortably. One of them was living in São Paulo and hardly set foot in Rio before the election, so efficient were the pastors in putting the vote together. The Universal Church shows a frankly pragmatic relation to politics, characteristic of a business empire expanding on many fronts. Apart from the police inquiries, there is a good chance the church will lose its TV network if the government refuses to authorize the transfer of the concession.[4] Political firepower is therefore essential for its daring entry into hitherto uncharted waters for non-Catholic religious groups.

A Protestant Caucus in the
Constituent Assembly

SCENE 2: *A Question of Balance*

I am at the airport on my way to Brasília to talk to Protestant congressmen. In the waiting room, whom should I spy but one of my targets? Introducing myself, I explain my intention to interview his colleagues in Brasília. Suddenly he pulls me up short with the remark, "Well, I think you're going to be disappointed." "Why?" I ask, stroking my beard in puzzlement. "Because there you won't find any bearded radicals," he replies. "Only balanced evangélicos, *of the center!"*

So far, we have talked mainly about the Pentecostals, going into some detail with regard to the organization and ethos of the main groups. This is partly because the confusing and less well-known Pentecostal world needs more introduction than do the historical Protestant churches originating in Europe or the United States. Moreover, tight sectarian organization means that political involvement will tend to be as blocs, requiring a certain understanding of the church's internal situation. However, no more than 60 or 65 percent of Brazilian Protestants are Pentecostal. Until very recently, the historical (i.e., non-Pentecostal) denominations were predominant numerically and more influential socially. Members of these churches made up the bulk of the modest Protestant parliamentary presence before 1986.

The Constituent Assembly of 1934, the first Brazilian Parliament elected by secret ballot (practically a sine qua non for Protestants to get anywhere politically at the time), had one Protestant member, a leading Methodist minister from São Paulo. His victory was due to the worries of the historical Protestant churches over growing Catholic influence in the government. The same Methodist was again the only Protestant representative in the Constituent Assembly of 1946 that restored democracy after the Vargas dictatorship. From 1950 to 1986, the number of federal deputies rose slowly, then oscillated between eight and fourteen. They were Presbyterians, Methodists, Congregationalists, and Baptists; some elected largely on a Protestant vote,

TABLE 3-1
Protestant Representation in the Chamber of Deputies

	Deputies from Historical Churches	Deputies from Pentecostal Churches	Total
Quantity during 1983–1986	12	2	14
Quantity during 1987–1990	15	18	33
Percent increase	25%	800%	135%

others less so; some enjoying the personal support of denominational leaders, others not; but all of them were candidates in their own name, without official endorsement from their own or any other church. Their parliamentary presence was discreet. In the executive sphere, a Presbyterian was nominated governor of a state in 1966 (the military regime had prohibited elections for governorships). In 1982, the first Protestant was elected to a governorship by popular vote. Meanwhile, Pentecostals were almost totally absent from the scene. There was no successor to the lone federal deputy (1962–1970) from Brazil for Christ until 1982. The two then elected were local initiatives, one from the Assemblies and one from the Four-Square, presaging later developments.

The picture alters abruptly with the 1986 election of a Senate and Chamber of Deputies that would function jointly in 1987–1988 as a Constituent Assembly. (See Table 3-1.)

At one fell swoop, the Pentecostals overtook the historicals and began to mirror their numerical predominance in the Protestant churches. (See Table 3-2.)

The Assemblies of God and the Baptists stand out, but with an important difference. The Baptists are the largest of the historical churches, but their seven congressmen were the result of spontaneous, uncoordinated campaigns. The Assemblies' representation, on the other hand, reflects a top-level decision. In April 1985, their leaders held an extraordinary meeting and agreed to elect a representative to the Constituent Assembly from each state, where possible one of their own members. The effort was so successful that in twelve states the Assemblies elected

TABLE 3-2
Protestant Churches Represented in the Constituent Assembly

Church	Number of Deputies
Pentecostal Churches	
Assemblies of God⁻	13
Four-Square Gospel	2
Church of Christ	1
Universal Church of the Kingdom of God	1
National Baptist Convention	1
Historical Churches	
Brazilian Baptist Convention	7
Presbyterian Church of Brazil	2
Independent Presbyterian	1
United Presbyterian	1
Christian Reformed	1
Congregational	1
Christian Evangelical	1
Adventist	1

their own people. The single state where they elected two representatives is the exception that proves the rule: The second deputy was Workers' Party candidate Benedita da Silva, whose campaign slogan of "woman, black and shanty-dweller" was not designed to appeal specifically to the church vote. Unlike her twelve colleagues from the Assemblies of God, she did not have (or need) the support of the church's state convention.

When we remember that the Assemblies are eighty years old and do not revolve around a charismatic figure, their political discipline is impressive. In part, this is due to their growing institutionalization: in the years preceding 1986, the General Convention had been restructured on a bureaucratic model and encouraged the previously inchoate state conventions to do likewise. Such developments were probably indispensable to the concerted effort that the national leadership undertook in 1986, inspired by the mystique of a constituent assembly that would, as they saw it, rewrite the country from scratch. In the absence of a unified personalistic leadership, this sort of structuring is essential for corporative political action. But it has to overlap temporally with the "totalitarianism" of the sect, that is, the capacity to control large areas of members' lives, including the ability of pastors to tell their flock how to vote, and a sufficiently strong church/world cleavage to prevail over competing political influences from outside. This is precisely what the bureaucratically structured historical denominations lack.

Table 3-3 shows that the Protestant members of the Constituent Assembly were relatively inexperienced as legislators or public administrators. This undoubtedly contributed to the negative public image they soon acquired. But we must distinguish between historicals and Pentecostals. The former were relatively experienced; it was the latter who were arriving at the federal level without political apprenticeship.

Although less experienced than their colleagues, the Pentecostals were not younger. The archetype of the new wave of Protestant politicians was a member of the Assemblies of God in his forties, inexperienced in parliamentary life at any level. This reflects the situation of ecclesiastically approved candidacies, for which it is necessary to have reached a certain age. The Assemblies have an apprenticeship ladder consisting of a long, slow series of promotions up to the pastorate, which is a strong means

TABLE 3-3
Political Experience of Federal Deputies Elected in 1986

	All Deputies	All Protestants	Historicals	Pentecostals
Never previously candidate for federal deputy	54%	57%	46%	66%
First legislative mandate at any level	30	39	20	55
Previous administrative posts (positions of trust) at municipal, state, or federal level	51	42	66	22

Source: Figures for "All Deputies" from Leôncio Martins Rodrigues, *Quem é quem na Constituinte* (São Paulo: OESP/Maltese, 1987), pp. 54, 55, 57, 62.

of social control in the hands of the rather elderly top rung. Only to a limited degree is the alternative route of a seminary education, leading to a pastorate in one's early twenties, now catching on. If this route became more widespread, the signs are that it would have a considerable effect on Assemblies politics, since it would encourage the emergence of a critical young clergy with a more sophisticated political theology. For the time being, the resistance of the Swedish founding fathers to anything more than on-the-job training for pastors in occasional short courses will inhibit this.[5]

The Pentecostal entry into politics in Brazil cannot be said, thus far at any rate, to offer a new route of political mobility for the ordinary poor believer. Instead, it is for men who have already stood out in church work and become paid or unpaid pastors, evangelists, singers, or presenters of Pentecostal radio and TV programs. (Other typical backgrounds for Pentecostal politicians are the wealthy businessman of financial influence in the church, and the son or son-in-law of one of the *pastores-presidentes*, virtual bishops who often have over a hundred churches under their control.) The sectarian mentality cannot easily accept an ordinary member who stands out in some non-ecclesiastical sphere, such as a trade union, and enters politics in an autonomous fashion with the support of other sectors of society. Such a person puts pastoral authority and sectarian socialization in jeopardy, and will therefore be ecclesiastically marginalized.[6]

Although the initiative to enter politics would seem to have come from the Pentecostals themselves, once they were there and had been "discovered," secular political actors such as the federal government were interested in their articulation. With this stimulus, some of the conservative deputies from the historical churches took the lead in attempts to form a Protestant caucus, which would be larger than all but two of the parties in the Constituent Assembly. Important ideological differences soon surfaced, since a minority of six out of the thirty-three could be classified as left or center-left. However, it was the majority tendency that achieved high visibility in the media, where it was portrayed as strongly conservative on economic, political, and behavioral questions and as ill prepared for public life, thanks to statements such as these from two Assemblies of God deputies: *"President Sarney is not to blame for a bad administration. Everything that has happened is in the Bible, and from now on, things are going to get worse."* and *"A woman has contractions with which she can defend herself from rape."* [7]

However, more important in tarnishing the Protestant deputies' reputation were the accusations that they made a practice of selling their votes. Needless to say, Protestants did not have a monopoly in such matters, but they stood out by their organization and fervor. The leading daily *Jornal do Brasil* led the way with a 1988 exposé that accused them of "making a profitable trade out of preparing the new constitution, by negotiating their votes in exchange for advantages for their churches, and often for themselves." [8] The list was considerable: government concessions for television channels and radio stations, nomination of protégés for federal posts, even large sums of money channeled through the Evangelical Confederation of Brazil.

The Evangelical Confederation had virtually ceased to function since the 1960s, due to political divisions among the historical churches that had dominated it. The Pentecostals had never taken part. In mid-1987, a group of Pentecostal deputies suddenly took it on themselves to resurrect the confederation. The new board claimed the right to receive a third of whatever resources the federal government channeled to the Catholic Church through the National Conference of Brazilian Bishops. The rebirth of the Evangelical Confederation was greeted with a storm of protest by some of the historical churches and cold indifference by others. It functioned only as long as there was government money coming in; once the Constituent Assembly had finished, the stream ran dry. The many regional offices that had been opened suddenly shut down, then the central office in Brasília, leaving a legacy of accusations over the final destination of the money.

The August 1988 denunciations of Protestant deputies in the Constituent Assembly became the Brazilian equivalent of the scandal over the television evangelists in the United States. Whereas in the United States the scandal occurred in the private sector, in Brazil, where the private sector is less lucrative, it erupted over the channeling of public funds. Protestant leaders who were already unhappy about the caucus in the Constituent Assembly joined in the protest against it. But the Assemblies of God, certain Baptists, and some other Protestant leaders came out in defense of the deputies, saying, "The enemy forces are envious because they can see Protestants gradually occupying the spaces they have a right to."[9]

When Brother Does Not Vote for Brother

SCENE 3: A Worthwhile Vote

At a meeting on Protestants in politics, a layman addresses the panel. "We are always being told that we should vote for Protestant candidates. But, so far, I haven't seen our politicians do anything worthwhile. Until I'm given some good reason to do otherwise, I shall continue to vote for non-Protestants." One of the panel members, a city councilor seeking reelection, replies with vehemence: "It's a tragedy when church members talk like that. Just think of it. If we didn't have any Protestant politicians, we wouldn't have any Bible Plazas, or streets named after pastors, or open Bibles on the presidential tables in our city councils, or the 'freedom of the city' for church leaders."

The 1988 municipal elections saw an unprecedented number of Protestant candidates, over a hundred in some municipalities, but relatively few were elected. The multiplication of candidacies divided votes and frustrated the political ambitions of many Pentecostal leaders. But were many Pentecostal voters refusing to support their own candidates? After the elections, the president of the Assemblies state convention in Minas Gerais recognized that the hierarchy had lost control of its members' votes. The reason? Not a rejection of the sort of politics practiced by the church's federal deputies, he argued, but the poor reputation of the major party associated with the Sarney government, the Party of the Brazilian Democratic Movement (PMDB), under which most of the Assemblies' candidates had run. This is not a farfetched analysis. Protestants do not vote just as members of a church, however "totalitarian" its pretensions; there are limits to the influence of Pentecostal leaders on their followers. They cannot prevail against widespread resentment of economic policies, let alone resurrect the reputation of a discredited government. The injunction to vote for a Protestant, and in particular for so-and-so, "who is our church's official candidate," can be very effective, but not under all circumstances.

In Search of an Anointed

SCENE 4: *Fanning the Fear of Persecution*

It is a few weeks before the presidential runoff election between conservative Fernando Collor and Workers' Party candidate Luís Inácio (Lula) da Silva. Propaganda is circulating among Pentecostals that a Lula government will persecute Protestants. I telephone the Evangelical Pro-Collor Movement in Brasília to ask for their prediction. They reply that they expect the great majority of the Protestant vote. I ask why, expecting to hear that Lula would endanger freedom of religion. The man gives a calm, reasoned analysis of how Lula's policies would lead to chaos. When I ask if they are not also worried about persecution, he replies, "Oh no, freedom of religion is guaranteed by the constitution."

In 1989, following a slow, controlled redemocratization, Brazil held its first presidential election in twenty-nine years. Protestants were highly visible even before the campaign, in the unsuccessful bid of the minister of agriculture, Iris Rezende, to get the nomination of the largest party, the PMDB. A charismatic populist, Rezende was mayor of the capital of the state of Goiás at age thirty-two, only to have his political rights taken away by the military. In 1982, he became the first Protestant to be elected a state governor. In 1986, President Sarney called him to the Ministry of Agriculture, where he became one of the few respected members of a very unpopular administration. For three successive years there were record grain harvests, each of which was celebrated with a thanksgiving service attended by the president.

The services became a bone of contention among Protestants, not with regard to Rezende's personal integrity but to the Sarney government's social policy. As a protest banner said: "In the land of superhunger, no one eats a superharvest."

Rezende was a member of the Christian Evangelical Church, a small non-Pentecostal group founded by British missionaries early in the century. At that time Goiás was fiercely conservative, and persecution moved a Protestant landowner to allow brethren to resettle on his land. Thus was born an entirely Protestant town, probably the only one in Brazil. Out of this unique environment came the Protestant who has gone furthest in politics.[10] Obviously one does not win mayoralties and governorships on the Protestant vote alone, and Rezende's posture has not always led to his being identified as "one of us" by all Protestants. But as the presidential elections approached, it became clear that he was the only Protestant with any chance, a fact that Pentecostal leaders were not slow to grasp. Thanksgiving services for record harvests had helped Rezende consolidate his image as the leading Protestant in public life. They also attracted Pentecostals, who attach great significance to the penetration of the public sphere (the quintessential "world" in all its negative doctrinal connotations), by ostentatious religious symbolism and conspicuous ritual performances. Hence the first action of the Protestant caucus in the Constituent Assembly had been to get an open Bible permanently placed on the presidential table. Another highly prized success had been to insert the name of God in the preamble to the new constitution, a victory made all the sweeter by the opposition of some of the communist deputies. As early as 1988, an influential Assemblies author wrote: "*Praising and thanking God, our brother Iris Rezende has been blessed . . . due to the prayers of thousands of believers who intercede for him, the efficiency of his leadership and the fact that he is 'not ashamed of the gospel.'* "[11]

Rezende was presented as an example of what a Protestant president could accomplish, not merely because he would be efficient and masses of believers would pray for him, but also because his very presence would be a mystical channel for God's blessing on Brazil. It is probably significant that this mystique developed around Rezende while he was in charge of agriculture, with all its dependence on the vagaries of climate and ecology. It was easier for the average Protestant to put good weather and absence of crop plagues into a theological framework than, for example, the dictates of the International Monetary Fund. Shortly before the party convention at which his fate would be decided, Rezende appeared at an Assemblies national congress. An Assemblies leader pledged to convince the entire nation "to support the man who has been used by God to produce superharvests." He then took up a powerful weapon in the Pentecostal armory: prophecy. "God has told me that an *evangélico* will be president. If you are chosen at the convention of the PMDB, then I already know the name of the next president of this country." [12]

With Rezende's defeat at the PMDB convention (and his decision not to leave the party and try another route), chances dimmed for a Protestant bloc vote. Eventually, a large segment regrouped around the front-runner, Fernando Collor. A dynamic young conservative, Collor was governor of a small state but had the support of Brazil's largest TV network. He presented himself as the scourge of the "maharajahs," civil servants in sinecures with enormous salaries. Cashing in on the poor image of politicians, Collor succeeded in presenting himself as an anti-politician. As the campaign drew on and it became clear that Collor was the only man with a chance of stopping a left or center-left victory, more and more Protestants flocked to his banner. They had been brought up on the ideology of Brazil's post-1964 military regime, and they were frightened by stories of the fate of believers in communist countries. This, however, was not the whole story.

The Making of the President

SCENE 5: *Calling the Devil by His Name*

With only two weeks to go to the first round of the presidential election, one of the front-runners is the Workers' Party candidate, Lula, who sends shivers down many a Protestant spine. On Reformation Day, October 31, during Lula's television slot, a Protestant speaks in the name of the Evangelical Pro-Lula Committee. The spokesman, far from being a theological liberal, is a product of the University Biblical Alliance, an Evangelical student movement equivalent to the Inter-Varsity Christian Fellowship in the United States. To leaders of the Church of the Four-Square Gospel, this is going too far. Calling the Devil by his name, they publish newspaper ads informing all their pastors to "orient their members not to vote for candidates of the left." Four are named specifically: Lula, the communist Roberto Freire, the left-wing populist Leonel Brizola, and the moderate social-democrat Mário Covas. "All left-wing ideology is totally opposed to the Gospel," the ads continue, denouncing the pro-Lula spokesman for "giving support to the communists in the name of the evangélicos." *Although the Four-Square leaders ban the spokesman from occupying their denomination's pulpits, a local pastor quickly invites him to do just that, thumbing his nose at the leaders' excess of zeal.*

The 1989 election provided a chance for left-of-center Protestants to register their discontent with the conservative, opportunistic image of the caucus in the Constituent Assembly.[13] Fishing for new allies in the Protestant pond, they started the Evangelical Pro-Lula Committee, which contrasted strongly with the Evangelical pro-Collor Movement. The latter was run by Pentecostal deputies and church leaders, and worked mainly among Pentecostal pastors, encouraging them to orient their flocks toward voting for Collor. He would combat corruption, they said, and had shown public sympathy for Israel.[14] He also desired to govern with Protestant help, and was the only candidate capable of defeating the "atheists and enemies of the Gospel" on the left. In addition to being portrayed as "God-fearing" (and Lula as an atheist), Collor was easy to present to the unpoliticized Pentecostal masses because of his emphasis on combating corruption, a useful bridge between the murky world of politics and familiar Protestant discourse on personal morality.

The pro-Lula movement, on the other hand, was composed of both ecclesiastical leaders and ordinary members, mainly of the historical churches, and appealed to the autonomous Protestant citizen. It tried to present a theological basis for reforms along the lines of Lula's proposal. A Protestant, they implied, could (and should) be on the left. The stress on Protestant identity as basic to their political choice was an attempt not only to change the public image but also to produce an effect within the churches.[15] The appearance of the movement's leader on Lula's television slot was the incident that most inflamed Protestant passions. This action was strongly criticized, since it served both to inform the Protestant community of the existence of fellow believers on the left and to warn the politicians that the Protestant vote could not be counted on as a solid bloc.

Despite these divisions, Protestant votes were probably decisive in the runoff. Initial results of my research among more than two thousand voters from various churches in several states suggest that Collor's advantage among the Protestant electorate was slightly larger than his slim overall margin of victory. In other words, among non-Protestant Brazilians, Lula actually had a majority of the votes.

Paying the Price?

Scene 6: *I Am Not a Drug Dealer, I'm an* Evangélico!

After the 1990 congressional elections, there are new faces among the Protestant federal deputies. Soon, a Baptist who was not elected on the religious vote is in all the headlines. His brother has been arrested for drug trafficking while carrying a false congressional identity card bearing the new deputy's signature. The latter claims his signature was forged and denies all knowledge of the affair. The signature is genuine, says expert opinion. Subsequent incidents continue to suggest his involvement in the drug traffic. A congressional committee demands his expulsion. "I'm not a drug trafficker, I'm an evangélico," *he declares, highlighting an identity it had not been his custom to stress. But his attempt to gain moral immunity fails. The days when a Protestant was presumed honest are past. On the eve of the secret vote in the Chamber of Deputies, the newspapers denounce a scheme by the Protestant caucus to close ranks and defend their brother in the faith, obliging a string of deputies to get up in Parliament and deny any such thing. One deputy even goes so far as to say that all of them will vote for his removal. In the end, the suspected drug dealer loses his seat by a small margin.*

In 1990, the Protestant federal deputies elected in 1986 were evaluated at the polls. Although only twelve of the thirty-three incumbents were reelected, many of them by reduced margins, several more were narrowly defeated and soon took office as replacements for deputies advancing to state or federal appointments. Other Protestants were elected for the first time. As of January 1992, the situation was as shown in Table 3-4.

The total is only slightly lower than in the previous legislature, but far below the triumphalistic predictions (fifty or seventy seats) of some church leaders. Pentecostal predominance has been confirmed, even more so if the three Lutheran deputies are placed in context. Religious representation in a parliament can be defined in terms of how deputies identify themselves or whether they practice their religion, but there will always be ambiguities. When a church has a clearly defined membership and a strong sense of community, reinforced by minority status, the problems are minimal. This is why we can say, for example, "There are twelve Protestants in the Brazilian Congress." But no one ever says, "There are 345 Catholics," because the difficulties (and sociological irrelevance) of such a statement are overwhelming. The three Lutheran deputies are a borderline case. Because their church arrived with German immigrants in the nineteenth century, it is a culturally defined identity. And at least one of them is nonpracticing. His Lutheranism is personally and politically irrelevant; his Germanness is not.

On the Pentecostal side, the presence of a deputy from the Christian Congregation, whose extreme opposition to politics has been commented on above, requires some explanation. The deputy is the owner of a radio station (an unlikely activity for a member of this media-rejecting denomination) with a completely Protestant program format. Thanks to the fame and leverage this earned him in the Protestant community, he won election on a totally religious vote. However, many of his colleagues state that he has no church affiliation at all, the name of the Christian Con-

TABLE 3-4
Protestant Federal Deputies and Senators

Churches	Number
Historical Churches	
Brazilian Baptist Convention	4
Lutherans	3
Regular Baptists	1
Methodists	1
Independent Presbyterians	1
Christian Reformed	1
Adventist	1
Total historicals	12
Pentecostal Churches	
Assemblies of God	12
Universal Church of the Kingdom of God	3
Four-Square Gospel	1
Christian Congregation	1
Total Pentecostals	17
Total of all Protestants	29

Note: There is just one senator, belonging to the Independent Presbyterian Church, partly because the number of votes needed far exceeds what the religious community can offer.

gregation being a mere label of convenience. If that is so, it is a stroke of genius, since it is the one church that would never bother to issue a denial. The deputy from the Christian Congregation is therefore a new type of politician: an entrepreneur with a totally Protestant market who invents a church affiliation to project himself politically.

The Assemblies of God and the Baptists continue to predominate, but a significant novelty is the forceful entry of the Universal Church of the Kingdom of God. Their selection of candidates is highly centralized: Bishop Macedo's personal choice. A strong factor in the church's evident voting discipline is the esprit de corps generated by media and police "persecution." The case has interesting implications for those who believe that the days of pastor-directed bloc voting by Pentecostals are numbered. Even if one group loses momentum, others wait in the wings. The extreme fissiparousness of Pentecostalism makes forecasting risky.

How did Protestant voters respond to their controversial caucus in Congress? It should be emphasized that in the late 1980s, politicians as a whole quickly disappointed popular hopes over the return to democracy. The result was a high rate of spoiled votes and defeat for many incumbents in the 1990 elections. Protestant deputies were defeated in roughly the same proportion as non-Protestants. But if we make the Brazilian media's usual distinction between Protestant "conservatives" and "progressives," dissociating the latter from vote-selling and unpreparedness for public life, the results are surprising: the "conservatives" returned to their seats at a higher rate than the national average, and the "progressives" at a lower rate. The only "progressive" reelected was the Assemblies of God dissident Benedita da Silva, with a considerably increased vote (and, she claims, an increased proportion of Protestant votes). Two other "progressives" have since returned to parliament as replacements.

Because Protestants are clearly part of Brazilian political culture, they may well have denied reelection to some of the caucus because they were disappointed at the lack of concrete results for themselves and their churches, not because they were shocked by media charges of vote-selling. In fact, we know little for certain about the motivations of Pentecostal voters, certainly not enough to affirm that between 1986 and 1990, new voting criteria penetrated the consciousness of a significant number. Other factors contributed to the defeat of Protestant incumbents. In 1990 there was no mystique of a Constituent Assembly to motivate pastors and their flocks. Moreover, the success of Protestant candidates in 1986 made it harder for Pentecostal leaders to control the 1990 flood of candidates inspired by everything from prophecies to cupidity.

New Christian Right?

SCENE 7: *No Latin American Comes to the Kingdom but by Neoliberalism*

Just outside Buenos Aires, some seventy Latin American Protestants from sixteen countries are gathered to discuss political participation. From time to time, someone mentions organizing Protestant political parties. Benedita da Silva of the Brazilian Workers' Party disagrees strongly. "The church should not become a ghetto; we must have a pluralist vision of society. We want everybody to be like us, but we're not all the same: we're Baptists, Presbyterians, Pentecostals . . . !" Afterward, a Paraguayan tells me that Protestants in his country are starting their own party. When I express doubt about its viability, he tells me they are all of one mind. That might be true in regard to separation of church and state, and maybe abortion, I reply, but what about economic policy? No problem there either, he says. What policy do you all agree on? I ask. Why, the American one, he replies. What other one is there?

Is the "generation of '86" that took Brazilian politics by surprise a New Christian Right à la the United States? There are resemblances, such as anticommunism, the preoccupation with sexuality and the family in the name of "Christian values," and the link between politics and Protestant presence in the electronic media. This last similarity is a rich vein awaiting deeper research. Brazil is quite possibly the second largest producer in the world of Protestant television programs. Canada and Europe have broadcasting systems that emphasize public service, impeding religious groups from buying time on a commercial basis. The rest of Latin America, which has systems oriented to the private market, relies largely on imported programs.[16] In Brazil, on the other hand, national television networks had developed by the 1970s, building on the communications infrastructure established by the military government, and they began a process of import substitution. The proportion of foreign programs fell from 60 percent in 1972 to 30 percent in 1983. At peak times, Brazilian television carries as low a proportion of imported programs as counterparts in France, Italy, and Britain.[17]

Protestant television followed the same route with only a slight lag. Except for a brief pioneering effort by Brazil for Christ in the early 1960s, Protestants had heretofore concentrated on radio. The older medium was considerably cheaper, required far less technical expertise, and was the main mass medium in the country until the late 1970s. Protestants tried television again only in the early 1980s, by which time American televangelists were already establishing a presence. Gradually, import substitution prevailed, assisted by the scandals involving Jim Bakker and Jimmy Swaggart. At present, on the Rio–São Paulo networks, most of which transmit over the entire country, there are ten to fifteen Brazilian productions and not one import.

Licenses for television channels have become valuable coin in the Brazilian political world; a significant number of congressmen and other politicians have them. It is important to remember that Brazil is in the first period of competitive politics since a modern communications network was created. The link between Protestant politicians and radio/television, whether as owners or programmers, may be no greater than for other definable sectors. What attracts attention is the contrast with the values of the secular culture industry, and the difference in strategy from the Catholics, *umbandistas*, and esotericals.[18] With the exception of the Catholic charismatics, all the latter groups try to permeate the values of the whole range of programs. The Protestants, on the other hand, produce separate programs oriented to evangelism. For Protestant politicians, media and politics are a two-way street: religious radio and television can be a route to public office, and political power can be a route to media entrepreneurship.

Despite similarities between the religious right in the United States and the Brazilian phenomenon, there are important differences. In economic policy, it is doubtful whether Protestant deputies can be classified in this way. Take the score given each member of the Constituent Assembly by the Trades Unions' Parliamentary Advisory Department (DIAP). The publication of these scores caused quite a stir nationally. DIAP used a scale of 0 to 10 to rate the votes of each parliamentarian on "ques-

TABLE 3-5
Trades Unions' Parliamentary Advisory Department Scores
of the Churches

All Deputies and Senators	All Protestants	Assemblies of God	All Pentecostals	Baptists	All Historicals
4.94	4.52	5.00	5.06	3.07	3.90

tions of interest to the workers."[19] A higher score meant a more left-wing orientation. The average for all members of the Constituent Assembly was 4.94; the average for all Protestants was 4.52. According to DIAP's criteria, in other words, Protestants voted slightly less favorably for workers. But the breakdown by denomination was surprising, given the predilection for labeling Pentecostals as more conservative than "historical" Protestants. (See Table 3-5.)

The Pentecostals turn out to have a much higher (more left-wing) score than the historicals, and slightly higher than the average for the Constituent Assembly. Taking into account the social origins of the great mass of Pentecostals, the score could be higher still. Even so, the voting record of Pentecostal deputies makes it rather difficult to label them generically as a religious right. Actually, the closest parallel to the North American religious right would be some of the Baptist parliamentarians. The Brazilian Baptist Convention still cultivates close ties with the Southern Baptists in the United States and is probably the most American-influenced of all the major denominations. The Protestant in Congress who defends the neoliberal ideal most vehemently is a Baptist.

The conservative reputation of the Protestant caucus in the Constituent Assembly stems from other issues than those examined by DIAP. (See Table 3-6.)

The motion granting a fifth year to Sarney was presented by a member of the Assemblies of God. It is said to have been worth several new licenses for radio stations and television channels. The vote against agrarian reform was widely attributed to finan-

TABLE 3-6
Selected Votes in the Constituent Assembly Not Included in DIAP
Score (in percent)

	All Members Present	Protestants Present
In favor of a five-year mandate for President Sarney	59%	75%
In favor of expropriation of productive land for agrarian reform	50	29
In favor of inclusion of "sexual orientation" in the phrase "no one will be discriminated against on the grounds of . . ."	28	7
In favor of the phrase "will protect life from its conception"	21	71
In favor of indissolubility of marriage	13	42

cial contributions from the landowner lobby; many Protestants changed their position at the last moment. The behavioral questions (abortion, homosexuality, and divorce) were the object of great Protestant interest from the committee stage.

Although the Brazilians concentrated on some of the same moral issues that have agitated the religious right in the United States, there are important differences. They have no coordinating agencies, like the Moral Majority, dedicated to elaborating political agendas and strategies and mobilizing grass-roots opinion. The brokers of the new Protestant politics in Brazil are not leaders of nondenominational agencies but controllers of ecclesiastical structures. Also, there are no sophisticated middle-class intellectual advisers like the pastoral agents in the Catholic base communities in Brazil. There is no project for society in any literature produced by the Pentecostal leaders or their politicians, and their congresses are singularly devoid of such discussion. This contrasts with the American religious right, which has a project going far beyond moral conservatism and channels a ground swell of public opinion through special nondenominational organizations. The aim is restoration of a threatened cultural ideal, because conservative Protestants feel they have lost control of a country with a Protestant founding myth. None of this exists in Brazil.

In parts of Latin America there is considerable influence of the North American right-wing theology-cum-ideology represented by "reconstructionism" or "dominion theology,"[20] which proclaims Christians' right to take control of countries and reconstruct them on (mainly Old Testament) "biblical principles for the government of the nations." This current of thought was represented at the meeting of Protestants in Latin American politics at Buenos Aires in October 1991, through people from several countries who were associated with North American entities such as Pat Robertson's Regent University, the Providence Foundation, and the Rutherford Institute. (Ironically, parts of the Old Testament that might seem highly relevant to Latin America, such as the jubilee law, establishing a return to a radically egalitarian landholding pattern every fifty years, did not figure in their thinking. Scripture was powerless against neoliberal economic principles.)

I have come across reconstructionism in Brazil, too, but in relatively marginal contexts. It seems to be influential mainly in the new wave of independent middle-class charismatic churches. These do not have the same relative weight among Brazilian Protestants as among their counterparts in some other countries, however. The religious contexts are very different: Brazil has an enormous Protestant field, with a relatively strong traditional middle-class penetration; some of the Central American countries had virtually no better-off Protestants until about the 1980s, and those who exist today tend to belong to the charismatic communities. This different overall picture, which weakens the relative force of the principled right in Brazilian Protestantism, also strengthens the principled left, as we shall see. And whereas in Central America the cutting edge of Protestant political involvement lies with middle- (or upper-) class elements, more trained by their upbringing and social location to think in terms of remolding the country, in Brazil it lies with the somewhat aged Assemblies of God leaders of humble origins, who have pulled themselves up by their bootstraps to lower-middle-class respectability. That does not mean that the principled right has no future in Brazil: It offers a ready-made project for Protestants in politics, capable of channeling idealism as well as of picking up the disillusioned flotsam of more purely church-centered and ill-defined political adventures.

The "Lost Decade" and Pentecostal Politics

SCENE 8: *We Are the Answer!*

At a conference of Protestant politicians, federal and state deputies, municipal councilors, and denominational leaders take turns speaking. Do we hear debate on national issues, analysis of Protestant participation thus far, specific proposals for the country's problems? No, all we hear is the repetition of statements such as "You and I have the answer"; "May God raise up in Brazil an anointed man"; "We are the answer"; "We are the salt of the earth." Not "we should be" but "we are." Shortly after the conference, the politician who organized it announces that he has found the anointed one: a thirty-eight-year-old rags-to-riches Baptist businessman with absolutely no political experience but with a "department of social action and evangelism" in his construction company that subsidizes poor churches all over the country, donates prefabricated buildings, and advises on evangelistic and social work. In 1994, he is to be the Protestant answer to Brazil's crisis.

Why did Brazilian Pentecostals enter politics in 1986 with such unprecedented and unforeseen force? To be sure, not all did enter politics. Of the six major groups listed at the beginning of this article, three clearly have become politicized: the Assemblies of God, the Church of the Four-Square Gospel, and the Universal Church of the Kingdom of God. A fourth, Brazil for Christ, is a likely candidate to follow suit; the now decentralized leadership, which initially reacted negatively against founder Manoel de Mello's personalistic politics, is planning action. The other two denominations, God Is Love and the Christian Congregation, remain indifferent to political competition. The former could change rapidly because it depends on the whim of one man, although the discrepancy with his previous stance would be apparent and would probably require some sort of supernatural bolstering. The Christian Congregation is very unlikely to modify its severe rejection of the "world," including politics, in the foreseeable future.

Whatever social factors explain the new face of Protestant politics in Brazil, the diversity of postures between denominations suggests that it must also be explained by strictly religious factors. The rays of political sun shining on each Pentecostal church are refracted differently by the various colors in the stained-glass window. One of the panes in the window is represented by the institutional interests generated over the years in each church. Another is the way each church sees itself, its idea of mission.[21] The conception of the church's mission is frequently a matter of internal dispute, however. Churches are not unequivocal bearers of fixed political postures; there are often factions within each church trying to change the coloring in that windowpane. Although organizations with sectarian characteristics tend to work with an ideal of unanimity, an oligarchical group such as the Assemblies of God produces frontier zones where strict conformity is not demanded. The eighty-year history, enormous size, and peculiarities of its trajectory have undermined the Assemblies' traditional apoliticism, which is giving way to corporate engagement. A more modern, liberal concept of responsible involvement by the individual citizen has yet to gain much ground.

Of course, there are more people in the pews now, and a certain degree of numerical growth is a sine qua non for electing people on the corporate vote of a single denomination.[22] But numerical growth is not a sufficient explanation; the Assemblies of God would certainly have taken Brazil for Christ's cue in the 1960s if it were. Size opens up possibilities for a certain type of politics; but the peculiar rhythm of each group will influence its reaction. There is no demonstrable relation between size and political participation, as if there were some sort of threshold that, once crossed, makes the step into politics as natural as planning another evangelistic campaign.

Still, numerical growth does have the effect of changing society's perception of Protestantism. Whatever its public image may be, a community of twenty million is not allowed to wash its hands so easily of the nation's destiny as is a community of two million. It cannot keep the same degree of social invisibility and irresponsibility, even if it does expect to be taken up to heaven tomorrow. Meanwhile, other social groups are searching for a single Protestant interlocutor, putting pressure on competing leaders to invent one. This is one reason for the founding of the Brazilian Evangelical Association in 1991, three years after the public scandal surrounding the Evangelical Confederation. But the association is the initiative of leaders with political sympathies stretching from the center to the left, of whom more anon.

The entry into politics is just one way Protestants are becoming more visible, moving into previously neglected spheres such as television, popular music, and sports. The social base for all this is the appearance in recent decades of a new kind of mass popular religiosity, a Protestant one. The sociological novelty is that this is the first popular religiosity in Latin America that does not even implicitly recognize the institutional hegemony of the Catholic Church. Not only does it have autonomy, as do Afro-Brazilian spiritists and the base communities to some extent; it also refuses to see itself as in any way subordinate, as having its "head in Catholicism," as is often said of the Afro-Brazilian religions.

Pentecostals have entered politics during a gradual, controlled return to democracy. Both the Sarney[23] and the Collor administrations have shown great continuity of faces and practices with the military regime. In need of new social bases, conservatives tried to enlist the Protestant members of the Constituent Assembly and played on simplistic anticommunism in the 1989 presidential campaign. Pentecostal politics can hardly be reduced to this, however. The initiative of the Assemblies of God in 1986 has other roots, even if we presume encouragement from secular politicians, for which I have no evidence. It would have been more traditional and controllable simply to continue soliciting Pentecostal support for outside candidates. There is always a risk for secular leaders in attracting cohesive religious groups into politics, since their particular style and demands may rock the boat you pull them into.[24]

The military regime of 1964–1985 never completely abolished parliamentary politics, but it greatly reduced its importance. When Congress regained space in 1986, much had changed. The military had quarreled with that traditional bulwark of authoritarian regimes, the Catholic Church, and had sought additional religious legitimation from the previously somewhat marginalized Protestants. Although the shift was not as spectacular as in Chile, the attention whetted the appetite of Protestant leaders.

Another change of the 1964–1985 period was the construction of a modern, nationwide communications network, especially in television. For most of the military regime, the private culture industry was dependent on this state-established structure and functioned under state censorship. Eventually, censorship slackened and the impact on social mores was great. This impact contributed to Protestant concern to have legislators of their own who would deal with such moral questions in the Constituent Assembly. These questions became more politicized than before, and Pentecostals were not the only Brazilians to express concern.[25]

Many writers have called attention to Protestantism's expansion in Latin America during the "lost decade" of the 1980s. But economically desperate people do not turn only to new religions, they also turn to new political actors. As traditional political actors lose credibility, they may be replaced by new ones who can mobilize the disillusioned through appealing to messianism and politicizing traditional moral concerns. The now-battered reputation for honesty that Protestants used to enjoy in Brazil helped them reach out to other constituencies, as may still be the case in countries like Guatemala and Peru. Then, too, the economic deterioration of the 1980s strengthened the informal economy, weakened political organizations based on the workplace, and increased the importance of the family and home, particularly of the women, who usually keep households together. The latter are the centers of radiation for Pentecostalism.[26]

Still another result of the "lost decade" is that it neutralized the traditional effects of conversion—the creation of a hardworking, honest, and frugal work force—on individual social mobility. This made Pentecostals more susceptible to the collective demands of the poor. At precisely that moment, redemocratization occurred, allowing freer expression of political currents and putting pressure on the ability of sectarian socialization to protect its members from other forms of politicization. The corporate project directed by the church leadership could then function as a preemptive politicization, protecting the sect's capacity for social reproduction. At a more immediate level, economic crisis weakened the churches financially, making access to public funds and favors even more attractive as an alternative to scarce private resources.

The "lost decade" also put strain on party structures, leading to the same loss of credibility that occurred in most Latin American countries. This has to do with the greater load that parties have been expected to carry in recent years as bridges between people and government, due not only to the economic crisis but also to longer-term processes such as urbanization and the spread of the mass media. In Brazil, we can add the effect of redemocratization: after the military had largely demobilized civil society, there were exaggerated expectations surrounding a return to competitive party politics.

Brazilian parties have little tradition (after each authoritarian period new ones are born) and are generally regarded as weak and nonideological, leaving them wide open to corruption and opportunism. Most Protestant politicians affect a disdain for parties, stressing the priority of personal integrity. Parties are a necessary evil. In contrast, Benedita da Silva, the only Protestant federal deputy in the Workers' Party, defends party discipline as a means of political growth and a brake on corruption. It is this same discipline (analogous to, and therefore competitive with, that of their own churches) that other Pentecostal leaders and politicians view as the great bane of the Workers' Party. But political dependence on prominent political figures does not merit the same censure among Pentecostals.

The Brazilian political system is relatively open to the political activities of sectarian religious groups, closer to the highly favorable American than to the unfavorable British system.[27] It has a federal structure, relatively open mass media, weak parties, and, above all, an electoral system in which deputies are elected with votes from an entire state rather than from a smaller electoral district, thus increasing the chances of a dispersed minority community. In the British system of one member for each electoral district, Protestant representation would fall overnight, and only those capable of constructing diverse political bases would survive.

All these external facilitating factors would have been of no avail if the churches had not been receptive. Pentecostalism had grown enormously in recent years, and it had grown in isolation from the historical Protestant churches. Although Protestantism in Latin America always works through a potentially unlimited number of autonomous groups, there are often countervailing tendencies that mitigate the isolation of each group. In these cases, Protestantism's more highly educated intellectual leaders, usually belonging to the historical churches, can often be heard within Pentecostalism, at least on certain matters, in a role vaguely similar to that of specialized "pastoral agents" in the Catholic base communities. But for various reasons, explained more in the next section, Brazilian Protestantism experienced an extreme splintering from the 1960s on. The explosion of Pentecostalism and its entry into politics occurred in this isolationist framework. As a result, Pentecostalism is more truly popular, in a sense, than the base communities, but also lacks the sort of specialized advisers who surround the latter's political activists.

Most Pentecostal politics in Brazil has been characterized by a firm rejection of any political position remotely connected with Marxism, although not necessarily by a firm adoption of neoliberal economics. Is the doctrine taught by the Pentecostal churches responsible for this posture? To a certain extent it is. Reading through the main Assemblies of God publication, *Mensageiro da Paz*, one sees the centrality of dispensationalist eschatology for their worldview. A certain lineup of forces is visualized for the

approaching end times, which leads to a geopolitical dualism that
rejects any noncapitalist ideal of society. The whole approach will
presumably undergo changes now that the Soviet bloc has col-
lapsed. Only nine months before the reunification of Germany,
O Mensageiro published an article that, on "biblical grounds,"
denied the possibility of such a thing. We must be cautious, however. Older sociological studies tended to portray apoliticism as
a necessary corollary of Pentecostal doctrine.[28] Such apoliticism
has turned out to be temporary, as conservatism may also prove
to be. Doctrinal systems are not straitjackets; rather, they are
large stores from which some products are purchased, others are
thrown out, and still others remain on the shelf, unused.

We cannot simply deduce political practice from religious
doctrine; various social factors intervene, such as social class,
educational level, professional interests of the clergy, and relative
position in the religious field. The relative location of each church
in the religious sphere is an important factor in its reaction to
political opportunities. In Europe, religious minorities historically tended to be left of center politically, due more to their
social position than to their doctrine.[29] In Latin America, where
sizable Protestant minorities are a new phenomenon, another
factor comes into play. The continent followed the pattern common to most Catholic and Orthodox countries: a monopolistic
church that, allied to autocracies, provoked the rise of a mili-
tantly atheistic left. Mass politics developed late in Latin America
with urbanization and industrialization, just as world Catholicism was moving from the right to the center and in some cases,
notably in Brazil, spawning a large Catholic left. Protestants thus
emerged as a political force in a context characterized by a secular
left and a progressive Catholicism. Being strongly anti-Roman, it
is not surprising that Brazilian Protestantism has so far tended to
enter politics further to the right. The desire to distinguish their
activity from that of the National (Catholic) Bishops' Conference
was a constant theme in the discourse of many members of the
Protestant caucus in Congress.

Another reason for Pentecostal opposition to any form of state
socialism is the class interest of many members who, since converting, have advanced economically or have at least had their

expectations raised. The prevalent ideology, that conversion with its attendant sacrifices will eventually lead to betterment, works against accepting a restriction on such possibilities in the name of a more egalitarian ideology. The interests of pastors are even more threatened; they tend to be among the main beneficiaries of the conversion process, a living demonstration of the message they preach. Not without historical reason, they fear that a left-wing regime would tamper with the free-market religious system in which they flourish.

Religious competition has heightened of late in Brazil, as illustrated by Catholic pronouncements on the "sects." In Rio de Janeiro, a "holy war" has broken out between *Umbanda* and the new Pentecostal groups, especially the Universal Church of the Kingdom of God. The increasing power of conservatives in the Catholic hierarchy has meant a return to a more clerical style in some dioceses, prompting some base communities to become independent Pentecostal churches. Amid this three-way rivalry, Pentecostal politics shows a desire for political power commensurate with their size and also a strategy for increasing church growth. Except for anticommunism, Pentecostal conservatism is less a matter of principle than a correct intuition of how to maximize returns. It is linked to the professional interests of the pastors, for whom institutional expansion is a matter of professional fulfillment and often of salary level. All things being equal, in a numerically expanding denomination the pastors will tend to be more conservative than the faithful, whereas in a stagnant or declining denomination they tend to be more progressive.

Pentecostal politicization has affected the leadership almost exclusively. The Assemblies, the Four-Square, and the Universal are all very clerical, in their different ways. Electoral politics offers a new form of personal and family mobility: many Pentecostal politicians are paid pastors, while others are sons or sons-in-law of pastors. Using David Martin's analogy of the pastorate as an escalator to be stepped onto, and in a later generation stepped off,[30] politics can be seen as another flight of the escalator, extending upward mobility not only financially but also in terms of social prestige.

Even so, a strong initial shove was needed to overcome the

culture of apoliticism in the Assemblies of God and the Four-Square. The Constituent Assembly did the trick, as it did for many minority social groups. It was a chance to rewrite Brazil, or at least to make sure others did not do so. Pentecostal leaders were motivated by two perceived threats: to religious liberty and to the family. There were rumors that the Catholic hierarchy would make an all-out bid to regain the status of official church, or at least win special treatment. A recrudescence of anti-Catholicism may seem anachronistic, but it parallels the rebirth of a less ecumenical spirit in the Catholic Church. Concern over the family, as reflected in debates over divorce, abortion, homosexuality, censorship, and drugs, was not just a theological fixation. It was also a correct intuition as to the locus of Pentecostal growth.

Surprisingly, there was no broader political project. Aside from religious liberty and the family, *O Mensageiro da Paz* commented only on issues involving religious symbols, such as whether God would be mentioned in the preamble to the new constitution. Hence, an unprecedented political activism occurred, but without the kind of vision for society that Protestant leaders have displayed at other times. The first such project was the mid-nineteenth-century hope of some Protestant pioneers and liberal Catholics for a reformation of the Brazilian church,[31] with profound implications for national identity. This was soon replaced by the alternative of transplanting existing Protestant churches from abroad, a denominational solution for a society that was not prepared for it.

Brazil's religious tradition was too monolithic to accept the American idea of a religious free-for-all. Whence Protestantism's early alliance with anticlerical forces, such as liberalism and Freemasonry, to free their supposed denominations from their local reality as sects. Missionaries presented Protestantism as the bearer of progress, education, and literacy. The Protestantization of the country was the route to development. This discourse has now been in crisis for some time, and in the Pentecostal churches it never caught on. Pentecostal leaders' politics, instead of being the future arriving for the nation, is somber, tinged with apocalyptic chaos, and little more than a church-growth strategy. They can countenance the use of politics in this instrumental way because they see their mission basically as expanding the frontiers of their group. Consider the following passages from a book by a leading Assemblies of God author that sold widely before the 1986 elections:

> If we elect *evangélicos* [as president, governor, deputy, etc.] we will without doubt be able to dedicate ourselves better to our task of evangelizing the country.[32]
>
> The taxes a believer pays . . . go to finance idolatry [Catholicism] and witchcraft [*Umbanda*]. . . . Each congressman . . . receives annually, in the federal budget, a certain sum. . . . See what a fabulous amount of resources could be helping our organizations in the social and educational sector.[33]

After the original Protestant project of a reform of the national church, later replaced by the attempted Protestantization of the nation through the importing of denominations, we have arrived at the growth of the sects with the help of direct participation in the political system.

Dissidents in the Fold: The Protestant Left

SCENE 9: *Communists and Bible-Thumping Progressives*

It is an unusual gathering, this pompously named First National Forum for Discussion and Understanding between Protestants and Progressive Parties. For one thing, among the speakers is the head of the Brazilian Communist Party. Another speaker is one of the leaders of the Workers' Party, a former guerrilla. On the Protestant side, there are deputies, church leaders, and intellectuals, all except one aligned with an evangelical rather than a liberal Protestant theology. Without meaning to offend, the Communist Party leader comes out with the old bourgeois view, so typical of many conservative Protestants, that "religion is fundamentally a private question." The Protestants at the meeting insist on precisely the opposite. The atmosphere of the forum, full of Protestants and non-Protestants, is nonetheless cordial.

A Baptist pastor has been asked to close the meeting. Choosing him was largely a tactical decision by the organizers, as he is a respected evangelist. But his style is completely out of step with what has gone before: instead of the calm intellectual, the traditional preacher; instead of the language of the political arena, the jargon of the evangélicos. *Some of the organizers wish the floor would open up under them. But this Bible-thumper who exhorts the Communist leader at his side to accept the Kingdom of God also criticizes the pietistic manichaeanism he learned at an American-run fundamentalist seminary. In 1989, he had risked his reputation and salary to sign manifestos supporting Lula, the Workers' Party candidate for president. It is his style, and not that of the university-educated speakers who preceded him, that will predominate if a really widespread Protestant progressive movement develops.*

I have outlined several common features of Protestant, and especially Pentecostal, politics. These include a concern to distinguish their product from that of the Catholic hierarchy and the base communities; anticommunism; a pragmatic conservatism aimed at maximizing concrete advantages; politicization of moral questions; and the ambition to insert religious symbols and ceremonies into the public sphere. But there is another current to be examined: the Evangelical Progressive Movement. These progressives are an example of what David Stoll has called "growing political differences among theological conservatives" as a result of the collision between numerical growth and the pauperization of the continent.[34] Their numerical inferiority is to some extent compensated for by an intellectual hegemony in the conservative theological camp.

To understand the possibilities for this movement, we need to look more closely at the trajectory of historical Protestantism. In 1932, the precursor of the Evangelical Confederation published a manifesto defending free education and legal aid, absolute freedom of thought, profit sharing, and a drastic reduction in military spending. The only Protestant member of the 1934 Constituent Assembly was elected by the Socialist Party. From 1955 to 1963, some of the historical churches developed an articulate left wing, in many respects more daring than anything in the Catholic Church at that time. However, in the 1960s, Protestant intellectuals were decimated by a wave of internal repression in many historical churches, especially the Presbyterian and the Methodist. Conservative denominational leaders were taking advantage of the general atmosphere of the country after the military coup in 1964. The Evangelical Confederation virtually ceased to function.

These events affected Brazilian Protestantism profoundly. The survivors of the intelligentsia regrouped in small ecumenical organizations. As a result of their bitter experiences and their new institutional basis, not to mention the ideological polarization of the country, they became separated from the Protestant masses by a theological abyss that prevented them from exercising any leadership. Today, the Lutheran and Methodist churches (and, to a lesser extent, the Independent Presbyterians) have theologically and politically avant-garde leaderships, but their grass roots rarely follow them. The Presbyterian Church of Brazil has remained in the hands of a stultifying orthodox leadership and suffered greatly from internal politicking. The Baptists never had such deep internal conflicts; a mildly left-wing minority was gradually removed from positions of influence in the seminaries in the 1980s. It is in this context of Protestant division and lack of intellectual leadership that the Pentecostal explosion occurred.

Since the mid-1970s, a new evangelical leadership and intelligentsia has begun to emerge, drawn mostly from university-educated people and some seminary graduates, and often based in parachurch movements. Although influenced by international developments such as the Lausanne Congress (1974), it is not a mere imitation. The proximity to misery and oppression, and the challenge of liberation theology, produced a commitment to "contextualizing" evangelical faith. Two organizations were especially prominent: the Latin American Theological Fraternity and the student movement known as the Aliança Bíblica Universitária. They were among the few Protestant entities in Brazil open to input from social scientists. As a result, an evangelical left became visible in the 1980s, assisted by the scandals over the Protestant caucus in the Constituent Assembly. For the 1989 presidential election, they formed pro-Lula and pro-Brizola committees. In 1991, some started a process of group affiliation with the Workers' Party, although not all the progressives identify with that option.

The new progressives represent a novelty in Brazilian Protestantism. Unlike older ecumenical organizations, they are theologically conservative in terms of the Bible, prayer, and conversion, and therefore much better placed to have an influence on ordinary Protestants. Unlike previous theologically conservative progressives, they are an articulate group that intends to be active not only in political parties and social movements but also in the churches.

The six progressives elected to the Constituent Assembly in 1986 came from elsewhere, but two of the three still in Congress are now in close contact with the Evangelical Progressive Movement, as are some state deputies. As for influence within the Protestant community, the key figure has been Robinson Cavalcanti, a practicing political scientist who led the pro-Lula campaign and is now affiliated with the Workers' Party. A product of the Aliança Bíblica Universitária and the Latin American Theological Fraternity, Cavalcanti has acquired wide influence through his 1985 book *Cristianismo e Política*. At first, his work was mainly pedagogical, awakening Protestants to political action in a mildly progressive direction. Then, in the late 1980s, he adopted steadily more defined left-wing positions. His trajectory, and the legitimacy his intellectual leadership has given, have moved a number of theological conservatives to take similar positions.

The Evangelical Progressive Movement was strong only relative to the past and to the rest of Latin America. It was hardly able to help more progressive Protestants win election to Congress in 1990, although it did help Benedita da Silva, who previously had few Protestant voters, to increase her total vote substantially. Progressives are not numerous enough to elect a deputy without help from the nonreligious vote. Few Protestants manage to unite this broad vote with a sufficient density in the transdenominational Protestant field, since the progressives of one denomination alone will be insufficient. The six progressives in the Constituent Assembly were not the result of this sort of combination.

The rise of a progressive movement, and especially the affiliation of an increasing number of evangelicals with the Workers' Party, may seem anomalous at this moment in history. In fact, the end of the Cold War has probably helped. On the left, it has ended militant atheism and forced parties to reevaluate policies and attitudes. After nearly winning the presidency in 1989, the Workers' Party is going through a purge of the quasi-independent Marxist groups within it. The old corporatism of the left, which sent shivers down Protestant spines even in the relatively moderate Sandinista regime, seems dead.

Among evangelicals, meanwhile, the end of the communist menace, the extreme unpopularity of the Collor government, the shift to the right of the Catholic hierarchy, and the growing maturity of the evangelical leadership facilitate the growth of progressive postures.

At the 1990 meeting of the Latin American Theological Fraternity, many members expressed their trepidation at the wave of neoliberal triumphalism in the continent. The effects of such policies in Latin America are very different from those in Western Europe, where more effective forms of citizenship have been constructed. "If it is true that communism has failed in the East," Robinson Cavalcanti states, "it is also true that capitalism has been a permanent failure for two-thirds of the world." Although what the Workers' Party means by "democratic socialism" is not clear, its main objectives are the democratization of the state, of property, and of income. The route to power is to be electoral, and there is to be an emphasis on ethics in public life.

Projections

The Evangelical Progressive Movement is still concentrated among historicals of a higher educational level. While it can hope to expand among the historical churches by means of its writings and debates, the main chance of penetrating the Pentecostal world is to hope that through a process of institutionalization, the criteria for leadership change substantially, permitting younger, seminary-educated people who are already influenced by progressive authors and speakers to come to power.

For the time being, the entry of the Pentecostal hierarchy into politics has unintentionally assisted the emergence of a progressive movement with a specifically Protestant identity and a desire to change the political face of the churches. There is no way of knowing where this will lead; after all, the brake on Catholic radicalization created by the authority of the Vatican does not exist in Protestantism. Dissident Protestants cannot be excommunicated, but they can be ostracized, which was the fate of the Protestant left of the 1960s. The current movement may well avoid a similar fate, for much the same reasons that the Catholic "popular Church" of the 1970s in Brazil avoided the fate of the "Catholic left" of the 1960s.[35] They took care not to transform the church into a political institution; did not abandon the church impatiently, even if this meant accepting a slower pace of change; showed more respect for popular religiosity, rejecting a secularized radical theology; emphasized the unity of the transcendent and immanent aspects of religion; and worked for the reform of other areas of pastoral practice. Some of the founders of the new Brazilian Evangelical Association (1991) are partial to the Progressive Movement. Although the Evangelical Association itself is broader, they see it as a chance to contribute to the transformation of the Protestant church as a whole. Just possibly, after the initial euphoria of political participation has worn off, the progressives who are well placed in the larger Protestant world will be able to provide elements for an ampler political project among Pentecostals.

From the 1991 Buenos Aires meeting of Latin American Protestants in politics, it would seem that only Brazil has a progressive evangelical movement of any size. It is important to ask why. Brazil is 40 percent of Latin America and has 50 percent of its Protestants. Neither its politics nor its Protestantism is very similar to those of a tiny Central American state. It is highly industrialized and urbanized, with a certain political and ideological sophistication, and does not have large indigenous ethnic groups. Its class structure is considerably more permeable than most of the continent's. The economic crisis is severe, but civil society has not disintegrated, as in Central America and Peru. Its middle-class Protestantism is older, denser, and more diversified; the Pentecostal predominance is not as overwhelming as in much of Latin America. There are probably over six million non-Pentecostal Protestants in Brazil, along with some thirteen million Pentecostals. Brazil has long outgrown the battles over church-state separation that still agitate other countries and maintain Protestant unity against a common enemy. Even if Catholicism still receives some institutional favors, it is hard for Protestants to feel really discriminated against. North American religious influence in Brazil is strong, but not as monopolistic as in Central America. Finally, the Brazilian Catholic Church was for many years the most politically progressive in the world, and this has affected Protestants. At the same time Brazilian Catholicism inspires some Protestants to become more conservative, it inspires others to emulation.

This overview of Protestantism and politics in Brazil has concentrated on the national, institutional, and parliamentary levels. Of course, much of the interaction between religion and politics does not occur at these levels. But the approach is justified, especially in redemocratized Brazil, where base communities and other social movements, so prominent in the fight against the dictatorship, have yielded in importance to the traditional institutions of parties and elections. It is through the latter institutions that Pentecostals made their spectacular entry into public life. Almost certainly, their influence will increase, with the possibility of affecting Brazilian politics profoundly in the next decades, when the Protestant share of the electorate may reach 20 to 30 percent. The prospects for internal change in Protestantism are thus not devoid of interest for ordinary Brazilians. Although the rags-to-riches businessman who is touted as a presidential messiah may prefabricate church buildings, he cannot prefabricate a political destination for Brazil's rapidly expanding Protestantism.

NOTES

Acknowledgements: The author is grateful for financial assistance from FAPESP (São Paulo State Research Foundation) and from the Programa de Dotações para Pesquisa da ANPOCS (Brazilian National Association for Postgraduate Study and Research in the Social Sciences), with resources from the Ford Foundation; and for institutional support from IDESP (São Paulo Institute for Economic, Social, and Political Studies).

1. Although large Catholic minorities survived in some Protestant countries after the Reformation, the Counter-Reformation saw to it that the reverse did not occur. Where sizable Protestant minorities exist today, they are of recent vintage. In no European country do they reach politically significant proportions.

2. There are, of course, gradations of poverty, and many studies have shown that most Pentecostal growth does not come from the very bottom rungs. Among denominations there are significant variations that reflect each group's evolution over time and differences in the initial product offered. Since the 1960s, the historical denominations have produced Pentecostalized breakaways of some size, notably the National Baptist Convention.

3. Another example is the name of the early split-off founded by Macedo's brother-in-law, the International Church of the Grace of God.

4. The organization of television in Brazil, perhaps halfway between the U.S. and British models, involves a mixture of market forces and government discretion.

5. Most of the (very occasional) more critical articles in the major publication of the Assemblies of God, *Mensageiro da Paz*, come from products of this alternative route. A student at the major seminary in Pindamonhangaba, who came up to me wearing a clerical collar and proudly introduced himself as a supporter of the Workers' Party, claimed that the majority of his fellow seminarians had voted for that party's candidate, Luís Inácio Lula da Silva, in the 1989 presidential election. The phenomenon of a critical clergy often gives the historical denominations a more left-wing image than their grass roots really correspond to. This is exemplified in Brazil by the Methodist Church and, to some extent, by the Lutherans and the Independent Presbyterians.

6. See the classic description of this in relation to Chilean Pentecostalism by Christian Lalive d'Epinay, *The Haven of the Masses* (London: Lutterworth Press, 1969).

7. Respectively, Matheus Iensen and Sotero Cunha; in *Aconteceu no mundo evangélico*, February 1988, pp. 4–5, and June 1987, p. 5.

8. *Jornal do Brasil*, August 7, 1988, pp. B6–B8.

9. *Aconteceu no Mundo Evangélico*, October 1988, p. 3.

10. One of the military presidents, Ernesto Geisel (1974–1979), was of German Lutheran descent, but nonpracticing. It is generally felt among Protestants that his case does not really "count."

11. Josué Sylvestre, *Os evangélicos, a Constituinte e as eleições municipais* (Brasília: Papiro, 1988), p. 70.

12. *Folha de São Paulo*, April 17, 1989, p. A5.

13. Although Protestants used to be stereotyped as fanatical and aggressive, they were also renowned for honesty. By 1989, the caucus in Congress and the money-raising tactics of some of the newer churches had shaken the reputation for probity.

14. This is related to "dispensationalism," a reading of the Bible that stresses the importance of the Jews in the scenario of the end of the world, leading to almost unconditional support for Israel.

15. The mere fact of a political option based on one's faith did not have to be expressed in a separate Protestant movement—as it was not, for example, in the case of those Protestants who supported Afif Domingos, the most outright defender of a neoliberal option.

16. Or else has a secularist tradition that does not readily allow religious television, as in Mexico.

17. Renato Ortiz, *A moderna Tradição brasileira* (São Paulo, Brasiliense, 1988), pp. 117–18; 201–2.

18. "Esotericals" refers to the current wave of mystical religion often known loosely as the New Age movement.

19. Departamento Intersindical de Assessoria Parlamentar, *Quem foi quem na Constituinte: Nas Questíes de interesse dos trabalhadores* (São Paulo: Cortez/Oboré, 1988.

20. See chapter 3 of David Stoll, *Is Latin America Turning Protestant?* (Berkeley: University of California Press, 1990).

21. This approach is parallel to that of Scott Mainwaring for the Catholic Church in *The Catholic Church and Politics in Brazil, 1916–1985* (Stanford, Calif.: Stanford University Press, 1986).

22. A church can, of course, exert an influence beyond its numerical size by sending its members out to conquer leadership positions in society and get elected on a nonreligious vote. But a sectarian group is unlikely to do this. It is possible that people in such leadership posi-

tions may stumble into the group as converts; this largely explains the atypical career of Benedita da Silva, the Workers' Party deputy from the Assemblies of God.

23. Sarney was the first civilian president after the military regime, but was not elected by popular vote.

24. Steve Bruce makes a similar point regarding the religious right in the United States in *The Rise and Fall of the New Christian Right* (Oxford: Clarendon Press, 1988), p. 56.

25. Antônio Flávio Pierucci, "As bases da nova direita," *Novos estudos CEBRAP* 19 (December 1987): 26–45.

26. See Stoll, *Is Latin America Turning Protestant?* pp. 317–19.

27. Cf. Bruce, *Rise and Fall*, p. 69.

28. Rubem César Fernandes critically reviews this stage of the study of Brazilian Protestantism in " 'Religiões populares': Uma visão parcial da literatura recente," *Boletim informativo e bibliográfico de ciências sociais* 18 (1984): 3–26.

29. The argument here is an extension of David Martin's theory for Europe in *A General Theory of Secularization* (Oxford: Blackwell, 1978). Examples of left-of-center minorities are the small Protestant community in France and its large Catholic counterparts in Holland, Switzerland, and Germany.

30. David Martin, *Tongues of Fire: The Explosion of Protestantism in Latin America* (Oxford: Blackwell, 1990), p. 64.

31. Following the sociology of religion, "church" here means an inclusive national body (like Anglicanism in Britain); "denomination" signifies a body that sees itself as one among many expressions of the true church, in the typical American context of religious pluralism and separation from the state; and "sect" refers to an exclusive body emphasizing separation from the world.

32. "Introduction" by Esaú de Carvalho, in Josué Sylvestre, *Irmão vota em irmão* (Brasília: Pergaminho, 1986), p. 24.

33. Sylvestre, *Os evangélicos*, pp. 62–64.

34. Stoll, *Is Latin America Turning Protestant?* p. 5.

35. Mainwaring, *The Catholic Church*, pp. 186–202.

4

Protestantism in El Salvador: Conventional Wisdom versus the Survey Evidence

Kenneth M. Coleman, Edwin Eloy
Aguilar, José Miguel Sandoval,
and Timothy J. Steigenga

PROTESTANTISM GREW strikingly throughout Latin America in the 1970s and 1980s. Estimating such growth is hazardous in the absence of firm national survey data, but the phenomenon is clearly embracing sizable segments of national populations. In Guatemala estimates of Protestantism as a percentage of the national population were in the range of 20 to 25 percent by the early 1980s, with more recent estimates approaching 30 percent.[1]

In Chile estimates of the magnitude of Protestantism were nearly as striking—somewhere around 21 or 22 percent by the early to mid-1980s. Also becoming heavily Protestant was Brazil's interior, where evangelization by the Assemblies of God met a receptive population. Estimates in the range of 16 to 20 percent of the Brazilian population as Protestant were common. Indeed, across South and Central America the growth of Protestantism was nearly ubiquitous.[2] In Colombia, Ecuador, Mexico, Paraguay, Uruguay, and Venezuela, the phenomenon was just starting, but discernible growth had already occurred.

The most dramatic political impact of Protestantism has been

An earlier version of this chapter appeared as "Protestantism in El Salvador: Conventional Wisdom versus Survey Evidence," by Edwin Eloy Aguilar, José Miguel Sandoval, Timothy J. Steigenga, and Kenneth M. Coleman, in *Latin American Research Review* 28, no. 2 (1993), pp. 119–40. Reprinted by permission.

in Guatemala. General Efraín Ríos Montt, who was "called to power" by junior military officers in 1982, used his eighteen-month reign to apply evangelical rhetoric to the task of counter-insurgency.[3] For no Guatemalan president has the office been literally quite such a "bully pulpit" as it was for Ríos, who sermonized every Sunday on radio and television. Overthrown in 1983, Ríos did not disappear from Guatemalan political life. He was campaigning vigorously in the 1990 presidential elections, only to be disqualified by a constitutional ban on past participants in palace coups. As of 1991, Guatemala once again had a Protestant as president, Jorge Serrano Elías, this time elected. Nothing illustrates the growing strength of Protestantism more dramatically than two Protestant presidencies—one military and one civilian—as bookends to the decade 1981–1991.

Neighboring El Salvador also has experienced the phenomenon. In the 1940s, the number of Salvadoran Protestants was estimated at less than 1 percent of the national population. By the late 1980s, serious public opinion research was yielding estimates in the range of 12 percent Protestant.[4]

Evangelical growth is so dramatic that throughout Latin America, Catholic authorities are decrying the "invasion of the sects," a label that lumps long-established Protestant denominations together with newer and more esoteric groups.[5] Underlying the denunciations is the suspicion that Protestant expansion is another form of North American imperialism. Many critics in the Catholic Church and on the left presume that the Central Intelligence Agency is bankrolling evangelism, to soften up popular resistance to U.S. foreign policy. Knowing more about who Protestants are and what they believe may help us assess the plausibility of such interpretations.

We seek not to explain the growth of Protestantism in El Salvador but, rather, to (a) describe the characteristics of Protestants, (b) examine the nature of their religious experiences, and (c) explore the implications of their religion for political attitudes and behavior. To do so, we employ survey data collected in 1988 and 1989 under the supervision of the late Father Ignacio Martín-Baró, S.J., director of the Central American University's Institute of Public Opinion Research (IUDOP).[6]

Two national surveys were employed for this purpose, with sample sizes of 1,065 and 1,303 respondents. The first sample, for a survey entitled "La religión para los salvadoreños," was interviewed between June 11 and 26, 1988, in seven of El Salvador's fourteen *departamentos*.[7] The second survey, entitled "Los salvadoreños y el nuevo gobierno de ARENA," was conducted between May 6 and 20, 1989, and covered all fourteen *departamentos*. Households were sampled, and one individual per household was interviewed. In both surveys, sampling in all departments included urban interviews in the *cabecera departamental* and rural interviews.[8]

Detailed sampling reports prepared by Martín-Baró and his associates at IUDOP provide much additional information, including preliminary analyses.[9] Perhaps the most useful datum in judging the quality of the survey is that refusals in the 1989 survey were 18.8 percent of the initial household sample, a strikingly low percentage for a country in the midst of a civil war.[10] We find these data to be of high quality, generated by researchers who were attentive to methodological probity under difficult circumstances. But readers of this article may judge for themselves, as copies of the sampling reports prepared by IUDOP are available.[11]

Sociological Characteristics of Protestants

Before examining the nature of the Protestant religious experience in El Salvador, it is worthwhile to consider some basic sociological characteristics. Two previous empirical examinations of Protestantism in Guatemalan village settings report that Protestants tend to be recruited from groups subject to extraordinary economic pressure, but that prolonged exposure to Protestantism tends to provide either motivations or behavioral propensities conducive to economic advancement.[12] These authors assert that Protestants may start out among the very poor, but in time some will attain greater economic security.[13]

Clearly, the survey data reported here are inadequate to assess such an hypothesis because the theory predicts movement over time while the data are synchronic. Yet as a first

Table 4-1
Monthly Income in *Colones*, by Religion

Monthly Income (colones)	Non-Affiliators (n = 156)	Protestants (n = 174)	Non-Practicing Catholics (n = 325)	Practicing Catholics (n = 355)
0	55%	54%	47%	51%
1–450	12	16	12	7
451–900	12	9	12	9
901–1,400	3	6	10	10
1,400+	17	15	19	23
Mean*	485 col.	407 col.	638 col.	727 col.
Median**	795 col.	700 col.	800 col.	1,100 col.
Standard Deviation*	1,151 col.	745 col.	1,272 col.	1,363 col.

*Calculated before collapsing data into four categories, including those with no income.
**Median income among those who earned some income (but excluding those with zero income).
$X^2 = 18.54$; $p = .0294$; d.f. = 12.

approximation to the issue, we can assess whether Protestants are socioeconomically distinct from holders of other religious beliefs. If not, that would suggest that Salvadoran Protestants had not yet, during the civil war of the 1980s, produced savings, investment, or other forms of entrepreneurial activity sufficient to yield socioeconomic differentiation.

In Table 4-1 we assemble part of the picture by reporting the monthly income of respondents.[14] Comparing Protestants with practicing and nonpracticing Catholics, and with those who profess no formal religion,[15] discernible differences can be detected. Protestants, on average, rank lower on socioeconomic variables than do Catholics and exhibit considerable similarity to nonaffiliators in their income profile.[16]

The most striking findings in Table 4-1 are that Protestants rank lowest in mean income (407 colones per month, including those with no income) and in median income (700 colones per month among those who earn some income), have the greatest homogeneity in income levels (note the lower standard deviation of 745 colones), and display the lowest percentage of respondents in the high-end income category. By contrast, the group ranking the highest on income profile is practicing Catholics, who display a mean monthly income of 727 colones and a median of 1,100 colones, followed by nonpracticing Catholics, with a mean of 638 colones per month and a median of 800 per month. In a finding that foreshadows subsequent results, Protestants resemble religious nonaffiliators more than any other group.

Another indication of how Protestants rank lower than Catholics is their educational profiles. Table 4-2 reports the years of formal education completed by Salvadoran respondents, according to religious category. Once again Protestants most resemble the religious nonaffiliators (mean of 5.8 years, versus 6.1 years for the nonaffiliators), while Catholics have more education, on average, with practicing Catholics being the most educated group of all (mean of 9.1 years, versus 8.5 years for nonpracticing Catholics).

As for occupation, in Table 4-3 we see that the familiar pattern continues to hold. Protestants and nonaffiliators tend to be concentrated more heavily in lower-status occupations. For example 58 percent of the economically active religious nonaffiliators are found in working-class occupations, as are 52 percent of the economically active Protestants. By contrast, only 40 percent of the economically active nonpracticing Catholics are employed in working-class occupations, and of practicing Catholics the total is a mere 24 percent working-class. At the other end of the scale, 23 percent of the economically active practicing Catholics hold professional jobs and 53 percent are in service occupations. The comparable figures among Protestants are 8 percent and 40 percent, and among nonaffiliators, 7 percent and 35 percent.

The sociological outline is clear. Salvadoran Protestants and religious nonaffiliators have lower education levels, occupy lower-status occupations, and earn less than Catholics, whether the latter are practicing or nonpracticing. Indeed, except for very marginal differences in occupational status, the similarity between Protestants and religious nonaffiliators is striking. Both groups are poor and generally educated only at the primary school level. The recruitment efforts of Salvadoran Protestants may well be directed toward this pool of poor, religiously non-

Table 4-2
Highest Grade Completed, by Religion

Years of Education	Non-Affiliators (n = 155)	Protestants (n = 174)	Non-Practicing Catholics (n = 325)	Practicing Catholics (n = 354)
None	23%	24%	15%	14%
1–6	41%	41%	24%	24%
7–9	11%	12%	13%	11%
10–12	11%	13%	29%	27%
13–21	14%	10%	19%	25%
Mean in Years*	6.1	5.8	8.5	9.1
SD in Years*	5.2	5.1	5.5	5.6

*Calculated before collapsing data into categories.
$X^2 = 75.37$; p = .0000; d.f. = 12.

affiliated individuals, although it would require other research methodoligies to confirm such a hypothesis. What is clear is the strong sociological resemblance of Protestants to the religiously unaffiliated.

The importance of these findings is suggested by comparing the Salvadoran Protestants so described with Daniel Levine's characterization of the Catholic ecclesial base communities (CEBs) in Venezuela and Colombia.[17] The CEBs are another attempt to reinvigorate religious community. Levine finds that the CEBs recruit from well-established urban barrios, not from recent invasion sites representing the poorest urbanites. The Salvadoran data, by contrast, suggest that Protestant recruitment may be taking place precisely among these lower strata. That is the inference that future longitudinal studies should pursue.

The Protestant Experience

Central to the Protestant vision has been the idea that a person's relationship to God can be direct, unmediated, and "bilateral." Reacting against a medieval church that was perceived as excessively hierarchical, bureaucratic, and dogmatic, Protestants over the centuries have stressed local initiative, popular participation,

Table 4-3
Occupational Status, by Religion

Occupation	Non-Affiliators (n = 151)		Protestants (n = 171)		Non-Practicing Catholics (n = 315)		Practicing Catholics (n = 336)	
	a	b	a	b	a	b	a	b
Professionals	4%	7%	4%	8%	7%	12%	12%	23%
Service occupations	19	35	19	40	30	48	28	53
Working class	33	58	25	52	25	40	13	24
Economically "inactive"	44	—	52	—	38	—	47	—
Totals	100	100	100	100	100	100	100	100

"A" column includes those who generate no income; "b" column excludes those who generate no income.
X^2 = 50.8; p < .0001; d.f. = 9, for comparisons of column a.
X^2 = 35.6; p < .0001; d.f. = 9, for comparisons of column b.

and "do-it-yourself" theology. While a multiplicity of Protestant denominations have emerged over the centuries, each with its own hierarchy and theology, there has been a "live and let live" character to the Protestant experience. Decentralization does not threaten the growth of Protestantism, nor do church schisms. Indeed, Protestantism grows by schism and decentralization.

Such characteristics have seemingly been replicated in the very recent spread of Protestantism in Latin America. The crux of the Protestant growth in the hemisphere in the 1970s and 1980s was that it affords the opportunity for decentralizing the religious experience. According to Thomas Bamat, Protestants tend to "create more egalitarian and participatory relations. They allow even the poorest people to assume leadership roles and to encourage emotional expression during liturgical services." [18] This point is reiterated by David Stoll, who argues that decentralization does not equal democratization, but it does create opportunity:

> It was not that the evangelical churches [of Latin America] were necessarily democratic: the most rapidly growing, such as the Assemblies of God in Brazil, could be very authoritarian. . . . But evangelical Protestantism opened up a whole new ladder of leadership possibilities. Theoretically, any male could reach the top, even if married and without formal training. For dissidents, there was always the possibility of joining another evangelical church or starting their own. For dissident Catholics confronting a local priest, there was often no place to go within the system. [19]

The Salvadoran data give us the opportunity to explore whether, in the middle of a protracted civil war, those who become Protestants have experiences that are more intimate, more "popular," and less "reactive" toward religious authority. In short, is there any evidence that Salvador's Protestants experience religion differently than do Catholics?

In certain ways the data suggest only marginal differences between Catholics and Protestants. Catholicism, for example, may be less hierarchical than commonly supposed. [20] Take the data

Table 4-4
Percentage of Respondents Who Know Their Pastor or Priest

	Non-Affiliated (n = 92)	Protestants (n = 173)	Non-Practicing Catholics (n = 323)	Practicing Catholics (n = 352)
Don't know cleric	80%	5%	42%	17%
Know "own" cleric	20	95	58	83

$X^2 = 214.8$; $p < .0001$; d.f. = 3.

reported in Table 4-4. The percentage who know their pastor/ priest among Protestants (95 percent) and practicing Catholics (83 percent) is quite high. While the results bespeak a slightly greater degree of intimacy among Protestants, the difference is not as vast as might be supposed.[21]

In Table 4-5, however, we find dramatic testimony to the nature of the Protestant experience. This table reports on whether respondents have ever been visited by a pastor or priest in their home. Protestants overwhelmingly (77 percent) report having received such visits, whereas the number of practicing Catholics who have been visited in their home by a priest is only 28 percent.

These data suggest that a high degree of "congregational intimacy" between religious authorities and believers is a distinctive feature of Protestantism and a likely source of its appeal.[22] Protestantism in El Salvador, as elsewhere in contemporary Latin America, appears to be a highly decentralized religious experience in which a driving force may well be the lack of hierarchy and the opportunity for neighborhood bonding to occur via in-home religious services.[23]

The pattern of intimacy is reinforced by the frequency of attending religious services (see Table 4-6). Protestants attend worship services twice as frequently as do practicing Catholics: 9.27 times per month versus 4.66 times per month. One-third of the Protestants (34 percent) attend more than ten services per month, with a significant percentage (12 percent) attending

Table 4-5
Percent of Respondents Who Have Been Visited at Home by Priest or Pastor

	Non-Affiliated (n = 86)	Protestants (n = 172)	Non-Practicing Catholics (n = 294)	Practicing Catholics (n = 341)
Never visited	91%	23%	84%	72%
Visited by cleric	9	77	16	28

$X^2 = 216.7$; p < .0001; d.f. = 3.

Table 4-6
Attendance at Religious Services: Monthly Rate

Services Attended	Non-Affiliated (n = 53)	Protestants (n = 168)	Non-Practicing Catholics (n = 295)	Practicing Catholics (n = 337)
None	76%	14%	45%	11%
1	11	4	12	5
2–4	8	29	38	60
5–10	4	19	3	16
11+	1	34	2	8
Total	100	100	100	100
Mean	0.87/month	9.27/month	1.58/month	4.66/month

$X^2 = 340.8$; p < .0001; d.f. = 12.

services daily. Such frequent attendance can certainly provide structure and discipline in the lives of the poor. In the best of cases, it appears to provide bonding and emotional support.[24]

If Protestantism is characterized by a strong commitment to a direct and unmediated relationship with God, then prayer ought to be intense among Protestants. Is that the case? The data in Table 4-7 suggest that Protestants indeed pray more frequently than do Catholics. The percentage praying more than once a day is about 30 percent of the Catholics and 57 percent of the Protestants.

In passing, we should note how intensely religious a society El Salvador is. Even among those professing no religious affilia-

Table 4-7
Frequency of Prayer, by Religious Affiliation

Incidence	Non-Affiliated (n = 152)	Protestants (n = 174)	Non-Practicing Catholics (n = 321)	Practicing Catholics (n = 352)
Less than daily	28%	1%	9%	3%
Once a day	47	42	68	67
Twice a day	7	15	8	17
Thrice a day	5	27	3	5
"At any moment"*	13	15	13	8

*The Salvadoran pollsters clearly interpreted this response as indicating the greatest frequency of prayer.
$X^2 = 257.6$; $p < .0001$; d.f. = 12.

tion, 72 percent assert that they pray at least once daily, and 92 percent of "nonpracticing" Catholics pray at least daily. Whatever legacies Catholicism has left in El Salvador, routine prayer is one of them. Protestantism may enhance that tendency, but it did not create it. Moreover, it does not appear to change the content of prayer greatly.[25]

But what about the content of belief? Do Protestants hold different theological beliefs than Catholics? Table 4-8 suggests that there are significant differences in the literalness with which Protestants and practicing Catholics interpret traditional Christian concepts. Note that 93 percent of the Protestants believe in an extraterrestrial heaven (versus 86 percent of practicing Catholics), and 75 percent of the Protestants believe in a metahuman hell, versus only 48 percent of practicing Catholics. Catholics, whether practicing or nonpracticing, are significantly more likely (34–35 percent) to believe in "a terrestrial hell" than are Protestants (14 percent).

Overall, Table 4-8 suggests that literal interpretation of many traditional Christian concepts is quite striking in El Salvador. For example, belief in miracles is widely diffused, ranging from a low of 79 percent among nonaffiliators to a high of 95 percent among both Protestants and practicing Catholics. Moreover, as many as 62 percent of the nonaffiliators believe in heaven, and 39 percent

Table 4-8
Belief in Traditional Christian Concepts

	Non-Affiliated (n = 153)	Protestants (n = 172)	Non-Practicing Catholics (n = 321)	Practicing Catholics (n = 349)
Believe in heaven*	62%	93%	70%	86%
Believe in metahuman hell	39	75	35	48
Believe in terrestrial hell	21	12	32	31
Believe in both kinds of hell**	3	2	2	4
Believe in miracles***	79	95	88	95

*$X2 = 73.8$; $p < .0001$.
**$X2 = 116.0$; $p < .0001$.
***$X2 = 45.1$; $p < .0001$.

of them believe in a metahuman hell.[26] So while the Protestant propensity toward literal interpretation of concepts traditional to Christianity is strong, such interpretations are widespread in Salvadoran society. Practicing Catholics share many beliefs with Protestants.

Aside from how Protestants and Catholics envision hell, do they interpret other religious concepts differently? Table 4-9 suggests another such area. The modal attribution of an ultimate purpose for religion among Protestants is that of "personal salvation" (40 percent of Protestants versus no more than 19 percent among any other category of respondents). In a context of poverty and protracted civil war, recourse to Protestantism might be interpreted as a conflict-aversive survival strategy, thereby enhancing the tendency to see personal salvation as the ultimate end of religion.[27] By contrast, as will be demonstrated in a subsequent section, Catholic believers are marginally, but significantly, more likely to endorse an activist church that confronts social injustice and tries to transform society as an agent of God on earth. Protestants, however, are more likely to seek to transform themselves, focusing on personal rather than societal salvation.[28]

Table 4-9
The Ultimate Purpose of Religion

	Non-Affiliated (n = 147)	Protestants (n = 173)	Non-Practicing Catholics (n = 324)	Practicing Catholics (n = 351)
Fomenting belief in God	31%	25%	37%	36%
Personal salvation	15	40	12	19
Other answers (9 categories)	54	35	51	45

$X^2 = 61.2$; p < .0001; d.f. = 30.

Judging from our data, the experience of Salvadoran Protestants can be summarized as follows: they participate in a home- and neighborhood-centered religious environment, characterized by familiarity with church authorities and intense religious practice. Protestants tend to be especially literal in their interpretation of traditional religious concepts in an environment where literal interpretations are common. And Protestants are highly likely to see religion as a route to personal salvation.

These being the characteristics of Protestantism in El Salvador, what indirect political effects are imaginable? The most widespread assumption is that Protestantism generates political conservatism. If Protestants exhibit ideologies of self-help via personal self-control, they are unlikely to endorse highly interventionist states as a solution to social ills. In this sense, they may be like other political conservatives. Since Protestantism generates such a strong sense of personal responsibility for improving one's own situation, it could undermine support for governmental intervention to improve social conditions.

Yet an alternative line of theorizing exists. Levine has noted the democratizing potential of decentralized religious communities, namely, the Catholic ecclesial base communities (CEBs). Since Protestantism shares some of the attributes of the CEBs, an analogous argument could be made: those who learn to interpret the world on their own via intensive Bible study might become politically emboldened and more capable of fulfilling the role of the proactive democratic citizen. In a different sense, David Martin suggests that Protestantism might enhance pluralism because it "represents an advanced form of social differentiation and can operate best where hitherto monopolistic systems are disintegrating."[29] Is it possible that the diffusion of Protestantism might unintentionally generate additional political space for a host of groups?

Political Implications of Religious Belief

Citizens evaluate the society that surrounds them as a preliminary step toward thinking about government. The degree of justice or injustice perceived will structure what citizens expect from government. At a minimum, we might assume that perceiving injustice is a necessary precondition for citizens to demand that government, or other agencies, such as the church, take an active role in restructuring society. If society is not perceived to be unjust, then neither government nor the church will be expected to change it.

How do Salvadorans perceive their society, and do the Protestants among them perceive society much differently than do other Salvadorans? In Table 4-10, we see that more than 70 percent of Salvadorans in all categories of religious belief consider the existing social system to be unjust. Protestants are most likely to see the existing system as just, but even so only 26 percent would characterize their society as "very just" or "somewhat just." So, while Protestants are somewhat more likely to see their own society in positive terms, perceptions of injustice nonetheless prevail among all Salvadorans, regardless of religion.[30] The potential for seeking assertive government is present even among Protestants.

Since the religious experience of Protestantism emphasizes intense interaction in very small units of worship, as well as personal salvation, how will Salvadoran Protestants interpret the proper role of the church? Will they see it as involved in rectifying the injustice that is so widely perceived? Or will such

Table 4-10
Perceptions of the Socioeconomic System of El Salvador

	Non-Affiliated (n = 131)	Protestants (n = 134)	Non-Practicing Catholics (n = 283)	Practicing Catholics (n = 311)
Very just	3%	10%	3%	2%
Somewhat just	15	16	16	14
Somewhat unjust	32	39	39	41
Very unjust	50	34	42	42

X^2 = 24.9; p = .003; d.f. = 12.

Table 4-11
Should the Church Prefer the Poor?

	Non-Affiliated (n = 131)	Protestants (n = 134)	Non-Practicing Catholics (n = 283)	Practicing Catholics (n = 311)
Yes	44%	42%	44%	43%
No	56	58	56	57

X^2 = 0.3; p = ns; d.f. = 3.

responsibilities be taken as individual rather than collective, for instance, "By taking care of myself, I take care of society by not becoming a burden to others"? Or do they perceive social injustice as immutable and incapable of being addressed?

One concept that has been much discussed in the post-Medellín era in Latin America[31] is the duty of the church to assist the poor. A recent strand of theology stresses the violence that poverty does to one's humanness, and therefore to one's capacity to relate to God. If that is so, then the role of the church in addressing poverty becomes a key issue. When Salvadorans were asked whether the church should "prefer the poor," individuals of all religious affiliations divided in the same way (Table 4-11). Roughly 42 to 44 percent favored the "preferential option for the poor," while 56 to 58 percent opposed such a posture by

Table 4-12
Should the Church Mediate Social Conflicts?

	Non-Affiliated (n = 131)	Protestants (n = 162)	Non-Practicing Catholics (n = 297)	Practicing Catholics (n = 333)
Yes	43%	24%	41%	51%
No	57	76	59	49

$X^2 = 31.2$; $p < .0001$; d.f. = 3.

the church. Those opposing preferential attention to the poor most frequently appealed to the equality of all human beings, presumably including equality before God. On this topic, then, Salvadoran political attitudes reflected a good deal of conservatism[32] in the late 1980s, regardless of religious affiliation. Slightly under half the Salvadorans surveyed endorsed a socially preoccupied church, but slightly more than half believed that the church should not accord special concern to the living conditions of the poor.

Yet the church could be active in other ways, such as mediating social conflicts. In Table 4-12, we see that here Protestants do differ, being less willing to endorse a role for the church in this regard. Two effects seem discernible in producing deviations from the 41 percent to 43 percent of individuals who otherwise might prefer an active role for the church.[33] Active Catholics are more likely (51 percent) to endorse a role for the church in resolving social conflicts, whereas Protestants are significantly less likely (24 percent). The reticence of Protestants to envision "the church" as an agent for conflict resolution is striking,[34] but perhaps equally important is that most Salvadorans do not see a productive role for the church in resolving social conflict. Apparently, conflict is so endemic and rooted in the Salvadoran experience that all Salvadorans find it difficult to envision human agents bringing it to an end, even agents purporting to serve divine ends. But Protestants are especially reticent. Indeed, they see the primary social role of the church as being to evange-

Table 4-13
Should a Christian Support the Guerrillas?

	Non-Affiliated (n = 144)	Protestants (n = 158)	Non-Practicing Catholics (n = 296)	Practicing Catholics (n = 334)
Yes	24%	13%	30%	33%
Don't know	13	10	10	10
No	63	77	60	57

$X^2 = 25.5$; $p < .0003$; d.f. $= 6$.

lize, that is, to incorporate more people and to influence them to do right.[35]

If Salvadorans believed that the church should not attempt to resolve social conflict, what did they believe in the late 1980s about the political implications of their religious commitments? One possibility is that, perceiving injustice, individuals would opt to support the guerrillas of the Farabundo Martí National Liberation Front (FMLN) and fight injustice through armed insurrection. Table 4-13 makes it clear that Salvadorans did not, on balance, believe that supporting the FMLN was a legitimate Christian option. Yet the difference between Protestants and Catholics was significant. Only 13 percent of the Protestants believed that Christians could support the guerrilla movement, while 33 percent of practicing Catholics could envision such support as appropriate. Individual decisions to pursue "liberation" via a religiously sanctioned commitment to revolution are more likely to emanate from Catholics than from Protestants. The latter were more apt to argue in follow-up probes that "all violence goes against God's will."[36] From such findings, readers might infer that Salvadoran Protestants endorsed the government's counterinsurgency campaigns. However, that was not the case. A poll after the 1989 presidential election by IUDOP reveals otherwise, as reported in Table 4-14. Here we see that virtually as many Protestants as Catholics favored negotiating with the rebels.[37] Indeed, the percentage of Protestants favoring

Table 4-14
What Should the New ARENA Government Do about the War?

	Non-Affiliated (n = 198)	Protestants (n = 161)	Catholics* (n = 895)
Negotiate	75%	79%	77%
Continue current course**	3	0	2
Increase military pressure	11	7	12
Other suggestions	11	14	9

*Catholics were not identified as practicing or nonpracticing.
**"Seguir peleando con el FMLN y tratar de ganar apoyo para el gobierno."
$X^2 = 10.8$; $p = .09$; d.f. = 6.

negotiation is marginally higher than in the other groups, and the percentage favoring militarization is marginally lower, both positions consistent with the belief that "all violence goes against God's will."

Another indication of Salvadoran Protestants' lack of belli-cosity can be found in Table 4-15. Here we see that Protestants are nearly as likely to favor making concessions to the FMLN to achieve a peace settlement as are other groups. Indeed, the major difference is that Protestants tend more toward neutral response categories (those found in parentheses), which might suggest a propensity to opt out of political conflict.

Protestants' lack of bellicosity is relative, to be sure. Like Catholics and nonaffiliators, Protestants are dubious about the wisdom of reducing the size of the army. But like other Salva-dorans, Protestants did wish to "purify" the army, presumably to retire or remove human rights violators.[38]

Finally, what are the partisan orientations, electoral experi-ences, and expectations for the political future exhibited by Protestants, Catholics, and nonaffiliators? At the time of the 1989 survey, power had just changed hands from the center-right gov-ernment of President José Napoleón Duarte, a Christian Demo-crat, to the government of Alfredo Cristiani, of ARENA, a party long suspected of committing human rights violations.[39] In the 1989 election ARENA received 53 percent of the valid vote, while

Table 4-15
Percent Endorsing Justifiable Concessions in Negotiations

	Non-Affiliated (n = 198)	Protestants (n = 163)	Catholics* (n = 897)
Reduce army to 1979 level	34%	23%	27%
	(33%)	(35%)	(26%)
New elections after cease-fire	37	23	29
	(25)	(31)	(20)
"Purify" the armed forces	68	68	73
	(24)	(25)	(21)

Note: Primary entry is percent endorsing a given particular concession. Entry in parentheses is the percent saying "I agree, more or less" or "Don't know." The row entries do not represent alternative answers to the same question, but the percentage indicating, in response to different questions, that a task should be attempted.
*Breakdown between practicing and nonpracticing Catholics is unavailable in this survey.
X^2 = 25.5; p < .0003; d.f. = 6.

the Christian Democrats dropped to 38 percent, and the newly recognized left offered candidates under the label of Democratic Convergence who garnered a modest 4 percent of the valid vote.

Significantly, Protestants are less conservative and linked to ARENA than some critics believed. Conspiratorial interpretations would have it that Central American Protestants are a tool of U.S. foreign policy. Yet in Table 4-16 we find that Salvadoran Protestants are less likely than Salvadoran Catholics to believe that the 1989 elections were honest. They also were less likely to vote than Catholics. But when they did vote, they were less likely to have voted for ARENA,[40] and less inclined than Catholics to believe that human rights violations would decrease under ARENA.

Such results hardly support a conspiratorial interpretation that the "invasion of the sects" functions as an instrument of U.S. foreign policy. As Salvadoran electoral processes were generally endorsed by the United States,[41] and were presented internationally as proof of the democratization of Salvadoran society, to find that poor Protestants expressed considerable doubt about the in-

Table 4-16
Elections, Parties, and the Political Future

	Non-Affiliated (n = 198)	Protestants (n = 161)	Catholics* (n = 891)†
Those believing elections honest[1]	40%	46%	59%
Those not voting[2]	55	44	37
Voters indicating[3]			
Vote for ARENA	33	31	40
Vote for PDC	7	14	10
Annulled vote	8	8	7
Vote is secret/refused to tell‡	39	41	34
Other	13	6	9
Those expecting human rights will be			
better protected by ARENA[4]	27	30	40

*1989 survey doesn't distinguish between practicing and nonpracticing Catholics.
†Number of cases varies between blocs in this table, being lowest in the third bloc (for whom voted) because overall electoral turnout rate was estimated (from self-reports) at 59 percent.
‡This was apparently the only item in the survey for which a high percentage of respondents refused to reveal their thoughts. We interpret this phenomenon as a well-placed insistence on the right of citizens to protect political privacy in a setting where violations of the secrecy of the vote have been commonplace, with tragic consequences. While such an insistence makes it difficult to calculate the Salvadoran vote, it does not indicate that the survey is invalid. These same respondents expressed a variety of views critical of the Salvadoran government and society, and they endorsed a number of policy proposals not then favored by the government. Clearly, then, Salvadorans were not intimidated from expressing their views. Surveys always have limitations—but the most important ones deal with the inability to capture the richness and nuances of views held by respondents. We see little evidence of intentional misrepresentation of views in these data.
[1]$X2 = 31.7$; $p = .0002$; d.f. = 6.
[2]$X2 = 21.3$; $p < .0001$; d.f. = 2.
[3]$X2 = 26.7$; $p = $ ns; d.f. = 8.
[4]$X2 = 17.0$; $p = .001$; d.f. = 4.

tegrity of the electoral process is striking. It is doubly so since they expressed significantly more doubt than did more highly educated and prosperous Catholics.

Were Salvadoran Protestants an effective tool of U.S. foreign policy, they should at least give credence to U.S.-arranged elections. But they did so even less than Catholics. Indeed, this suggests an inversion of the "common knowledge" about politico-religious alliances in Central America. Rather than Protestants being a "tool of the United States" and confronting a "radicalized" Catholic Church, the reality is closer to a situation in which poor Protestants doubted the integrity of electoral processes and the possibility of reform, while (generally) more affluent Catholics were willing to take a chance on the possibility that U.S. pressure for electoral reform could produce meaningful outcomes. Whatever the political implications of Protestantism in El Salvador, they do not include an especially close association with the governing right-wing ARENA party or with the electoral processes that brought it to power.

Our results suggest a complex picture of what Protestantism implies for political attitudes among Salvadorans. Most Protestants perceive injustice in Salvadoran society, as do most Salvadorans. But most Protestants do not endorse an especially assertive church, one that intervenes on behalf of the poor or mediates social conflicts. Only 24 to 42 percent of Protestants feel comfortable with a vision of the church that seeks to restructure human society so as to do God's will. The more dramatic the social application of Christianity, such as supporting the guerrillas, the less comfortable most Protestants feel.[42]

At the same time, it is clear that Salvadoran Protestants are not simply agents of the militaristic right. Protestants, like all Salvadorans, wanted to see a negotiated settlement to the war that has devastated the country so tragically since 1979. They saw the need to make concessions to the guerrillas slightly less clearly but in roughly the same terms as did other Salvadorans. Nor are Protestants especially enthralled with ARENA. As best as can be inferred from a post-1989 election poll, Protestants were less sanguine about the electoral process, about ARENA, and about the political future under ARENA than were Catholics.

Conclusion

What do these two surveys from the Central American University's Public Opinion Institute (IUDOP) reveal about the origins, beliefs, and political implications of Salvadoran Protestantism? The data from IUDOP reveal that Protestants are recruited from the poorest and least educated elements of Salvadoran society. Clearly less well off and less well educated than local Catholics, Salvador's Protestants most resemble religious nonaffiliators in sociological terms. Both groups come from the poorest strata of society. Contrary to Weberian visions of a Protestant Ethic lifting poor converts into higher social strata, our data give little sign that Protestantism has led to upward social mobility in El Salvador.[43]

Conservatism is indeed implicit in the worldview of Salvadoran Protestants. But it is not always doctrinal conservatism, and is not fully grounded in distinctive beliefs about theological topics or political objects. Rather, it is the kind of conservatism associated with personal discipline, with minding one's own business, with trying to solve one's personal problems rather than the world's. Constantly under political and economic pressure in an environment of protracted civil war, the understandable reaction of many Salvadoran Protestants was to mind their own business. Indirectly, that may imply a less activist church. But if the immediate effect of Protestantism is to turn inward, this can also be understood as a way of summoning one's strength for imposing order on a disorderly world. The shared experience of regular interaction in a congregational community mobilizes emotional and moral resources. In this sense, Protestantism becomes a survival strategy.

Is this avoidance of the world? Does it suggest political withdrawal? Not necessarily. Salvadoran Protestants are drawn from the ranks of the poor. But more Protestants vote than do the equally poor Salvadorans who remain religiously nonaffiliated, so Protestantism is not necessarily an electorally demobilizing experience. Protestants *do* reject violence as a form of political action: they reject association with guerrillas, but they also favor negotiation between the FMLN and the government, although they do not necessarily see the church as an appropriate broker between the parties. Protestants may feel particularly comfortable with representative democracy, in which citizens participate as individuals, but less comfortable with the notion of the church as corporate actor.

The overall pattern of belief and behavior suggests a generally consistent orientation of changing social structures by changing people. Protestants do see injustice in the world that surrounds them, but they believe that people must change in order to address social evils. That implies a need to evangelize, so as to change more people. But it also implies a need to assure themselves that change really has occurred, which requires intense religious practice. The intensity of religious practice increases the chance that declaring oneself an evangelical will actually lead to behavioral change. It can also lead individuals to assume new roles and competences.[44]

Certain theorists have suggested that potential for cultural change is inherent in the spread of decentralized religious authority in Latin America. Writing of the Christian base communities, Levine notes that the creation of "confident, articulate, and capable men and women from a hitherto silent, unorganized and dispirited population" via religious association may "demystify authority by giving the tools of association to everyone, making the effort legitimate in religious terms and thus fostering the growth of a truly independent civil society."[45] David Stoll makes a similar argument about Protestantism.[46] We concur regarding the Protestants of El Salvador.

Under very specific circumstances, organized poor people, including Protestants, may decide to challenge authority structures. To identify those circumstances would take us well beyond this study.[47] But we do believe, as does the Reverend Joe Eldridge, that Protestants, reflecting on biblical texts, can decide that they need to press public authorities for help.[48]

Yet Salvadoran Protestants are distinguished primarily by their lack of political uniqueness. They are not political apologists for the right. Nor are they supporters of the insurrectionary left. They vote more frequently than some but less frequently than others. Their votes in 1989 seemed to be neither highly distinct from nor more conservative than those of Catholics.[49] Given the fears attending the diffusion of Protestantism in Central America, the most striking feature of our findings is how similarly Salvadoran Protestants, Catholics, and nonaffiliators assess the troubled political environment of their country in the late 1980s.

These findings help to put the "invasion of the sects" into perspective. The diffusion of Protestantism in El Salvador may be a cultural challenge, but it is not overtly political. Rather, Protestantism has provided a strategy for emotional husbandry and personal survival in one of the most difficult environments for the poor in this hemisphere. If so, perhaps it is not really "alien" to the Salvadoran experience.

NOTES

Acknowledgments: This study is dedicated to the martyrs of El Salvador's José Simeón Cañas Central American University (UCA): Julia Ramos and her daughter, Celina; Father Ignacio Ellacuría, rector; Father Ignacio Martín-Baró, vice rector and director, University Public Opinion Institute (IUDOP); Father Segundo Montes, dean of social sciences; Father Juan Ramón Moreno; Father Joaquín López y López; and Father Amando López. No conventional expression of gratitude can do justice to the sacrifice made by these individuals who died on November 16, 1989, precisely because they were committed to academic integrity, religious tolerance, and political reconciliation in El Salvador. In presenting a secondary analysis of data collected under the supervision of Father Martín-Baró at IUDOP, we acknowledge the immense achievement of those who engaged in the scientific study of public opinion under conditions of civil war and constant threat. Our responsibility is to replicate, as best we can, the care and prudence that so marked the scholarship of Martín-Baró's IUDOP. Via continuing analysis of data that IUDOP collected, fellow scholars can perhaps help to sustain the commitment of Father Martín-Baró and his colleagues to hearing the testimony of the poor. See notes 6 through 10 for further information on the IUDOP surveys.

The authors also wish to thank Héctor Avalos, Charles L. Davis, Virginia Garrard-Burnett, the Reverend James E. Goff, Jonathan Hartlyn, David L. Lowery, Gary Marks, Catharine Newbury, James Penning, Lars Schoultz, Donald Searing, Jurg Steiner, David Stoll, and James W. White, as well as five anonymous reviewers for a professional journal, for helpful comments on this chapter.

1. Timothy R. Evans, "Percentage of Non-Catholics in a Representative Sample of the Guatemalan Population," paper presented at the World Congress of the Latin American Studies Association, Crystal City, Va., April 4–6, 1991, provides a careful empirical assessment of the diffusion of Protestantism in Guatemala based on a 1990 survey in three departments. His estimate is a cumulative total of 30 percent Protestant.

2. See David Stoll, *Is Latin America Turning Protestant?* (Berkeley and Los Angeles: University of California Press, 1990), 3–10, 333–38.

3. See ibid., 180–217; Virginia Garrard-Burnett, "Protestantism in Rural Guatemala, 1872–1954," *Latin American Research Review* 24, no. 2 (1989): 127–42; and Timothy J. Steigenga, "The Protestant Role in State-Society Relations in Guatemala, 1871–1989" (M.A. thesis, University of North Carolina, Chapel Hill, 1991), pp. 37–48.

4. The 1 percent figure comes from Everett A. Wilson, "Sanguine Saints: Pentecostalism in El Salvador," *Church History* 52, no. 2 (1983): 189. Our examination of twenty-two surveys conducted by the Instituto Universitario de Opinión Pública at the Universidad Centroamericana José Simeón Cañas in San Salvador revealed estimates that fell mainly in the range of 10 to 14 percent, with the single most common figure being 12 percent. Stoll reports estimates, from varying agencies, of 12.13 percent, 12.78 percent, and 14 percent for 1985. Stoll, *Is Latin America Turning Protestant?* pp. 335, 337, 333.

5. See Stoll, *Is Latin America Turning Protestant?* pp. 1–24, 39–41.

6. By agreement with Father Martín-Baró, all twenty-two of the surveys conducted prior to his assassination are on deposit with the Institute for Research in Social Science at the University of North Carolina at Chapel Hill. All analyses reported herein were completed by the authors. Sole responsibility for their accuracy rests with the authors.

7. The first sample included two departments judged by IUDOP to be "low conflict" settings (Ahuachapán and Santa Ana), four departments judged to be "high conflict" settings (Usulatán, San Miguel, Morazán, and Chalatenango), and the capital city of San Salvador. In the fall of 1989, the Farabundo Martí National Liberation Front (FMLN) carried an offensive to previously untouched upper-class neighborhoods of the capital city. This led to the reprisal attack on the Central American University that took the lives of Father Martín-Baró and other university personnel. San Salvador would not previously have been described as a "high conflict" zone.

8. Urban interviews were distributed across five social strata: (1) upper and upper middle (11.6 percent [1988], 7.6 percent [1989]);

(2) middle middle (15.8 percent [1988], 15.0 percent [1989]); (3) lower middle (21.9 percent [1988], 25.2 percent [1989]); (4) working class (18.4 percent [1988], 19.9 percent [1989]); and (5) marginal urbanites (7.2 percent [1988], 12.4 percent [1989]). The remaining interviews were with rural dwellers (25.3 percent [1988]; 20.0 percent [1989]).

A potential source of bias in the samples is that they overrepresent the urban population. Given war conditions, no national census was undertaken in 1990. Therefore, lacking certain knowledge of the percentage of urban dwellers in El Salvador, it makes little sense to weight the cases in these samples to adjust them to fit (un)known national parameters. What we can do, however, is examine whether the distribution of our central independent variable, religious affiliation, varies by urban and rural environments. We find no systematic relationship. For example, the 1988 survey reveals that the three provinces with the highest percentage of Protestants include the western, mountainous rural department of Santa Ana (26.4 percent Protestant), the underpopulated east-central department of Usulatán (20.4 percent Protestant), and San Salvador, the capital city (16.0 percent). Certain other rural departments have much lower percentages Protestant (Chalatenango: 5.0 percent; Ahuachapán: 9.9 percent). As noted previously, the national average is best estimated, from all twenty-two surveys undertaken, at 12 percent Protestant. Because Protestantism is growing in both urban and rural areas, and the correlates of Protestantism appear to be the same in rural and urban settings, we conclude that oversampling urban areas is *not* an important determinant of the findings of this study.

9. For example, the average age of interviewees was 36.5 years (1988) and 37.6 years (1989), with standard deviations of 15.0 and 15.3 years, respectively. Mean educational level was 7.9 years (1988) and 7.6 years (1989), with a standard deviation of 5.6 years (1988) and 5.3 years (1989).

10. As a contrast, in seventeen surveys conducted between 1975 and 1991 by the National Opinion Research Center in Chicago, the average refusal rate was 17.2 percent, including some rates as high as 20 to 21 percent. See National Opinion Research Center, *General Social Surveys, 1972–1991: Cumulative Codebook* (Chicago: National Opinion Research Center, 1991), pp. 705–6. Other reports of major surveys in the United States indicate refusal rates in the 20-percent range as being common. Charlotte Steeh, "Trends in Nonresponse Rates, 1952–1979," *Public Opinion Quarterly* 45 (1981): 40–57; Giovanna Morchio, "Trends in NES Response Rates," memo to Board of Overseers, National Elections Study (Ann Arbor: University of Michigan, 1987).

11. Contact José Miguel Sandoval at the Institute for Research in Social Science, University of North Carolina at Chapel Hill, Chapel Hill, N.C., 27599-3355.

12. James D. Sexton, "Protestantism and Modernization in Two Guatemalan Towns," *American Ethnologist* 5 (1978): 280–302; Sheldon Annis, *God and Production in a Guatemalan Town* (Austin: University of Texas Press, 1987).

13. Such findings support theories of the effects of Protestantism that date back to the work of Max Weber, collected in Max Weber, *The Sociology of Religion* (Boston: Beacon Press, 1963).

14. In Table 4-1, an initial category of "no income" is complemented with categories that roughly correspond to quartiles. Hence, zero income to 450 colones represents the bottom quartile, between 450 and 900 represents the second quartile, and so on.

15. As we shall note in a subsequent section, nonaffiliators generally believe in God but apparently not in the institutional church.

16. The major difference is in the relatively greater incidence of "high-income" nonaffiliators versus "high-income" Protestants. Table 4-2 also reveals a cluster of "high-education" nonaffiliators. We infer that the "high-income" nonaffiliators are likely to be university-educated skeptics who have routes to income other than the self-abnegatory routes available to poor Protestants.

17. Daniel Levine, "Popular Groups, Popular Culture and Popular Religion," *Comparative Studies in Society and History* 32, no. 4 (1990): 718–64.

18. Quoted in Stoll, *Is Latin America Turning Protestant?* p. 29.

19. Ibid., pp. 36–37. Still, both ibid., p. 309ff. and Levine, "Popular Groups," note that Catholic ecclesiastical base communities share some of the qualities of Protestantism: strong emphasis on participation, Bible reading, and theological interpretation from below. Both may also open up opportunities for women, given the emphasis on Bible-reading. Participation in either forum may stimulate poor women to demand assistance in developing literacy skills, and more prosperous women to seek leadership roles. Other features of Protestantism may not be found in the base communities, however.

20. If Levine, "Popular Groups," pp. 742–44, is correct. Much of the appeal of the base communities derives from their emphasis on "Protestant-like" qualities: meetings in homes, emphasis on prayer and direct communication with God, and the provision of opportunities for women.

21. Yet statistical significance in this table is highly influenced by the stark contrast between practicing Catholics and Protestants on the one hand and nonpracticing Catholics and nonaffiliators on the other. This gap may serve, more than anything else, to validate the labels. Nonaffiliators and nonpracticing Catholics should not know "their" pastoral agent well, since they do not have one. This finding is wholly expected. By contrast, the similarity between Protestants and practicing Catholics could have been otherwise.

22. The fact that Protestant churches often begin as livingroom operations and expand very slowly to occupy larger churchlike buildings is one source of the frequency of "home visits" by Protestant pastors, as is the tendency toward church formation by schism. One's pastor may be one's neighbor who has started the congregation (or even the denomination) via livingroom services, which then rotate from house to house. In commenting on an earlier version of this manuscript, Héctor Avalos, who now holds a Ph.D. in religious studies but was once a "boy preacher" for an evangelical sect in another Latin American country, reported that "in my former church, the frequency of a cleric's visits was also a measure of his/her work performance by members." Personal communication, November 15, 1991.

23. Sigifredo Bieske, a German Protestant missionary to Costa Rica, stresses the importance of family-centered recruitment strategies in his *El explosivo crecimiento de la iglesia evangélica en Costa Rica* (San José, Costa Rica: EDUCA, n.d. [ca. 1990]), pp. 18–21, 115–16. And in our own study, 18 percent of Protestants who reported having converted from Catholicism attributed their conversion to "home visits" by evangelists.

24. "When people attend church services three, four, or five times a week," states Joseph T. Eldridge, once a Protestant missionary to Honduras, "they either come to love their fellow worshipers or to dislike them. If the former, then bonding and real community grows—the kind of self-confident community that may even begin to challenge authority on occasion. If the latter, then individuals may leave to join or to found another congregation . . . and Protestantism per se is not necessarily impaired." Informal presentation, Chapel of the Cross, Chapel Hill, N.C., February 14, 1991.

25. Additional analyses indicate that between 43 percent and 52 percent of all prayers pertained to personal welfare, regardless of belief category (nonaffiliators, Protestants, nonpracticing and practicing Catholics). Six percent of Protestants and 10 percent of practicing Catho-

lics prayed for an end to the civil war. Seventeen percent of Protestants and 23 percent of practicing Catholics prayed to give thanks for all their blessings. In sum, the content of prayer seemed roughly similar.

26. Some readers have expressed much interest in the conceptual distinction between a "metahuman hell" and "terrestrial hell." This distinction was imposed by the original survey researchers, for whom such theological distinctions were, no doubt, commonplace. A "metahuman hell" refers to a place not on this earth, while a "terrestrial hell" refers to a human existence so painful that it might be conceived as the equivalent to doing penance. "Metahuman" hell is the traditional Christian conception. To think of a terrestrial hell would be to reinterpret the conventional understanding.

27. See Steigenga, "The Protestant Role," for this interpretation of the spread of Protestantism in neighboring Guatemala.

28. As David Stoll is at pains to argue, Latin American Protestantism is a complex and internally differentiated phenomenon. So there may well be Salvadoran Protestants with a strong orientation to righting social wrongs and transforming human society. The Lutheran Church upholds such an orientation in Salvador, according to Jorge Cáceres, "The Churches in El Salvador: From Prophetism to Mediation," paper presented at the World Congress of the Latin American Studies Association, Crystal City, Va., April 4–6, 1991.

29. David Martin, *Tongues of Fire* (London: Basil Blackwell, 1990), p. 294.

30. It is perhaps important, however, that among Protestants who see injustice, a higher percentage attribute the existence of injustice to "God's will" (12 percent) or to "disobedience to God" (7 percent) than among other religious groups. Such orientations might well indicate an acquiescent orientation toward existing social injustice (from data analyses unreported in text).

31. That is, after the 1968 meeting of the Latin American Conference of Bishops in Medellín, Colombia, at which a call was made for the Catholic Church to exhibit a "preferential option for the poor."

32. Here we are defining conservatism as reticence to use social organization in efforts to remedy distributive inequalities.

33. That is, if nonreligious groups are taken as a baseline, 43 percent of nonaffiliators would endorse church activism in social conflicts and 41 percent of nonpracticing Catholics would endorse such activism.

34. There is some ambiguity in the key concept in the question. This

item refers to "the Church." Respondents could have interpreted the item to refer to (a) all churches, (b) the Catholic Church as the dominant church, or (c) "my church," be it Catholic or Protestant. With the current survey instrument, we are unable to discern the referents that respondents invoked. A few items did ask for evaluations of the Catholic Church. Those items are less pertinent to the point of our study, and hence have not been analyzed. But for the record, 32 percent of Salvadoran Protestants evaluate the work of the Catholic Church in Salvador as "very good" or "good," while 25 percent evaluate that labor as "bad" or "very bad," with the remaining Protestant respondents offering neutral evaluations.

35. Roughly 60 percent of other Protestants hold this view, versus 39 to 45 percent of the other groups under study.

36. By a margin of 36 percent among Protestants to 21 percent among Catholics and 26 percent among nonaffiliators; $X^2 = 45.5$, $p = .002$.

37. Throughout 1990 talks were held under the auspices of the United Nations, leading to the participation of the left in 1991 legislative elections for the second consecutive time under the label of Convergencia Democrática (Democratic Convergence). In those elections, Democratic Convergence won 12 percent of the vote, the Christian Democrats 28 percent, and ARENA 44 percent. Talks resumed after the 1991 elections and eventually led to the successful negotiation of a peace accord under the direct supervision of outgoing Secretary-General Javier Pérez de Cuellar, which began to be implemented in the early months of 1992.

38. The issue of reducing the size of the army is not merely theoretical. One central issue in 1991 negotiations between the FMLN and the ARENA government was the FMLN proposal to "follow the Costa Rican model" by abolishing the Salvadoran armed forces. That proposal was not accepted, but significant restructuring did become a major part of the peace agreement.

39. The former U.S. ambassador to El Salvador, Robert White, has accused the ARENA founder and a former army intelligence chief, the late Roberto D'Aubisson, of being the intellectual author of the assassination of Archbishop Oscar Romero in 1981.

40. The high percentage of voters who refused to reveal their vote makes such an inference hazardous. At least, the percentage of nonreporters was about the same (more than 30 percent) among all religious categories. Whatever measurement error this creates appears to be random across common social categories. In a separate multivariate analysis not reported here, neither age, years of education, gender, income,

occupation, nor religion predicted the response "the vote is secret and need not be revealed."

41. The elections were criticized as "demonstration elections," in which civil liberties are insufficiently respected to permit bona fide readings of the public will but that serve the purpose of justifying further foreign assistance by the U.S. government. See Edward S. Herman and Frank D. Brodhead, *Demonstration Elections: U.S. Staged Elections in the Dominican Republic, Vietnam and El Salvador* (Boston: South End Press, 1984).

42. The same generalization can be made for Catholics, but the relative degree of endorsement for church activism, or for heroic personal attempts to right social wrongs via participation in a revolutionary group, is significantly higher, even if still low in absolute terms.

43. With synchronic data, unfortunately, we cannot empirically discount the possibility that the Protestants under study might have been even poorer than the religiously nonaffiliated prior to conversion. Given that both groups include many who approach extreme poverty, we find such a possibility unlikely.

44. One of the most important roles is that of reading the Bible aloud, a skill many women lack. Participation in a congregation may, therefore, lead to the acquisition of skills that empower. See also Stoll, *Is Latin America Turning Protestant?* pp. 318–19; and Elizabeth Brusco, "The Reformation of Machismo: Asceticism and Masculinity among Colombian Evangelicals," paper presented at the International Congress of the Latin American Studies Association, Crystal City, Va., April 4–6, 1991, on the ways in which Protestantism may redefine gender relations.

45. Levine, "Popular Groups," pp. 718, 758–59.

46. Stoll, *Is Latin America Turning Protestant?* pp. 314–17, 329–31.

47. But Wayne Cornelius, "Urbanization and Political Demand-Making: Political Participation among the Migrant Poor in Latin American Cities," *American Political Science Review* 68, no. 3 (1974): 1125–46, provides an excellent overview of the conditions necessary to encourage political demand-making by the poor.

48. Eldridge, in his informal presentation, told the story of how, in the midst of a sermon about Christ on the cross, biblical references to thirst prompted an outburst of concern about the lack of water in the surrounding Honduran squatters' settlements. This led to petitioning of public authorities, who actually responded to the problem.

49. A perfectly valid question is whether apparent differences are truly a result of Protestantism or whether other independent variables

(including low income), highly correlated with Protestantism, might be the "true cause" of the variations observed. A four-page technical report showing that the results hold up under multivariate analysis is available from Kenneth Coleman, Institute of Latin American Studies, University of North Carolina at Chapel Hill, Chapel Hill, N.C. 27599-3205.

5

The Reformation of Machismo: Asceticism and Masculinity among Colombian Evangelicals

Elizabeth Brusco

THE CHURCH IS a large, plain building of simple cinderblock. From the outside, during the day, it would be easy to pass without identifying it as a church—it could be a warehouse squeezed under the subway tracks along with gas stations and tiny corner stores. At night, the waves of singing and shouting from within draw streams of people carrying Bibles. At each door, a woman wearing a dark skirt, white blouse, and yellow banner across her chest greets the congregation members as they enter. Inside there are no candles or crosses, no identifiable altar—again little to distinguish this large, echoing room as a church. On the raised stage in the front are a hefty table and several ornate velvet and mahogany chairs that look like thrones. Occupying the chairs are four or five serious-looking men dressed in suits, who occasionally rise to read a Bible verse, lead a prayer, or make an announcement. There is a telephone on the table, and one of the men is absorbed in a long conversation.

For the most part, the service seems to be running itself. The prayer, once started, takes off in as many directions as there are individuals in the congregation. Many toss and turn, dancing in the spirit. Others are raptly speaking in tongues. Some simply kneel and sob. The majority of the several hundred people at the meeting are female. The sisters with the yellow banners are active on the floor of the church, moving about to direct a prayer, teach a lesson, and take up the collection. There are about fifty of them, all dressed the same. On a bulletin board in the lobby of the church a list of home prayer meetings and Bible studies is posted, each with the name of the woman who will lead the session. The church is Iglesia Juan 3:16 in the Bronx, the largest Hispanic Pentecostal church in New York City.

This was my introduction to the realities of Pentecostalism among Latin Americans, an interest that became the focus for my dissertation fieldwork in Colombia during 1982 and 1983. My research in Colombia concentrated on how conversion to evangelical Protestantism has affected the domestic lives of converts. I found that Colombian evangelicalism reforms gender roles in a way that enhances female status. It promotes female interests not only in simple, practical ways but also through its potential as an antidote to machismo, the emphatic masculinity so widespread in Latin America.[1]

The assertion that evangelicalism serves the interests of women, and allows them a kind of prominence they are denied in the wider society, has been made before. One locus of such interpretations has been the North American frontier, where circuit-riding preachers and revivals helped women domesticate their men. The numerical preponderance of women in evangelicalism in the United States, Latin America, and elsewhere has been widely documented.[2] Many scholars have recognized that women occupy significant positions within the formal organization of these churches to a much greater extent than in other wings of Christianity. The way in which women also gain prominence through the less institutionalized "authority of personal charisma" in evangelical churches has been given much attention.[3] Finally, scholars have noticed that women are often the first to convert to Pentecostalism.[4]

Unfortunately, such impressive data have had a tendency to fall out of the final analysis.[5] Instead of focusing on the central position of women in evangelical life, scholars pass on to what they regard as more important factors, explaining the success of Pentecostalism at a "higher" or more encompassing level than the household. As a result, women are pushed to the periphery of the problem, as they so often have been in social analysis.

James Sexton's interpretation of Protestant conversion in Guatemala provides a good example of how women become marginal to a phenomenon in which they are actually central. According to Sexton:

> The social marginality model may be applied more appropriately to understanding why women seem to be attracted to Protestantism in larger numbers than men. Traditionally they have held socially less fulfilling positions than men, and they see Protestantism as a new avenue to personal satisfaction and accomplishment.[6]

I call this the "bridge club" explanation, because it leaves women as peripheral to church life as a ladies' bridge club is to political and economic life. By proposing separate explanations for male and female involvement in evangelical churches, Sexton misses the crucial ways in which the entire experience is shaped by the gender system. Sexton's approach also leads to the erroneous implication that Protestants are male. This is clear in his conclusion: "Protestants also are associated with other kinds of material and nonmaterial changes. That is, they more often work in nonagricultural occupations, they are more often legally married, *their wives* are measurably more educated than Catholic wives."[7] This perception contradicts his own data, which show the voting membership of the largest Protestant congregation in the Guatemalan community he studied to be 63 percent female and 37 percent male.[8]

Explaining the evangelical movement in terms of marginality has the effect of removing women from a central place in understanding evangelical growth. Women always seem marginal if we look for explanations in the social domains from which they are systematically excluded: formal politics, public economic structures, church hierarchies, and so forth. Explaining their involvement in a religious movement by the fact that it provides a kind of prominence they are denied in the public realm requires that we avoid thinking too deeply about the functions of religion. Going beyond this kind of explanation will suggest how religious change can both redefine the domestic realm of the household and have implications for the public realm.

This chapter will look at evangelical Protestantism from the female point of view. Such is, after all, the point of view of the bulk of evangelicals, and it will help us understand how Protestantism can effect social change in ways that heretofore have been ignored.

Practical and Strategic Consequences of the Movement

To highlight the remarkable success of Colombian evangelicals in altering resistant gender roles, it will be useful briefly to compare the approaches of fundamentalist and revolutionary movements to gender oppression. Both kinds of movements stress collective interests over individual ones, and they make goals explicit in a way that is unusual in everyday life. And both fundamentalism and revolutionary programs can fuse male and female values in unusual new ways. In African liberation movements, women in the military and in decision-making bodies joined with men in the struggle to create a new and just society.[9] A similar unity of purpose characterized the sexes during the Cuban revolution. However, the prominence of women in revolutionary movements is often eroded after the latter come to power and establish the new structure. While the resulting legislated reforms look good on paper, even the most vigorous efforts to promote gender equality often fail to bring about real changes in male and female behavior, particularly in the family and household. Although many would argue that the "private" world of the family is ultimately shaped by wider political forces, the intimate world of courtship patterns, marital roles, and who washes the dishes seems to be one of the most conservative areas of life, or at least one of the areas that is most difficult to police.

Regarding Colombian Protestantism as revolutionary might seem farfetched. The Colombian evangelical movement has hardly campaigned for legislation to protect women's rights; indeed, it would not be surprising for it to oppose such action, much as its North American counterparts opposed the ERA. Superficially, evangelical churches bear little resemblance to what we would consider a feminist movement. Insofar as evangelicalism in Colombia enhances the quality of women's lives, it accomplishes this only within the bounds of traditional structures. Such movements are quite common in the literature on women's collective action across cultures. There are two kinds of movements, according to a useful distinction by Maxine Molyneux.[10] The first, based on women's "practical interests," is directed against some encroachment on their ability to fulfill traditional obligations. The result is a narrowly focused mobilization like a consumer boycott. The second kind of movement is based on women's "strategic interests." It aims to revise the sex/gender system, and results in a broad form of mobilization that looks suspiciously like Western feminism. Paradoxically, Colombian evangelicalism most resembles the latter type of movement.[11] To understand how, let us first consider some of the practical advantages that evangelical Protestantism confers on women, then turn to the more "strategic" elements of evangelicalism in Colombia, that is, how it revises sex role behavior.

My data on Colombian evangelical households support the conclusion reached by other analysts of Latin American Pentecostalism: that conversion of both a woman and her spouse improves the material circumstances of the household. Quite simply, no longer is 20 to 40 percent of the household budget consumed by the husband in the form of alcohol.[12] Ascetic codes block many of the other extrahousehold forms of consumption that characterize masculine behavior in Colombia, such as smoking, gambling, and visiting prostitutes. Furthermore, an emphasis on marital fidelity for both partners prohibits a man from keeping other women outside his marriage, so a man's limited resources are no longer split among two or more households dependent on his wage.

To the women with whom I worked in Colombia, it is very clear how Pentecostalism serves their practical interests, and they often comment on it. Yet the tangible improvement in the lives of women and children is only one indicator of a much more remarkable trend. With conversion, machismo, the culturally shaped aggressive masculinity that defines the male role in much of mestizo Colombia, is replaced by evangelical belief as the main definer of expectations in husband-wife relations. The *machista* personality and the male role defined by evangelical Protestantism are almost diametric opposites.[13] The ideology of evangelicalism condemns aggression, violence, pride, and self-indulgence while providing positive reinforcement for peace-seeking, humility, and self-restraint. This applies to male as well as female members. Especially for men, conversion often entails the replacement of an individualistic orientation in the public sphere with a collective orientation and identity in the church and home. One outcome of conversion, then, is that the boundaries of public-male life and private-female life are redrawn and the spheres themselves are redefined. The relative power positions of the spouses change. This is not to say that women now have power over their husbands. In evangelical households the husband may still occupy the position of head, but his relative aspirations have changed to coincide more closely with those of his wife. This last fact is key to the analysis of Colombian Pentecostalism and, I believe, constitutes a change of revolutionary proportions.

The numerical preponderance of women in Pentecostal churches, along with the fact that they often occupy leadership positions, has not prevented some researchers from concluding that women's place is still structured to be beneath that of men.[14] They point out that Pentecostal churches rarely allow women in the higher leadership roles. Yet it is just as important to remember the parallel nature of male and female organizations within these churches; hence women in fact lead their own organizations. Nor should we assume that the women's organizations are less important than male-controlled ones. Indeed, in some cases they are equal to, or more active and influential than, their male counterparts. Even more important, when men in positions of leadership share the same values and aspirations as women, they are usually not operating against the latter's interests.[15]

It is abundantly clear to me why those men occupied the ornate chairs on the stage of Juan 3:16 while the sisters effectively ran the services from below. The success of the movement in the terms I am outlining depends on its not being perceived as a way women are gaining supremacy and control over men.[16]

This is what makes the evangelical movement so attractive to women and so successful in improving their lot: instead of trying to revolutionize the public realm, which would be necessary for women to have greater access to jobs and male income, let alone have their interests taken seriously by male power holders, Protestantism reorders the participation of men and women in the private realm. It places the private realm of home and family at the center of both women's and men's lives. Success for men in the public sector in terms of jobs, education, and so forth becomes subsidiary to success in this revalued private realm. Status achievement is reinterpreted in terms of family-oriented values, fulfilling the role of the good provider.

The shift in patterns of status acquisition and consumption illustrates the point. In Colombia, mestizo male status and consumption patterns tend to be individualistic. That is, a man's clothes, his watch, are for his use only. Because of the separation of male and female spheres, between *la casa* (the house) and *la calle* (the street), a man can enhance his status without reference to the state of his household. With conversion, and the breakdown of sex segregation that accompanies it, the condition of the home becomes crucial to the status of men as well as women. Status becomes acquired cooperatively through consumption and investment strategies for the family as a unit.[17]

Asceticism among Colombian evangelicals usually does not lead to capital accumulation, because of the generally tenuous resource base of most households. Still, the transformation of consumption patterns can contribute to upward mobility. Household consumption can include income-generating purchases, such as a house or land, livestock, a car or truck, and, most important, education for the children. It is important to note that such investment is distinct from individual entrepreneurship because it is household-based.[18] That is, the household is acting as a corporate group, and although a profit motive may be at work, the form the investment takes is influenced by its consumption orientation. In other words, goods like houses, land, cars, and

livestock all have use value for household members as well as
market value as commodities. Such consumption patterns may
not create new economic opportunities in the sense of having a
transformative effect on the economy. Yet they often help particular families achieve upward mobility, or at least greater financial
security.

Upward mobility for many evangelical families is based on
the education of children for professional careers. A common
pattern for Colombian couples is to experience financial success
through entrepreneurial activities, then spend money on educating their children to bring their social status into line with
their new economic status.[19] But for Protestant families and extended kin groups, educating children is the *means* by which they
achieve class mobility. Many evangelicals from peasant backgrounds have become physicians or agronomists, careers that
can be achieved as the result of diligence in one's studies and that
require a far smaller degree of favoritism and pull than would
be necessary in business dealings. Such professions can also be
practiced without the obligatory drinking and socializing that
is the cultural norm for business transactions in Colombia. It is
therefore no accident that Colombian evangelicals have achieved
upward mobility through the professions more often than as
entrepreneurs.

Protestantism as a Form of
Female Collective Action

One of the biggest problems faced by feminist reformers in the
United States and elsewhere is that while a woman's role is redefined to allow her greater freedom in terms of jobs, education,
and political participation, male roles do not automatically ac-
commodate themselves to this changed situation. The result of
expanding women's roles is that women end up working a double
day. But imagine if male and female values were the same.

It is hard for North American feminists to see the changes
that result from evangelical conversion in Colombia as involving anything that could be called "liberation." Yet one of the

hard-won lessons of contemporary feminist anthropology is that "woman" is not a universal category, nor are women's problems and interests uniform across cultures. True to its cultural origins, Western feminism has emphasized individual freedom. In a typology of female collective action, Temma Kaplan displays the typical bias.[20] She labels certain movements as emerging from "female consciousness," then argues that they differ from true feminism by valuing social cohesion over individual rights, and quality of life over access to institutional power. I prefer Molyneux's distinction between "practical" and "strategic" forms of women's collective action, mentioned earlier, because it tends not to be as culture bound.

Antagonism toward the family has been a frequent bone of contention between Western and Third World feminists. Women in developed countries find the traditionally assigned family roles problematic because these conflict with new goals of career, individual self-fulfillment, public recognition, and power. But if Western feminists see the family as a locus of oppression, Third World feminists tend to see it as their main source of security. Whether the family is a source of oppression, or of power and security, is a question that has to be addressed empirically rather than interpreted in terms of the differing values that feminists bring to the subject. At this time in Colombia, changes in the family that work to the advantage of women are of keen interest to them.

Many women's collective movements have been organized around regaining basic rights that are being infringed by modernization and social change.[21] Despite ethnographically documented antagonism between the sexes in many traditional societies, women's roles in such societies generally complement those of men, and women's needs and status are safeguarded by implicit cultural rules within a shared system of values.

The last century of modernization in Colombia provides a particularly powerful example of disruption of these traditional safeguards as a result of the divergence of male and female value systems. The transition to a cash economy, proletarianization, and widespread migration to urban centers make women's access to resources increasingly tenuous. One outcome is that women become dependent on whatever income they can extract from men on the basis of persuasion, instead of being able to insist on formally recognized rights. At the same time, the economy is strongly biased against women workers.[22] When a man abandons his wife and children, it dramatizes the rupture of female and male values and has devastating economic consequences for those who remain behind. The high rate of abandonment in Colombia would be unthinkable in a society where a man's values and goals are realized through his attachment to a family. When women work, a larger portion of their earnings is spent on the family, whereas a much larger part of a man's income is spent on personal consumption.[23] Severe competition among women for men and a great deal of mystification of each sex by the other, and of the male-female relationship in general, is another symptom. Finally, the commoditization of sex is manifest on both sides. This runs a continuum from married women who reward their husband's contributions to the household with sexual favors and punish his failure to provide by withholding; to women who enter a series of relationships with men depending on their ability to provide income; to prostitution.

Conclusion: Some Broader Considerations

In Colombia, the template of evangelical Protestantism is helping men and women redefine their roles around the institution of the family. It may well be helping women (and some men) in more practical ways than feminist reform movements have, at least to date in this particular context. Yet evangelical Protestantism is not just practical but strategic, in that it seeks to redress underlying gender inequalities. That it accomplishes this through the transformation of male as well as female roles is the key to its effectiveness. This is an achievement that Western feminism, despite its mighty labors, cannot claim to have achieved to the same degree.

I am not arguing that born-again religion serves the same function in all times and places. Where there is less sex segregation, less female dependency, and a more individualistic orientation for both men and women, such a movement would not improve women's status—it would probably never get started. Perhaps my interpretation is relevant only where religious conversion challenges the kind of aggressive maleness illustrated by machismo. Still, we already have compelling case material from areas far removed from Latin America, where culture change has disrupted the articulation of male and female worlds, showing Pentecostal ideology serving the same function. Not long ago, among the Telefolmin people of Papua New Guinea, a Baptist revival movement took on the ecstatic features of Pentecostalism. Among the Christian converts who led the revival, women played a key role, often manifesting shaking fits that were attributed to possession by the Holy Spirit. During the trances, the Holy Spirit made known his wishes that all Telefolmin convert to Christianity and that the old Telefol religion be abandoned, including the all-important rituals of an esoteric men's cult. The Holy Spirit also demanded, through a female in trance, that egalitarian relations between men and women be established and that conjugal ties and nuclear family obligations take priority over men's duties in their cult. As a result of the revival, over a dozen cult houses were destroyed or desecrated. Not coincidentally, the Telefolmin were being affected by the transition to a cash economy, which probably included an increase in female dependency on male wage labor.[24]

Finally, I would like to make a point about the role of evangelical Protestantism in institutionalized politics. As scholars in this volume and elsewhere are pointing out, we must stop assuming that born-again religion in Latin America has "easily predictable political implications."[25] In Colombia, where the state maintained, until recently, a concordat with the Vatican granting the Roman Catholic Church special privileges, there is a notable absence of evangelicals in political offices above the local level.[26] Yet even if Latin American evangelicals begin to capture political power, it will not nullify their low-key but (one hopes) long-term impact on the gender system. In particular, the schismatic nature of the evangelical movement may protect it from becoming exclusively a vehicle for male political interests. The movement works best through small groups that are based on personalistic ties, and its tendency to keep reproducing such groups through schisms when a church gets too large will continue to encourage broad-based, grass-roots involvement by women.

NOTES

Acknowledgments: The bulk of the field research was carried out in two areas of Colombia: the capital city of Bogotá and the rural municipality of El Cocuy in the northern reaches of the Department of Boyacá. Fieldwork in Colombia was supported by grants from the National Science Foundation, the Wenner-Gren Foundation for Anthropological Research, and the Institute for Intercultural Studies. I am grateful to these organizations for having made the study possible. I would also like to thank Donna Kerner and Susan Wolf for their comments on drafts of this paper.

1. The argument presented here has been elaborated in a larger work. See Elizabeth Brusco, *The Reformation of Machismo* (Austin: University of Texas Press, forthcoming 1994). I use the terms "Pentecostalism," "evangelicalism," and "fundamentalism" interchangeably in this chapter because the process I am discussing seems to prevail in various denominations despite other differences among them. This also reflects the common identity that *evangélicos* in Colombia share in the face of the Catholic predominance.

2. See, for example, Kendall Blanchard, "Changing Sex Roles and Protestantism Among the Navajo Women in Ramah," *Journal for the Scientific Study of Religion* 14 (1975): 43–50; Salvatore Cucchiari, "Between Shame and Sanctification: Patriarchy and Its Transformation in Sicilian Pentecostalism," *American Ethnologist* 17, no. 4 (November 1990): 687–707; Cornelia Butler Flora, *Pentecostalism in Colombia: Baptism by Fire and Spirit* (Cranbury, N.J.: Associated University Presses, 1976); Vivian Garrison, "Sectarianism and Psychosocial Adjustment: A Controlled Comparison of Puerto Rican Pentecostals and Catholics," in Irving I. Zaretsky and Mark P. Leone, eds., *Religious Movements in Contemporary America* (Princeton: Princeton University Press, 1974), pp. 298–329; Lesley Gill, "Like a Veil to Cover Them: Women and the Pentecostal Movement in La Paz," *American Ethnologist* 17, no. 4 (November 1990): 708–21; Felicitas Goodman, *Speaking in Tongues: A Cross-Cultural Study*

of Glossolalia (Chicago: University of Chicago Press, 1972); Rosemary Ruether and Eleanor McLaughlin, eds., *Women of Spirit* (New York: Simon and Schuster, 1979); James Sexton, "Protestantism and Modernization in Two Guatemalan Towns," *American Ethnologist* 5, no. 2 (1978): 280–302.

3. Elmer T. Clark, *The Small Sects in America* (New York: Abingdon Press, 1937); Flora, *Pentecostalism in Colombia*; Nancy Hardesty, Lucille Sider Dayton, and Donald W. Dayton, "Women in the Holiness Movement: Feminism in the Evangelical Tradition," in Rosemary Ruether and Eleanor McLaughlin, eds., *Women of Spirit* (New York: Simon and Schuster, 1979); Walter J. Hollenweger, *The Pentecostals* (Minneapolis: Augsburg Publishing, 1972); Anthony LaRuffa, *San Cipriano: Life in a Puerto Rican Community* (New York: Gordon and Breach, 1971); Rosemary Ruether, "Introduction," in Rosemary Ruether and Eleanor McLaughlin, eds., *Women of Spirit* (New York: Simon and Schuster, 1979); William J. Samarin, *Tongues of Men and Angels: The Religious Language of Pentecostalism* (New York: Macmillan, 1972).

4. Goodman, *Speaking in Tongues*; LaRuffa, *San Cipriano*; Sidney Mintz, *Worker in the Cane: A Puerto Rican Life History* (New Haven: Yale University Press, 1960).

5. For a discussion of this problem in the anthropological study of myth, see Edwin Ardener, "Belief and the Problem of Women," in Shirley Ardener, ed., *Perceiving Women* (New York: John Wiley and Sons, 1975).

6. Sexton, "Protestantism and Modernization," p. 284.

7. Ibid., p. 297. Emphasis added.

8. Ibid., p. 293.

9. For example, see the discussion of Angola, Mozambique, Guinea-Bissau, Zimbabwe, and Namibia in Stephanie Urdang, "Women in National Liberation Movements," in M. Hay and Sharon Stichter, eds., *African Women South of the Sahara* (London: Longman, 1984).

10. Maxine Molyneux, "Mobilization without Emancipation? Women's Interests, State, and Revolution," in *Transition and Development*, Richard Fagen et al., eds. (New York: Monthly Review Press, 1986).

11. This stance may seem far afield from much feminist thinking about Christianity, and about fundamentalism in particular. To quote some particularly imposing ancestors, Elizabeth Cady Stanton said, "The Bible and the Church have been the biggest stumbling blocks in the way of women's emancipation." More recently, but no less forcefully, Mary Daly stated, "A woman's asking for equality in the church

would be comparable to a black person's demanding equality in the Ku Klux Klan." See Mary Daly, *Beyond God the Father: Toward a Philosophy of Women's Liberation* (Boston: Beacon Press, 1973), p. 6. However, some feminist historians are reclaiming women's involvement in evangelicalism as a precursor of the suffrage movement and the first wave of feminism in the United States. See, for example, Barbara Epstein, *The Politics of Domesticity: Women, Evangelism and Temperance in Nineteenth Century America* (Middletown, Conn.: Wesleyan University Press, 1981).

12. When Fals-Borda recorded the household budgets of several families in a rural district in Colombia, he found that about 20 percent of earnings were spent on beer. This doubled during holidays, to 42.1 percent of the household budget. See Orlando Fals-Borda, *Peasant Society in the Colombian Andes: A Sociological Study of Saucío* (Gainesville: University of Florida Press, 1962).

13. The term "machismo" was coined by North American social scientists and journalists and, although derived from the Spanish "macho" (male), is not itself a Spanish word. In the literature it is used with a wide range of often contradictory meanings, some emphasizing male self-confidence and some, male self-doubt and insecurity. I use it here to refer to the complex of male behaviors that my Colombian informants call "machista" (the Spanish adjective form). These include excessive drinking, violence against women, chronic infidelity, abdication of domestic responsibilities, and a general identification with the world of the street rather than with the home. "Machista" in Colombia means something other than "macho." Mothers often enjoin their sons to be *macho*, that is strong, stoic, dependable, and decisive, but never to be *machista*.

14. See Cucchiari, "Between Shame and Sanctification"; and Gill, "Like a Veil to Cover Them."

15. Here I would like to make reference to some of the recent work on the topic of resistance. James Scott has argued that we need to broaden our notion of resistance to include acts and beliefs that challenge the structures of inequality in a more covert and less risky fashion than open confrontation. See James Scott, *Weapons of the Weak: Everyday Forms of Peasant Resistance* (New Haven: Yale University Press, 1985). Emily Martin leads us in a similar direction by enumerating some of the many forms that consciousness and resistance may take, along a continuum from acceptance to rebellion. See Emily Martin, *The Woman in the Body: A Cultural Analysis of Reproduction* (Boston: Beacon Press, 1987).

16. I. M. Lewis has interpreted women's possession cults such as the

Egyptian *zar* as "thinly disguised protest movements directed against the dominant sex." Insofar as they protect women from the exactions of men, and are useful in manipulating husbands and male relatives, he believes they "play a significant part in the sex-war in traditional societies and cultures where women lack more obvious means for forwarding their aims." Lewis sees the same process occurring in Christian contexts and quotes Ronald Knox, who said, "From the Montanist movement onwards, the history of enthusiasm is largely a history of female emancipation, and it is not a reassuring one." See I. M. Lewis, *Ecstatic Religion* (Harmondsworth, U.K.: Penguin Books, 1971), p. 31.

17. It is interesting to compare the status acquisition patterns associated with the machismo complex with those outlined by Ehrenreich with regard to the male "breadwinner" role in the United States. In the latter case, supposedly the middle-class male's only avenue to prestige was through the consumption patterns of his family. See Barbara Ehrenreich, *The Hearts of Men* (Garden City, N.Y.: Anchor Books, 1983).

18. For many reasons, the wholesale application of the Weberian thesis concerning the development of capitalism in sixteenth-century Europe to the Colombian case is inappropriate. Most important is Colombia's position on the dependent periphery of a world system characterized by an unequal distribution of power. See Max Weber, *The Protestant Ethic and the Spirit of Capitalism* (London: Allen and Unwin, 1982 [1930]). Other factors include the nature of Colombian class stratification, the role of the traditional Colombian oligarchy in monopolizing resources, the concern with status differentiation among lower- and middle-class people that belies actual economic class position, and the current economic and political ramifications of the illegal drug trade.

19. Norman Whitten, "Strategies of Adaptive Mobility in the Colombian-Ecuadorian Littoral," *American Anthropologist* 71 (1969): 228–42.

20. Temma Kaplan, "Female Consciousness and Collective Action: The Case of Barcelona 1910–1918," *Signs* 7, no. 3 (1982): 545–66.

21. For example, see Augusta Molnar's study of women in western Nepal. The present analysis may not be relevant to situations of missionization of indigenous peoples where the traditional economy and sex/gender system are still relatively intact. Augusta Molnar, "Women and Politics: The Case of the Kham Magar of Western Nepal," *American Ethnologist* 9, no. 3 (1982): 485–502.

22. See, for example, Rubbo's excellent account of how this process accompanies proletarianization in the Cauca Valley of Colombia, as

huge sugarcane plantations displace peasant subsistence agricultural-
ists. Anna Rubbo, "The Spread of Capitalism in Rural Colombia: Effects
on Poor Women," in Rayna Reiter, ed., *Towards an Anthropology of Women*
(New York: Monthly Review Press, 1975), pp. 333–57.

23. For a similar situation among Mexican workers, see Lourdes
Benería and Marta Roldán, *The Crossroads of Class and Gender: Indus-
trial Homework, Subcontracting, and Household Dynamics in Mexico City*
(Chicago: University of Chicago Press, 1987), p. 120.

24. See Dan Jorgensen, "Telefolmin Follow-up," *Newsletter, Cultural
Survival Inc.* 4, no. 2 (Spring, 1980).

25. David Stoll, *Is Latin America Turning Protestant? The Politics of
Evangelical Growth* (Berkeley: University of California Press, 1990).

26. Colombia is the only country in the world whose government
still maintains a concordat with the Vatican that gives the Catholic
Church special privileges. The Catholic Church in Colombia has a reputation throughout South America as being especially powerful and influential in national life. Evangelicals comprise a minority that, as recently
as the 1940s and 1950s, was violently persecuted. Despite this fact, the
evangelical movement has grown rapidly since the 1960s. The movement is now estimated to have over a million adherents, about 4 percent
of the national population.

6 Shifting Affiliations: Mayan Widows and Evangélicos *in Guatemala*

Linda Green

THE VILLAGE OF Be'cal lies on the windward side of a six-thousand-foot ridge, the cane-and-adobe houses partially hidden among cornfields. A visitor is struck immediately by the beauty of the landscape. Yet the lush green hillsides shimmering in the morning light, and the blue-gray mist lingering low in the valleys most afternoons, belie the poverty of the 150 families who live here. Doña Juana, along with thirty-five other widows, is waiting in front of the small Catholic chapel for a relief group to arrive. Representatives of this small church-based project will distribute a pound of beans, a pound of dry milk, and a liter of oil to each woman. Dressed in the colorful hand-woven blouses and skirts of Be'cal, the women kneel in the shade of a blooming bougainvillaea tree, talking in small groups while their children play. This will be the second of three food distributions for widows. "Perhaps they aren't coming today," some begin to murmur. They have been waiting for over an hour. A short distance away, perched on the ridge above them, are several men with rifles. This is the local civilian patrol in charge of guarding the village. Strangers are not allowed to enter without permission from the army commander in the nearby town. When asked what they are guarding against, the men reply halfheartedly, "la subversión." When pressed as to where subversives are to be found in this apparently peaceful landscape, the men refer nervously to the demands of the local military garrison.

Doña Juana says that not all the widows of Be'cal have agreed to participate in the project. "They don't want handouts," she says. At first she, too, was reluctant, until her daughter, also a widow, became so ill that she could no longer work. Seven years ago Juana became a member of the Prince of Peace, a church that believes in the power of the Holy Spirit, speaking in tongues, and faith healing. On the advice of neighbors she joined Prince of Peace to help her son Pedro, who was drinking heavily. The pastor prayed for him time after time, until he began to sober up. Now Pedro doesn't drink anymore.

Juana said she was a Catholic before the violence, when her second husband was alive, but the Church doesn't have specific prayers to help men stop drinking. A Catholic priest told Juana simply to trust in God. Juana is preoccupied by the illness of her daughter, who has lost so much vitality that she is unable to walk, eat, or work. According to Juana, her daughter suffers from *susto* (literally, "fright"), prompting her to go to a Mayan prayer-maker (or priest) for help. Juana is especially concerned because her first husband died from *susto* some years ago. Her second husband was kidnapped in 1982, when heavily armed strangers in civilian dress came to the house and took him away. No one knows why. He never returned, joining the innumerable Guate-malans who have been "disappeared" by government-backed death squads.[1]

Today Mayan communities in the western highlands of Guatemala are in disarray. Towns and villages have been rav-aged by decades of the slow violence of structural poverty and, since the late 1970s, by a brutal counterinsurgency war. Pro-found social transformations have taken place. Two visible signs of structural change are civil militias imposed by the army in 1982 and the prevalence of fundamentalist Protestant churches in rural communities.[2] Historically, civil institutions such as the Catholic Church, Protestant missionaries, and schools have acted as ideological proxies for the state in Mayan communities, but their ability to shape everyday life in accordance with Western values has been limited. As a result, the state has repeatedly resorted to coercion to achieve its ends. This has taken various forms, including compulsory labor drafts, debt peonage, military conscriptions, and, more recently, kidnapping, massacres, and civil patrols.

Evangelical churches had been growing steadily but unspectacularly for decades when, in the 1980s, the murder of a dozen Catholic priests and hundreds, perhaps thousands, of lay leaders sent a flood of Catholics into evangelical meetings as a haven from repression. In some areas whole villages converted at once. The village of Ri bey (discussed below) is a case in point. Before the violence Ri bey had a population of seven hundred people, mostly (if only nominally) Catholic. Today there are three hundred people, and all refer to themselves as *evangélicos*. By the late 1980s evangelical leaders were claiming over 30 percent of the national population and predicting that, if growth rates remained high, Guatemala would become the first Protestant country in Latin America. The recent proliferation of evangelical churches has invited renewed speculation about their possible connections with the Guatemalan power structure, dating from Justo Rufino Barrios, the Liberal caudillo who first invited Protestant missionaries to Guatemala in the 1870s, to General Efraín Ríos Montt, the born-again military dictator who ruled the country in 1982–83.[3] Catholic leaders responded with accusations that evangelical missionaries from the United States were working hand in glove with the Guatemalan army and buying converts with handouts.[4]

During the 1980s some academic literature and reports in the popular press on evangelical conversions in Latin America focused on the connection between the U.S.-based Christian missions and their relationships with conservative political regimes north and south of the Rio Grande.[5] The direct linkage of the state coercive apparatus with fundamentalist missionaries in Guatemala is justifiable in the wake of the brutal counterinsurgency campaign of 1980–84 and "the peculiar program of state supported evangelization."[6] Yet on closer inspection, explanations for the phenomenal growth rates in Guatemala are not so easily categorized. Recent anthropological work has documented shifts in religious affiliations in several areas prior to the onset of political violence.[7] While fear and intimidation have been important accelerators of membership growth in evangelical congregations, they do not explain ongoing participation.[8]

In this chapter I address the question of what a shift to fundamentalism might mean for women survivors of the violence who, for one reason or another, have abandoned their exclusive allegiance to traditional or orthodox Catholicism. I suggest that by the 1980s Protestant evangelicalism—and particularly the fundamentalist and Pentecostal strains—was uniquely situated to offer a religious alternative to people who have experienced rapid and radical social change as a result of political violence and whose communities have been fractured by years of privation. Evangelical churches, although never dominant in rural Guatemala, have been present for decades. Fundamentalism in these instances is not so much a religion of repression, although initially it was for many, nor the religion of advancement, as it has been for a few, but a "religion of survival," a refuge from suffering and a space in which the women are able to reclaim some personal control over their lives. In this way the women of Chicaj are utilizing a panoply of responses to the seemingly intractable economic misery and ongoing state repression.

The Reorganization of Community

Guatemala has been described as the country of "eternal spring and eternal tyranny."[9] To tourists who hurtle along the Pan-American Highway en route to Lake Atitlán and the famous market at Chichicastenango, the landscape is stunning. The hills, the softness of the sky, and the outline of trees create an unforgettable image—this is the Guatemala of eternal spring. Along the way travelers glimpse Indian men bent low under the heavy loads they are carrying. They see Mayan families in brightly colored clothing, laboring over the plots of broccoli and snow peas that have sprung up amid the traditional fields of corn. These are the Kakquikel Mayas, descendants of the civilization that built the famous temples of Tikal and Palenque and Copán. For the tourists they are a picturesque metaphor of a simpler way of life, free from the demands of the modern world.

The reality for the majority of Kakquikel Mayas who live in the towns and villages near the highway is very different. They live on the darker side of modernity. Rather than enjoying the promised benefits of progress and technology, they experience the degrading underside of capitalist economic relations, a repressive state, and environmental devastation. They live in grinding poverty; the average life expectancy is forty-five years; 60 percent of the children die of preventable diseases, such as diarrhea, influenza, and measles, before the age of five; and nine out of ten children are malnourished. Most household heads earn an income of less than U.S. $300 per year.

It is a three-hour walk over rugged mountain paths from the village of Be'cal to the *municipio* of Chicaj, the site of the local civil government, the military garrison, and the weekly market. One Catholic priest lives in Chicaj and is responsible for a parish with a combined population of over thirty thousand people. He celebrates mass in Chicaj daily. Although there are small chapels in most of the villages, with only one priest to look after the large population, mass is rarely said in the villages. People must walk to town to attend mass. During the worst years of state repression, one priest was killed and another was forced to abandon his duties. The intimidation persists. At Christmas Eve mass in 1989, twenty-five soldiers suddenly entered the church, soon after the service had started. They occupied three middle pews on the men's side, never taking their hands off their rifles, then left abruptly after the sermon.

Most of the inhabitants of Be'cal continue to identify themselves as Catholics, but since the 1980s increasing numbers of people have started to attend Pentecostal services in several churches that have sprung up locally. The presence of evangelical groups in the communities is not new; what has changed is the number of different sects in the towns and villages. In some villages there may be three or four churches competing for worshipers. The Catholic Church, too, is comprised of splinter groups: the traditional religious brotherhoods (*cofradías*), the orthodox Catholic Action (*acción católica*) and the charismatic renewal (*la renovación*). Although Padre Miguel of Chicaj tries to

maintain close ties with the *cofrades*, the catechists, and the charismatics, tensions persist. Now only a few Catholic men from the
village of Be'cal participate in the *cofradía* that assumes responsibilities in Chicaj for processions in honor of the saints. If a man
chooses to participate, he must move into town for at least part of
the year to perform the necessary and often costly duties. Other
men, members of the orthodox Catholic Action movement, assist
Padre Miguel with his pastoral duties. More recently charismatic
groups have sprung up in Chicaj, providing a "Catholic alternative" to Pentecostalism. A group of young men, members of
Catholic Action, started a musical group. They play electronic
instruments at local religious celebrations and sing songs similar to charismatic hymns in order, they say, to provide God's
house with music and to do something for the pueblo and the
Church. For the most part there continues to be a polite tolerance
among the different groups. Mayan priests also remain active
in the area. They are often sought to perform *costumbre* (Mayan
customs and rituals) and healers are sought for their efficacy in
treating illness such as *susto, nervios* (nerves), and the healing of
fractured bones.

Most evenings in Be'cal competing loudspeakers from the Assemblies of God, the Church of God, the Prince of Peace Church,
and the charismatics broadcast familiar songs to the handful in
attendance. The chapels are rough-hewn, furnished with simple
wooden benches and lit by candles. They stand in sharp contrast
to the colonial-style Catholic Church that dominates the town
square in Chicaj. In the evenings six or eight congregants, mostly
women, will gather with the local pastor to pray in Kakquikel.
The pleas of the women are modest, asking for help with their
daily woes. The pastor admonishes them to forgo the rituals and
practices of Mayan beliefs and to obey the men—pastors, civil
patrol heads, military commanders—in authority over them.

The people of Be'cal are poor. Extended families live close to
each other in small cornstalk or adobe houses, and help each
other with planting and harvesting. Decisions of importance are
usually made jointly and by consensus. Most families have only
a few acres of land on which to grow corn and beans. They must

supplement their incomes with work on the large plantations of the south coast, local projects such as road construction, petty commerce, cutting and selling wood, or participating in development projects. Going to the plantations is usually the choice of last resort. Wages on the south coast for harvesting cotton, coffee, or sugar are only U.S. $1–2 per day. People often return sick with malaria or one of the other infectious diseases endemic to the lowlands, and with little or no cash to show for their efforts.

According to Carol Smith,[10] the Department of Chimaltenango probably receives more development aid per capita than anywhere in the *altiplano*, yet rather than alleviating the precarious economic situation in which most people live, conditions continue to worsen. U.S. Agency for International Development (USAID)–funded projects, which provide the bulk of development aid in the department, focus on nontraditional export agriculture, itself a component of larger structural adjustment strategies. Such agriculture, however, rather than ameliorating rural poverty, is having the opposite effect. The net result, according to a study by Peter Rosset,[11] is growing inequality. Access to land, credit, technology, technical assistance, and markets varies considerably according to the size of landholdings, thus favoring the wealthy over the poor. Social differentiation, food insecurity, overuse of land, deforestation, and a growing rural proletariat are the realities that have characterized economic life in Chimaltenango since the late 1980s.

For the widows of Be'cal the situation is even more precarious. Many of them are dependent on the goodwill of development projects for handouts or as buyers for their weaving. For some this is the only way to earn the cash they need for food and fertilizer, but they rarely earn more than U.S. $5 every two weeks, hardly enough to keep them in the staple food of black beans, let alone other necessities. The women returned to Be'cal after the worst phase of the violence. Although many had lived for a year or two in the towns or the capital city, where there are more economic opportunities, most chose to return. Juana wants her children to be raised in their own community, where they can grow corn, speak their own language, and follow a familiar rhythm of life. "For the *indígena*, life is community and collectivity," she says. "To live in the pueblo or city is to struggle alone."

Christianity, the Corporate Community, and Capitalism

Here I turn briefly to an analysis of social and historical factors that have helped to shape the present situation. Historical considerations place the recent tide of conversions to Protestant evangelicalism in rural communities within a framework that elucidates local explanations of complex social realities. As W. George Lovell[12] has noted, "Three elements essential to groups' survival, recur and figure prominently (for the Maya): land, community, and an attachment to place." Understanding the "cycles of conquest" to which Mayas have been subjected (since the sixteenth century)—"conquest by imperial Spain, conquest by local and international capitalism, and conquest by state terror"—contextualizes the strategies used by Mayas to survive.

The connections between politics and Christianity can be traced back to the Spanish conquest. Mayas were forcibly relocated into nucleated settlements—the forerunners of today's *municipios*—where they underwent the dual processes of colonialization and Christianization.[13] The Spanish clergy organized men into *cofradías*—religious brotherhoods—that structured religious devotion and provided priests an income in exchange for their services. The Catholic clergy were active in rural community affairs during the colonial and early postindependence period. Yet the Catholic Church never succeeded in remaking rural communities ideologically. During the Spanish colonial period, even though traditional rituals and customs were forbidden, public worship led by *cofrades* continued to be infused with Mayan moral and cultural principles.[14]

The arrival of Protestant missionaries in the late nineteenth century heralded the beginning of a new Christian era in Guatemala. Although the first missionaries were few in number and exercised limited influence at the local level, they were the beneficiaries of substantial state support.[15] The Liberals, who came to national power in 1871, were determined to wrench the country from its colonial past, and their policy included destroying the political and economic foundations of Catholic Church influence in state affairs.[16] Export agriculture based on large-scale coffee production was the economic cornerstone of Guatemala's entry into modernity. Protestantism was the theological justification for the imposition of conditions necessary for "progress" to flourish.[17] The interplay between capitalism, Christianity, and politics helps to explain in part the profound changes that have reshaped Mayan communities and culture since the 1870s.

The rise of capitalist productive relations began slowly around the middle of the nineteenth century and accelerated during the 1880s, after the Liberals took power. The turn of the century ushered in a wholly new set of social relations for Mayas. Guatemalan coffee production developed on large tracts of land, much of which were seized from Mayan coastal and piedmont communities. Some lands were plundered when communal property rights were abolished in favor of private holdings in 1877 through the enactment of an agrarian reform law. Large tracts were turned over to foreign investors and the rural bourgeoisie.[18] Coffee production and profits were dependent upon an exploitable labor force. Through a corvée labor system known as *mandamientos* and debt peonage, plantation owners had easy access to Indian labor. Work on the coffee plantations had a devastating impact on the traditional local economy. Each year plantation work took people away from their subsistence plots, making it difficult to tend their land properly and thus leading to low yields. A vicious cycle was created. Low yields made it more difficult to meet subsistence needs and more necessary to go into debt to survive, and debts meant working on plantations. For the first time large numbers of *ladinos* (non-Indians) moved into Mayan communities as representatives of state power.

Indian responses to these changes were resistive although subdued in comparison to clashes in the early republican years.[19] Opposition took several forms: outright rebellions, attempts at juridical settlements of disputes, and restructuring of community boundaries through existing social institutions. The Mayas closed

ranks. After the expulsion of the Catholic clergy from their communities, Mayan religious celebrations and rituals thrived. The
political-religious *cargo* system became the central institution of
social organization.[20] The *cofradías* (saint societies) were responsible for economic, political, and religious aspects of community
life. The age-graded *cargo* system of authority and responsibility
controlled a system of land inheritance by installments, ritual life
centered on fiestas, public service appointments, and community dispute resolution.[21] Power resided in the hands of elderly
patriarchs, and young men advanced only gradually in prestige,
influence, and independence. The political-religious hierarchy
provided a mechanism for communities to maintain a degree of
social equilibrium in face-to-face relations through power sharing
and through slowing the process of the accumulation of wealth.
Ethnic distinctions between Mayas and ladinos were sharply
drawn during this period. Ladinos moved into rural villages as
representatives of the Liberal state and rural bourgeoisie, placing
the Mayas in a directly subordinate position. As a result, class
distinction became muted and ethnic tensions surfaced.

In the early decades of the twentieth century, some Mayas
abandoned traditional forms of worship to adopt religious practices centered on the tenets of Protestantism. Recent work on the
missionary efforts of Presbyterians in Quetzaltenango attribute
the rapid rise in evangelical membership during this period to
the disruptive effects of the coffee boom.[22] By 1923 efforts in rural
areas of Quetzaltenango, Retalhuleu, and Suchitepequez were
yielding a steady stream of converts. A network of indigenous
lay preachers were offering *cultos* (worship services) in local
languages to residents of villages, *aldeas* (hamlets), and *fincas*
(plantations). Thomas Bogenschild notes that those prone to conversion were from communities most affected by the social and
economic transformations of the period. The development of
coffee production, the construction of roads, and military con-
scription displaced economic practices and forms of social organization in the entire western region. The expansion of the Presbyterian mission was rapid and notable in those communities
most disrupted by the changes.

Diaries and correspondence of one of the early mission workers provide a picture of poverty and despair among those seeking affiliation with the church.[23] Bogenschild suggests that impoverished Guatemalans in the region turned to Protestantism not for reasons of social mobility but for basic survival needs. As indigenous workers were coerced into debt, many abandoned their participation in the traditional cargo system. On *fincas* and in rural areas, this abandonment of traditional forms resulted in severe loss of corporate social control. Lacking a strong hierarchy of town elders to punish locally defined deviant behavior, many converts turned to the church to provide social control. Missionaries, for example, became involved in settling disputes involving inheritance rights, rights to property, and local feuds. The only other option for the villagers was the state legal apparatus, which in practice did not recognize the juridical rights of Mayas.

Although little formal historical work has been done on the Department of Chimaltenango, it is known that the Central American Mission began working in the region during the first decades of the twentieth century. It operated a seminary in Panajachel in which the Presbyterians played an active role, and anecdotal data suggest close ties between the two groups. The Chimaltenango region appears to have been undergoing related processes of social transformation. J. C. Cambranes[24] cites a 1900 document by a political chief in the Department of Chimaltenango who reports, "Of the ancient communal lands, there is not one small area which is not private property." Given the congruences of economic and social transformations and terms of institutional efforts on the part of the Central American Mission, Kakquikel responses may have been similar to those of the peoples of the Quetzaltenango region.

By the 1950s Catholic traditionalists of the *cofradías* were being challenged by orthodox Catholics and Protestant missionaries in many *municipios* of the highlands. Processes set in motion during the previous three decades had a profound impact on *cofradía* political and religious positions within communities. Douglas Brintnall[25] suggests that the abolition of debt peonage in 1934 and freeing Mayas from the burdens of forced labor in 1944 allowed agricultural innovations long held in abeyance to take place. In his study of the town of Aguacatán in the Department of Huehuetenango, Brintnall found that Mayas with more valuable land were able to devote time and surplus to cash-cropping of garlic and installation of irrigation systems. This led to a greater degree of economic differentiation among Mayas in the communities than previously existed. Some lands became more valuable as a result, and served to undermine the logic of land inheritance by installment, the basis of the political-religious cargo system. Moreover, these changes eroded the economic underpinnings of ladino domination and Mayan subordination. By the late 1940s younger Mayan men were involved in peasant leagues, political parties, and the agrarian reform law committees, assuming position of power and authority customarily reserved for community elders.[26]

Catholic Action, which represented orthodox Catholicism, was promoted by the archbishop of Guatemala City during the period 1944 to 1954 to ward off a perceived threat of communism. The revolutionary government had banned clergy from involvement in political and labor issues. In this anticlerical environment the archbishop promoted orthodoxy among lay Catholics, and sought to compensate for the shortage of priests, by organizing Catholic Action groups and training men to work as catechists. The *cofradías* were already in decline, for their political authority was being subverted by economic transformations. Catholic Action, by challenging the legitimacy of the *cofradías*, introduced another element of factionalism into villages.

Some of the foreign diocesan priests and nuns who arrived in large numbers in Guatemala during the 1950s became involved in small social welfare projects along with pastoral duties. They instructed lay workers in spiritual practices grounded in Catholic orthodoxy and encouraged involvement in agricultural cooperatives, health care facilities, and literacy campaigns. The spiritual dimension of Catholic Action challenged the religious practices of *costumbre* and age-graded authority, and its social emphasis on universal equality questioned subordination based on ethnicity.[27] As class tensions were subsumed within a discourse of ethnicity among Mayas and between Mayas and ladinos, conflicts escalated.[28]

In the 1960s many second-generation lay catechists became politicized in some regions of the highlands.[29] They assumed leadership roles in popular democratic organizations that gained considerable momentum after the devastation wrought by the 1976 earthquake. The catechists, along with Catholic priests and nuns, influenced by liberation theology, worked among the rural poor in a spirit of cooperation and in hopes of social justice. Meanwhile, evangelicals were doggedly toiling among the Mayas in some of the same communities. Their memberships were growing slowly but steadily.

By the late 1970s community factionalism brought about by economic, political, and religious changes exploded into social chaos. In the early 1980s, to squelch a growing insurgency, the Guatemalan army unleashed a reign of terror directed against not only guerrilla combatants but also the unarmed civilian population, whom they were trying to organize. It became politically dangerous in many areas to be labeled a Catholic. Throughout the western highlands staggering numbers of people died, or were disappeared or displaced, most of them Mayan Indians. Hundreds of communities were razed, and their inhabitants were forced to flee for their lives. In the department of Chimaltenango, a scant fifty miles from the capital city, at least 20 percent of the population was displaced between 1981 and 1983.[30] Many did not return to their villages for several years. Other communities were split apart, then resettled under the watchful eye of the military.

The political violence hit the Chimaltenango area in two waves. From 1976 to 1980 people were kidnapped and killed selectively. Later, during the scorched earth phase of the war, villagers ran for their lives as the army killed people indiscriminately. Houses were leveled, crops burned, animals killed. Kakquikeles began to repopulate the area slowly in 1983 and 1984. The violence had reached into communities in unexpected ways.[31] A sense of trust—the basis of community—was severely undermined. The presence of the army, continuing incursions by guerrilla columns elsewhere in the region, the civil militias, spies, denunciations, death lists, and innuendos created deep apprehensions and anxiety. Today, no one can be sure who is who, who can be trusted. People are afraid to speak about the terror and fear that permeate their lives. The silence adds more fear to the instability.

One mechanism of social control instituted by the army during this period was the civil patrol, a mandatory system of community surveillance.[32] One of the widespread structural effects of the civil militia is its entrenchment at the local level through the subordination of "traditional" village political authority to the military commander. Its presence has created a climate of fear, intimidation, and suspicion that at times has turned petty feuding into a conduit for vigilante justice. By 1990 civil patrols had been abandoned in less contentious areas of the highlands, but in the rural villages of Chicaj patrol service continued to be obligatory. Social bonds based on trust, stability, and structure have been destabilized. In a seeming state of order and control, the civil militias create social chaos.

Shifting Affiliations

I first met Maria in 1989, when she was twenty-five years old, five years after her husband, José, was killed in front of her and her two children. She lives with her mother and sister-in-law, also widows, in Ri bey, a small village of three hundred people. All three women regularly attend the services of the Church of God. A year after we met, Maria asked my field assistant and me to help her baptize her latest child, only a few months old. At first I was bewildered. Why couldn't she make the arrangements herself? It turned out that Maria wanted to baptize the child in the Catholic Church, just like her two older children, to make her strong and healthy. The baptism was a protective blessing for the child's well-being here and now, not about cleansing the soul of original sin for salvation in the next life. Yes, she said, there are baptisms in the Church of God, at the age of decision (around ten years old), but that is not what she wanted. Catholics bless children soon after birth, like the young corn blessed soon after harvest. We set up the baptism for her, but not at the local parish. It was not that the priest would have objected—he did not—but that Maria knew some of her evangelical neighbors would protest. Maria continues to attend the Church of God worship services in her village. While it is politically expedient for widows in some villages to go to services, it is also something more.

The nightly services allow women a safe haven to participate in communal activities. Most women comment they are *muy alegre*, that they provide pleasurable diversion with the clapping, shouting, and praying. Church members also help each other, work together to build houses, plant and harvest corn. *Cultos* provide a place and space within which to rebuild a sense of trust and community. And many of the women are widows who have little access to male labor. In some cases the women are replacing family labor-sharing with fictive kin ties, owing to the loss of family members to the violence or to hostilities over religion and politics within families. Perhaps there are actual conversions among these women and attending these services is in no sense bad faith on their part. Maria, like many others, is first of all seeking solace, a sense of wholeness in a community fragmented by war and modernity.

Several months after the 1976 earthquake, Doña Antonia's husband, Felipe, was "disappeared." Suddenly, at the age of forty, she was alone with eight sons ranging from fifteen to four years old. To this day no one knows why Felipe was kidnapped. He had borrowed money on his land the year before, to purchase a truck, and after his death the truck and the land were lost. Antonia moved with the children to town, where she wove and made tortillas to support her family. Four years later she joined the local Church of God. She speaks enthusiastically of taking part in and belonging to the group.

In 1987 Antonia joined with other widows in town to organize an informal Christian group that interprets the Bible in a radically different way than the Church of God. The women talk about their suffering and sorrows, and they look for ways in which they can work together to change their situation. Antonia says she sees no contradictions between the two forms of Christianity. The widow's group seeks ways to redress social injustices, while the church services "*se calma mi corazón*" (soothe my heart). Since the day her husband was kidnapped, Antonia says she has been very sad, and her head aches with worry. Most of the widows refer to their sufferings in terms of bodily pains. They relate the headaches, gastritis, ulcers, and *nervios* to the day their husbands were kidnapped or killed. Like her late husband, Antonia's oldest son has a drinking problem and at times becomes violent. She moves between the widows' and church groups, seeking refuge and hope.

Taking the reports of missionaries at face value, anthropologists have not always distinguished between affiliations and conversions, that is, identifying oneself with a religious group and experiencing the kind of personal transformation that evangelicals preach. In the case of the Mayan widows, the distinction between conversion and affiliation, between identity and membership, is obviously significant. Although there has been a dramatic rise in evangelical church memberships in rural communities, the Mayan women's religious affiliations are neither fixed nor static, nor do changes in membership necessarily represent their rejection of Mayan cosmology. Christian religious affiliations, which may be multiple, are in part survival strategies that emerge from their lived experiences. As such, religious mobility between Christian churches is the women's response to profound social upheavals. These Mayan women are neither dupes of false consciousness nor fickle opportunists but deeply involved in shaping their lives.

The moral and social foundation of these communities has been deeply shaken by political conflict and economic misery. Upheaval has undermined local indigenous institutions that until recently controlled social dissonance. Previously the *consejos de los ancianos* (community council of elders) was the local body that punished deviant behavior. Now the women turn to evangelical churches to help them with some of their social problems. While Pentecostal sects are dividing households and neighbors with their patriarchal, individualistic ideology of sin and salvation, they are simultaneously filling social vacuums created by the destruction of families and communities. The women I know talk about the deep divisions in their communities, about the breakdown of the social bonds of trust and tradition. Most lost not only husbands but also fathers, sons, and brothers to the violence. Poignantly, the same women recall the traumas of living with men who drank and turned violent. Without husbands, many continue to face the same problems with the few men left in their families. Women point to the prohibition of alcohol use by the *evangélicos* as an attractive feature of "conversion."

They seek relief from their sufferings that are the result of both political violence and economic structures that have led to a wearing down of community norms. Rather than a turning away from Mayan values, these evangelical affiliations, in spite of their fire-and-brimstone discourse, provide Mayan women and their families with a mechanism to recapture control over their lives, however contradictory such a statement may seem. Women are trying to regain a sense of community, sharing, group undertakings in a respectful and dignified way, so emblematic of Mayan culture.

Although evangelical churches may fill some of the social gaps resulting from the disarray of community structures, the fact that women move back and forth between the churches suggests that the new groups meet women's needs only partially. The fluidity with which the women cross religious boundaries points to the pragmatic approach they have adopted as they struggle to meet exigencies. They see no particular epistemological contradiction in this mobility. The women make their choices from available options, trying to recapture piecemeal elements of community— trust, cooperation, communalism—through permissible institutions in a militarized society.

NOTES

Acknowledgments: The field research on which this article was based was conducted in three geographically contiguous *municipios* of the Department of Chimaltenango. I use the fictitious name Chicaj to refer to all three *municipios*, and Be'cal and Ri bey as pseudonyms for the *aldeas* where I worked. My intention is to provide a modicum of protection for the people with whom I worked. In 1991 the situation in Chicaj remained politically charged. This essay has benefited greatly from the insightful comments of Tom Bogenschild, Peri Fletcher, Margarita Melville, Mary Beth Mills, Jim Quesada, Nancy Scheper-Hughes, José Sotz, David Stoll, and two anonymous reviewers. The research was sponsored by the Institute for International Education (IIE) Fulbright Scholars Program.

1. According to Americas Watch, *Guatemala: A Nation of Prisoners* (New York: Americas Watch, 1984), since the mid-1960s over forty-five thousand people have "disappeared" in Guatemala.

2. I distinguish between the terms "evangelical," "fundamentalist," and "Pentecostal" by drawing on the typologies used in David Stoll, *Is Latin America Turning Protestant? The Politics of Evangelical Growth* (Berkeley: University of California Press, 1990), 4. "Evangelical" refers to any non-Catholic Christian. "Fundamentalist" signifies any Protestant who cites Scripture as the ultimate source. "Pentecostal" refers to one who subscribes to mystical forms of Protestantism based on the belief in the power of the Holy Spirit.

3. Ríos Montt is an elder in the born-again California-based Church of the Word. During his presidency some of the worst human rights violations in the hemisphere took place, according to an Amnesty International report, *Guatemala: Massive Extrajudicial Executions in Rural Areas under the Government of General Efraín Ríos-Montt* (London: Amnesty International Publications, 1982)

4. Stoll, *Is Latin America Turning Protestant?*

5. Examples include Sheldon Davis, "Guatemala: The Evangelical Holy War in El Quiché," *Global Reporter* 1, no. 1 (1983): 9–10; Enrique Domínguez and Deborah Huntington, "The Salvation Brokers: Evangelicals in Central America," *NACLA Report on the Americas* 18, no. 1 (1984): 2–36; "The Rise of the Religious Right in Central America," *The Resource Center Bulletin* (Albuquerque, N.M.) no. 10 (Summer/Fall 1987); Mary Westropp, "Christian Counterinsurgency," *Cultural Survival Quarterly* 7, no. 3 (1983): 28–31. Stoll, *Is Latin America Turning Protestant?* and David Martin, *Tongues of Fire: The Explosion of Protestantism in Latin America* (London: Basil Blackwell, 1990), are notable exceptions in recognizing the diversity among evangelical forms. Among anthropological works that have added to our understanding of evangelical Christians are two noteworthy collections: Jane Schneider and Shirley Lindenbaum, eds., "Frontiers of Christian Evangelism," *American Ethnologist* 14,

no. 1 (1987); and Lynn Stephen and James Dow, eds., *Class, Politics, and Popular Religion in Mexico and Central America*, Society for Latin American Anthropology Publication Series 10 (Washington, D.C.: American Anthropological Association, 1990).

   6. See Thomas E. Bogenschild, "The Roots of Fundamentalism in Western Guatemala," paper presented at Congress of the Latin American Studies Association, Meetings, Crystal City, Va., April 4, 1992; and Stoll, *Is Latin America Turning Protestant?* p. 191, for a discussion of Operation International Love Lift in the Ixil Triangle and other development projects financed by FUNDAPI, the development arm of the Church of the Word.

   7. See June Nash, "Protestantism in an Indian Village in the Western Highlands of Guatemala," *Alpha Kappa Deltan* (Winter 1960): 49–53; Douglas Brintnall, *Revolt Against the Dead: Modernization of a Mayan Community in the Highlands of Guatemala* (New York: Gordon and Breach, 1979); Benjamin Paul, "Fifty Years of Religious Change in San Pedro La Laguna, a Mayan Community in Highland Guatemala," paper presented at the American Anthropological Association, Chicago, November 1987; Sheldon Annis, *God and Production in a Guatemalan Town* (Austin: University of Texas Press, 1987); Kay Warren, *The Symbolism of Subordination: Indian Identity in a Guatemalan Town* (Austin: University of Texas Press, 1978); Ricardo Falla, *Quiché rebelde* (Guatemala City: Editorial Universitaria de Guatemala, 1980).

   8. Andrés Opazo Bernales, "El movimiento protestante centroamericana. Una aproximación cuantitativa," in Luis E. Sawande, ed., *Protestantismos y procesos sociales en Centroamérica* (San José, Costa Rica: EDUCA, 1990), 13–37, based growth rates on number of evangelical congregations rather than on "conversions," and noted an overall growth rate of 8.3 percent for Guatemala as a whole between 1980 and 1987. What is interesting is that the data are broken down by departments. Of the twenty-two departments, Chimaltenango ranked twelfth, with the number of congregations growing by 82 percent, about the national average. What is striking is that the top-ranked department is Totonicapán, which sustained relatively little violence, growing by 2,286 percent during the same period. El Quiché, the hardest hit by the war, declined in number of congregations by 8.6 percent. The data contradict implicit assumptions that the area with the greatest violence would exhibit the greatest church growth.

   9. Jean-Marie Simon, *Guatemala: Eternal Spring—Eternal Tyranny* (New York: W. W. Norton, 1987).

   10. Carol Smith, "The Militarization of Civil Society in Guatemala:

Economic Reorganization as a Continuation of War," *Latin American Perspectives* 17, no. 4 (1990): 8–41.

11. Peter Rosset, "Non-traditional Export Agriculture in Central America: Impact on Peasant Farmers." Working paper no. 20. University of California, Santa Cruz, 1991.

12. W. George Lovell, "Surviving Conquest: The Maya of Guatemala in Historical Perspective," *Latin American Research Review* 23, no. 2 (1988): 25–57.

13. The *municipio*, long considered by anthropologists as the basis of Mayan community, was an outcome of colonial state policy. Mayas were forcibly relocated from "natural" units of clan lineages to colonial settlements under administrative control. See Robert M. Hill and John Monaghan, *Communities in Highland Maya Social Organization: Ethnohistory in Sacapulas, Guatemala* (Philadelphia: University of Pennsylvania Press, 1987).

14. Nancy Farriss, *Maya Society Under Colonial Rule* (Princeton: Princeton University Press, 1984).

15. See Bogenschild, "Roots of Fundamentalism," for a discussion on the legal protection and nonmonetary support offered by the Liberals to the early Presbyterian missionaries and Central American Mission.

16. Catholic Church properties and investments were confiscated, foreign clergy were expelled, religious orders were disbanded, and priests were not allowed to hold public office.

17. Virginia Garrard-Burnett, "Positivismo, liberalismo e impulso misionero: Misiones protestantes en Guatemala, 1880–1920," *Mesoamérica* no. 19 (1990): 13–31.

18. David McCreery, "State Power, Indigenous Communities, and Land in Nineteenth Century Guatemala, 1820–1920," in Carol A. Smith, ed., *Guatemalan Indians and the State, 1540–1988* (Austin: University of Texas Press, 1990), 96–115, notes that the geographic location of the communities and demographics heavily influenced the degree of dispossession and displacement. Many communities in the highlands lost vast tracts of land, especially those located away from the village site, but most were left with some *ejido* (public) land on which to subsist. In areas of prime coffee cultivation, however, many local inhabitants were forced to become resident workers or day laborers. It was not until the early twentieth century that population increases exerted substantial pressure on communal land resources throughout the highlands.

19. See Robert Carmack, "The State and Community in Nineteenth

Century Guatemala," in Carol A. Smith, *Guatemalan Indians and the State, 1540–1988* (Austin: University of Texas Press, 1990), 116–40.

20. See Eric Wolf, "Closed Corporate Peasant Communities in Mesoamerica and Central Java," *Southwestern Journal of Anthropology* 17, no. 1 (1957): 1–18.

21. Bogenschild, "Roots of Fundamentalism." The elders resolved community disputes involving land, inheritance rights, adultery, and other forms of "illicit" behavior.

22. See ibid.

23. Ibid., citing the Burgess family papers, housed in the Presbyterian Historical Society (Philadelphia) under Record Group 201. According to Bogenschild, the mission was able to provide a rudimentary yet important social support network for individiuals displaced or dispossessed by Liberal development policies.

24. J. C. Cambranes, *Coffee and Peasants in Guatemala* (Guatemala City: University of San Carlos of Guatemala, 1985).

25. Brintnall, *Revolt Against the Dead*.

26. Jim Handy, "The Corporate Community, Campesino Organizations, and Agrarian Reform: 1950–1954," in Carol A. Smith, ed., *Guatemalan Indians and the State, 1540–1988* (Austin: University of Texas Press, 1990), 163–82.

27. Warren, *Symbolism of Subordination*.

28. Arturo Arias, "Changing Indian Identity: Guatemala's Violent Transition to Modernity," in Carol A. Smith, ed., *Guatemalan Indians and the State, 1540–1988* (Austin: University of Texas Press, 1990), 230–57.

29. See ibid. For a more controversial reading of Catholic involvement in popular, democratic, and revolutionary movements, see David Stoll, "Between Two Fires: Dual Violence and the Reassertion of Civil Society in Nebaj, Guatemala" (Ph.D. diss., Stanford University, 1992).

30. Smith, "Militarization of Civil Society."

31. No one knows how many people were killed, but it is difficult to find anyone in this area who has not lost at least one family member or friend.

32. Americas Watch, *Civil Patrols in Guatemala* (New York: Americas Watch, 1986). See also Victor Montejo, *Testimony: Death of a Guatemalan Village* (Willimantic, Conn.: Curbstone Press, 1987); and Benjamin Paul and William Demarest, "The Operation of a Death Squad in San Pedro La Laguna," in Robert Carmack, ed., *Harvest of Violence* (Norman: University of Oklahoma Press, 1988), 119–54.

7 Religious Mobility and the Many Words of God in La Paz, Bolivia

Lesley Gill

ON ANY SUNDAY afternoon, one may walk along the Avenida Buenos Aires, through the commercial hub of central La Paz's Aymara Indian neighborhoods, and encounter any number of itinerant preachers, prognosticators, vendors of religious paraphernalia, and storefront churches brimming with the faithful. A man on a street corner predicts the imminent end of the world and advises passersby to prepare for Judgment Day. For only a few pesos, a Pentecostal preacher will channel the healing powers of God to the sick by a touch of his hand. An Aymara woman seated on the sidewalk sells pictures of the Pope side by side with llama fetuses for use in indigenous rituals. Further up the avenue, voices and music spill into the street from a makeshift church, as believers inside raise their hands toward heaven to receive the empowering forces of the Holy Spirit.

Nowadays similar scenes are continually played out in other parts of the city, especially in neighborhoods where large numbers of rural Aymara Indians have established their homes. As social transformations have undermined the power of the official state religions, Catholicism, and of those groups long aligned with it, new opportunities have arisen for a variety of religious organizations—evangelical Protestants of various sects, Mormons, Jehovah's Witnesses, Seventh Day Adventists—to recruit converts and challenge the dominance of the Catholic Church. Although Catholicism has coexisted in uneasy tension with indigenous beliefs and practices for centuries, the proliferation of so many new fundamentalist organizations has turned La Paz into a vibrant religious marketplace where practitioners of various sorts compete for the souls of Bolivians.

The new marketplace of souls has sprung up in a society that, through the 1980s, hovered on the brink of chaos. It spreads among people who feel helpless because their lives have been disrupted by hyperinflation, unemployment, and tantalizing new symbols of consumption that remain completely out of reach. Familiar institutions—the family, political parties, unions, communities, and the state—are unable to overcome a pervasive sense of despair. The new churches capitalize on this sense of powerlessness. Out of a crumbling social order, they hope to erect a particular notion of the truth as more authoritative than competing versions, permitting them to distinguish idolatry and paganism from "religion."[1]

Yet even as impoverished city dwellers flock to the new faiths, their commitment is not always as great as their mentors desire. Indeed, in La Paz there is considerable religious mobility, whereby men and women shift loyalties over the course of their lifetimes[2] and may even maintain more than one religious affiliation at the same time. An individual can be born and raised a Catholic, convert to evangelical Protestantism by joining the Assemblies of God, then move to the United Pentecostal Church, which offers a slightly different twist to the fundamentalist message, and finally revert to folk Catholicism. At any point in the process, the person may also consult a *yatiri* (indigenous diviner and healer) about a variety of misfortunes. As poor urban dwellers selectively adopt different beliefs and practices, they create forms of popular religiosity not anticipated by any of the competing sects and organizations.[3]

This chapter examines the process of religious mobility in La Paz.[4] Since the 1960s, the fragmentation of rural landholdings, urban migration, political instability, economic depression, deindustrialization, and the rise of the cocaine trade have reordered personal relationships. Consequently, peasants and urban migrants increasingly confront the world as individuals rather than as members of communities, unions, neighborhoods, and even families. They are thus forced to create new networks and reactivate preexisting ones to deal with steadily declining standards of living. Changing religious affiliation is one part of this process. Contrary to conventional assumptions, tumultuous social changes have prompted Bolivians less to develop firm loyalties to new groups than to embark on a series of religious experiments whose outcome remains unclear.

Religious beliefs and practices are an inherently relational phenomenon. They not only form part of the way people conceptualize the supernatural and ensure a favorable association with it, but also express how men and women define themselves in relation to their experiences and to other people. Given the growing atomization of social life, it should come as no surprise that the ideology of many new religious organizations, particularly those espousing Protestant fundamentalism, emphasizes individualism and self-sacrifice as a means of personal improvement.[5] Yet as people change religious identities, they also develop new ties of solidarity with some individuals even as they distance themselves from others.[6]

The new social bonds and associated religious beliefs may offer relief from the circumstances that repeatedly confound their lives, but they do not provide lasting solutions to the overwhelming psychological and economic burden of poverty. Not surprisingly, the relief that people feel is likely to be temporary, and at times ambiguous. Individuals thus move on to experiment with other religious groups or drop out of organized religion altogether. In the process, they redefine religious ideas and ritual practices in the context of their changing personal experiences.[7]

Changing religious affiliation is therefore an integral part of the inventive and contradictory process of social change in a city where the lower class must struggle every day to survive. It includes both conversion—a personal ideological transformation—and affiliation, which encompasses varying forms of membership or participation in a religious group (as Green notes in Chapter 6). To comprehend this process, we must first appreciate the manner in which religion became a matter of individual choice, albeit a choice structured by the shifting balance of power between competing class and ethnic groups. To this end, we must explore how the Bolivian revolution of 1952 changed religious practice in La Paz, reordered social life, and paved the way for the "invasion of the sects."

Parting the Waters

One day early in the twentieth century, Francisco Calderón, a peon on the Hacienda Cotana, was seized by the estate's administrator, locked in a room, branded, and beaten within an inch of his life for practicing witchcraft. The administrator, José Sardón, had discovered a bundle of items used in witchcraft—including glass, excrement, lemons, and alcohol—behind the hacienda house. He deduced that Calderón, a well-known indigenous diviner, was plotting to kill him. Calderón repeatedly denied the accusations, claiming that the culprit was most likely his estranged wife, who had taken up with a man on a neighboring estate. Sardón was not convinced. The specter of witchcraft, to say nothing of the fear of Indians plotting against him, so rattled the hacienda administrator that he summoned all of the Aymara peons to the chapel, where he made a spectacle of Calderón and obliged them to pray to the Christian God.[8]

During the first half of the twentieth century, the rural oligarchy and its minions ruled Bolivia in close alliance with the Catholic Church. Non-Catholic beliefs were suppressed, sometimes violently. The latter presented individuals with a vision of the world and the supernatural outside the parameters set by the Catholic hierarchy, and therefore threatened the status quo at least implicitly. On many haciendas, chapels stood next to the country homes of the landlords. During religious festivities and life-cycle events, the power of the priests and the landlords acted together to maintain the status quo. Similarly, wealthy urban families strengthened the paternalistic ties of obedience and protection that bound household servants to them by sponsoring marriages, baptisms, and other events. By so doing, they had their benevolence publicly sanctified by a priest in the presence of God.

Under the aegis of this holy alliance, indigenous beliefs and practices were persecuted, as they had been for centuries in periodic campaigns to "extirpate idolatries." They developed under the domination of Catholicism, which also was refashioned by continuous interaction with indigenous beliefs and customs. Similarly, Protestant and other non-Catholic groups, who struggled to establish themselves in Bolivia in the first half of the twentieth century, also faced substantial hostility from entrenched interests. The Seventh Day Adventists came to Bolivia as early as 1907, the Four-Square Gospel Church arrived in 1929, and the Assemblies of God was founded in 1946; but they all languished during their first decades in the country.[9] Such groups were dominated by foreign missionaries who could not communicate with the majority of Bolivians in their own languages, Aymara and Quechua, and showed little understanding of their problems. It should come as no surprise that they had little success converting the local population.

The 1952 national revolution changed all this. One of the most sweeping agrarian reforms in Latin American history abolished the haciendas that had so encroached on corporate Indian communities. The reform also outlawed the system of unpaid labor (*pongueage*) that had long been associated with landed estates. Although the Catholic Church was not directly affected by the post-1952 reforms, the demise of the rural oligarchy considerably undermined its power. Besides breaking the power of the oligarchy, the revolution produced new patterns of upward and downward social mobility that restructured social life. As peasants and urban servants gained independence from their former patrons, the revolution opened new possibilities for religious recruitment.

In the city, the ideology of paternalism that had structured domestic service gradually gave way to a servant-employer relationship that was more contractual and sporadic.[10] Servants perceived paid household labor as a temporary occupation that they could use as a stepping-stone to the urban labor force. In the countryside, many peasants became independent landowners for the first time. New towns emerged on the altiplano, as marketing patterns shifted to compensate for the void left by the hacienda owners.[11]

Meanwhile, the commercialization of the economy, combined with the renewed expression of class antagonisms and ethnic conflicts, gave rise to new insecurities. Even though domestic servants enjoyed greater freedom from their employers than previous generations of household workers, they had lost many of the material benefits of paternalism without receiving greater social security from the state. Other workers faced similar problems. Nor did the post-1952 state provide peasants with technical and financial assistance, thus contributing to the stagnation of the rural economy. Population growth and inheritance fragmented landholdings, forcing peasants to migrate in search of additional sources of income. Many left for La Paz, where they created squatter settlements on the steep slopes overlooking the city center. Between 1950 and 1987, La Paz grew from 321,063 inhabitants to nearly 900,000. El Alto, a satellite city on the high plateau surrounding the center, grew from 11,000 to over 350,000 inhabitants in the same period.[12]

Besides hoping to achieve what they called progress, that is, improving their economic situation, urban migrants often said they wanted to "civilize themselves." This entailed getting an education, learning Spanish, and, especially for women, dressing well. Indeed, some early migrants who settled in La Paz during the 1960s and 1970s did manage to prosper by establishing themselves in commerce. They became meat sellers, truck drivers, and wholesalers of various sorts, and resided in the neighborhoods of Ch'jini and Gran Poder. Most migrants did not enjoy such good fortune, however. They remained trapped in domestic service, street vending, part-time construction work, and other low-paid, insecure occupations.

Their situation grew steadily worse through the 1980s. Following years of political instability and fiscal mismanagement, inflation shot into the stratosphere, generating daily, sometimes minute-by-minute, price increases. Bolivian currency became worthless. People discovered that the only way to keep pace with inflation, which by conservative estimates culminated at an annual rate of 14,000 percent in the mid-1980s, was to obtain U.S. dollars flowing into the country through the illegal but lucrative cocaine trade. Meanwhile, prolonged drought in the highlands and flooding in the lowlands drove still more peasants into the cities, where their survival depended more than ever on a cash income.

The government's response only aggravated their plight. In 1985 the administration implemented a series of fiscal austerity measures backed by the International Monetary Fund. Although inflation halted almost overnight, thousands of people lost their jobs, wages were frozen, and cutbacks in state spending led to further erosion of public education, health care, and urban transportation. Faced with an increasingly desperate situation, and having nowhere to turn except a perilous future in the cocaine trade, many Bolivians were ready to listen to new religious messages.

Indeed, some found it almost impossible not to believe. In the absence of regular employment and a state-funded safety net for the poorest inhabitants, the possibility that a benevolent, superior power might not exist was simply unimaginable for most of La Paz's shantytown dwellers. Helping them to deal with their feelings of insecurity were over 124 religious groups vying with each other and the Catholic Church.[13]

Evangelical Protestants have been the most successful in recruiting converts,[14] even though, compared with Brazil and Guatemala, the impact of evangelical Protestantism in Bolivia is less.[15] They claimed 244,000 converts, or 4 percent of a national population of six million, in the mid-1980s, but this figure is conservative and has grown.[16]

Unlike the Mormons and Baha'is, who found most of their converts among the middle class, evangelicals enjoyed the greatest success among peasants, lower-class urban dwellers, and rural migrants. Their growth curves began to swing upward in the 1960s. The Assemblies of God began a program of "total evangelization" in 1967, and a decade later boasted six hundred preaching centers with over twenty-seven thousand members. In 1965, five hundred local churches from thirty-six established denominations began an Evangelism-in-Depth crusade that ended with over nineteen thousand professed converts.[17] Still other groups arrived in the country.

The ecstatic forms of worship associated with Pentecostalism quickly took hold in urban squatter settlements, where the presence of the Catholic Church was nominal at best and often nonexistent. Catholic clergy found themselves poorly prepared to minister to impoverished urban dwellers for a number of reasons. Years of specialized religious training required for the priesthood, and a declining number of men interested in devoting their lives to the Catholic Church, produced a constant shortage of priests.[18] Whether priests were foreign or Bolivian— and 85 percent were foreign[19]—they came from a different social background than their parishioners and typically lived in isolation from the latter's problems.

Protestant evangelicals rapidly filled the gap. They won more converts by expanding into neighborhoods where the institutional Catholic presence was weak than from wresting believers away from the Church in areas where it was dominant. Long periods of training were not necessary for aspiring leaders to propagate the evangelical message. Local men who received "the calling" set up their own storefront churches with the support of small groups of followers. Some of the most successful Pentecostal churches were established by local men who broke away from missionary control. Such leaders developed their own particular interpretations of the Scriptures and could conduct worship services in Aymara, if they needed to communicate with new migrants from the countryside. Splits and regroupings distinguished the spread of the new religious groups, a process often aggravated by divisions on the national and international scenes.[20]

Under military rule from the mid-1960s to the early 1980s, the Bolivian state directly intervened in religious affairs. A series of pro-U.S. military regimes facilitated the entry of evangelical Christian organizations into Bolivian society in order to curb the influence of liberation theology, which the military labeled communist.[21] With the return of elected government in 1982, new regulations required religious groups to state their beliefs, have at least fifteen hundred members, and possess their own building in order to operate legally. But in practice, little changed; the rules were ignored, and new groups simply affiliated temporarily with better-established ones.

The intense competition between many sects, the Catholic Church, and indigenous practitioners ensured that religious dogma was constantly debated, as each group sought to erect its version of religious truth to the exclusion of all others. On the eve of Pope John Paul II's visit to La Paz in 1987, Pentecostal preacher Luis Camacho issued a stern warning to his flock. "Some people have to receive God's representatives from Rome," he roared, "but we [the Pentecostals] have God with us all the time, because we have opened ourselves to the Holy Spirit. For the same reason, we don't worship pieces of wood [representations of the Catholic saints] and appeal to intermediaries [the saints] who supposedly stand between mankind and God. That is idolatry!" He went on to describe how the Devil ran rampant through Catholic convents and monasteries, how they were rife with fornication and homosexuality, and how dead fetuses were regularly discovered in the nuns' quarters.[22]

Camacho went on to warn his congregation of a rival version of Pentecostalism, represented by another church located just a few blocks down the street. "We believe that Jesus Christ is the true God and without Him there is no salvation," he told members. "Some [other Pentecostals] believe in a trinity. They see God as three people and try to impose this false vision onto others. But there is only one God and his name is Jesus Christ."[23] He went on to characterize indigenous beliefs as idolatrous because of the absence of Christ.

The pope was more than willing to do battle with the likes of Luis Camacho. He condemned the false doctrines of the "sects" and went on to assail liberation theologians, who form a small left wing of the Bolivian Catholic Church, for failing to bring the traditional teachings of the Church to Bolivians. He also warned city dwellers not to stray from the straight and narrow moral path. According to the pontiff, practices such as *sirwiñacu*, an indigenous form of trial marriage, were immoral; Catholic men and women could live together only within the bounds of holy matrimony.[24]

How, we might ask, do immigrant Aymaras take part in this aggressive and divisive world of religious combat? In order to answer this question, we must examine the manner in which religious identity arises from changing and often contradictory life experiences.

The Making of a Religious Identity

Religious identity must be thought of as a dynamic, continually evolving process that takes place over an individual's entire lifetime. In La Paz, shifting religious affiliation occurs within the context of rapid change that has altered personal relationships in the immigrant Aymara neighborhoods and moved men and women to seek new explanations for their problems, reevaluate their personal identities, and establish a new sense of self. Affiliating with an organized religion is just one of a number of ways that people try to establish bonds in this crisis-ridden milieu and construct new explanations of their personal history. Aymara immigrants have to contend with the stigma of their rural Indian origins as they struggle to forge new identities and build supportive networks in the city. Worship services offer them an institutional base for developing significant ties to other people. Churches also provide rituals and beliefs to validate these social bonds, creating a new sense of community. Confronted with an overwhelming situation, immigrants turn to organized religion at different times in their lives. They do so with varying degrees of conviction and commitment, in the hope of finding spiritual comfort. For women, in particular, organized religion represents one of the most common ways of developing new relationships, because they find it harder than men to acquire emotional support and economic security once they move outside kin networks.

Many people subscribe to more than one religious dogma at a time. Most have been baptized Catholics at birth, then converted to another religion, usually evangelical Protestantism, without completely forsaking their Catholic heritage. Vacilia Choque is such an individual. She is a thirty-six-year-old Aymara market woman who migrated to La Paz shortly after marrying at the age of seventeen. Choque's husband works as a part-time mason, and she sells clothing in the vast urban market known as Miamicito (Little Miami). Choque describes herself as a Catholic, having undergone a Catholic baptism in the rural community where she was born. Several years after settling in La Paz, she began to attend an evangelical Protestant church called Cristo es la Respuesta (Christ Is the Answer). She was deeply moved by its message, and attributes her recovery from a serious illness to the intervention of the Protestant God. According to Choque:

> I was in the hospital and cried and cried, pleading with the Señor [God] to save me. Then one night—it must have been three o'clock in the morning—He called my name and said, "Don't cry. Your Father is here. I am going to help you." And just like that, He cured me with His words. It was really tremendous.

Over ten years later, Choque still recalled the events of that night in vivid detail. She continued to attend the worship services at Cristo es la Respuesta, despite the opposition of her husband, who described the church as "nonsense" and maintained that he would go dancing to hell on Judgment Day.[25] Yet Choque still defined herself as Catholic, even though she was uncertain where she stood and could not participate in folk Catholic fiestas because of the high cost of food, alcohol, and other ritual items that made reciprocity impossible for her. As she explained the apparent contradiction: "I am a Catholic because I have been baptized and everything, but I have not been receiving the [Catholic] message lately. Also, with everything so expensive I can't afford to go to fiestas and drink and dance. That's just how my life is."

In addition to people like Choque, who apparently hold contradictory beliefs at the same time, other people move between religious organizations over the course of their lives. Their participation reflects an ongoing process of association and distancing with their class peers, as they seek to address personal misfortunes, overcome the disintegrating effects of economic crisis on their lives, and, if possible, advance both socially and economically. These resulting religious trajectories may be very different for men and for women. They also may have very different meanings for the relatively well-to-do than for those who are less well off.

Some men are able to use religion as a vehicle for upward mobility more effectively than are women. They not only enjoy more opportunities within organized religion for full-time careers than women, but also encounter greater possibilities for crafting religious practices to fit their personal economic agendas. In a community on the Bolivian altiplano studied by Gilles Rivière, for example, a rising group of merchants gained control of the folk Catholic system of rotating religious positions and used it to strengthen a network of patron-client relationships crucial to their entrepreneurial endeavors. At the same time, large numbers of *comuneros* (community residents) converted to Pentecostalism to distance themselves from the resulting exploitative relationships.[26]

The evangelical churches springing up in the countryside and in La Paz are invariably organized by men, who, according to evangelical strictures, are the only ones entitled to preach the word of God. Women may play important roles in various female organizations set up within the churches and during periodic home visits, but they cannot fashion a career and earn a livelihood from the church. The successful male preacher, in contrast, may attract enough followers and contributions to support himself and his family. The religious trajectory of Pentecostal pastor Nestor Vargas illustrates how men can use religious conversion for personal advancement.

Nestor Vargas was born sometime in the mid-1940s in a rural community located forty kilometers from the city of Oruro. He was baptized a Catholic and participated in the community's folk Catholic rituals while growing up. His association with Pentecostalism began in the 1960s, after he migrated to La Paz and his young son fell sick. Vargas and his wife took the child to a folk healer for treatment, as they were accustomed to do in the countryside when a serious illness arose. When treatment failed, they decided to seek the assistance of a Pentecostal church, on the advice of friends who spoke to them of the healing powers of the Protestant God. The church's pastor laid his hands on the sick infant, and the child eventually recovered. This experience so moved Vargas that he and his entire family decided to convert.

The church that they joined was called the Pentecostal Assembly of God, a local affiliate of the well-known denomination headquartered in Springfield, Missouri. When a split developed in the congregation in 1970, over the issue of missionary control, Vargas was outspoken in his opposition to continued association with the mission. Other members were still comfortable with the dependent relationship, so Vargas seized the initiative, rallied dissenters, and led them out of the church. But he did so only after securing a promise from some "Chilean brothers" to help organize a new church. The Chileans were from the Pentecostal Methodist Church, noted for its support of Chilean dictator Augusto Pinochet. Although the Chileans could not offer any financial assistance, they did provide educational materials and gave the fledgling church some preliminary guidance.

This is how Nestor Vargas launched his career as a Pentecostal preacher. Over the next decade, his group moved from one site to another. By 1988, the church occupied a choice location on the busy Avenida Buenos Aires, where it represented the center of a loosely knit coalition of similar churches scattered throughout the country. The La Paz congregation counted some 130 members, most of them lower-class, rural immigrants. The man who had consulted folk healers for medical cures was using his position as a Pentecostal preacher to pass judgment on the "superstitions" and idolatrous practices of rural Aymaras, whom he periodically tried to convert during forays to the countryside.

In the life of Nestor Vargas, we can appreciate the importance of religious conversion in shaping an individual's future life, as well as the contradictory implications of such a transformation. On one hand, the experience of conversion encouraged Vargas to transcend his previously narrow, self-interested approach to life. It taught him the awesome power of God and provided something that went beyond himself. On the other hand, conversion to Protestantism enabled Vargas to further his considerable personal ambitions. As he moved from one affiliation to another, he defined himself in opposition to the beliefs and practices that he used to hold, redefining himself in relation to others as he consolidated a new social position. In the end, Vargas enjoyed social prestige and economic comfort considerably above what he had experienced as an impoverished migrant.

Needless to say, most men who come to La Paz have not been able to parlay a religious conversion into social and economic advancement. Women are precluded from such religious careers altogether. Yet women greatly outnumber men in many of the new religious groups in La Paz; their participation in worship services and other church activities may be three to four times greater than that of their male brethren. The rigid, puritanical rules of most congregations allow women to develop greater self-esteem because abusive male behavior, such as drunkenness and sexual harassment, are controlled.[27] The bonds that they develop with other believers often replace ties with kin left behind in the countryside, or marital relationships that have ended through divorce, abandonment, or death. Their decisions to move from one church to another emerge from changing life circumstances in the city around them and within their own households.

Margarita Ticona is a fifty-four-year-old widow who has never converted to Protestantism but has had experience with three different religious organizations. She migrated to La Paz with her family in the early 1970s, after her late husband, a tin miner, became sick and could no longer work. The family could not survive on the husband's pension from the mining company, so Margarita began selling food in front of the Bolivian Workers' Central union hall in downtown La Paz to earn additional income. She also sought occasional work as a laundress to make ends meet. Her husband died soon after the family resettled in La Paz, leaving Ticona with four children to raise.

Although Ticona had lived her entire life as a folk Catholic, now she began to listen more closely to the messages of the various religious practitioners who plied their trade on the streets of her neighborhood. One day a pastor from a Protestant church came to her home and offered a free meal to anyone who wished to attend worship services in his church. Ticona decided to send her fourteen-year old daughter, who subsequently developed a regular association with the group. She was supportive of her daughter's involvement, because she felt that the church exercised a strong moral influence over the young woman during a vulnerable time of life. Ticona herself decided to visit another evangelical congregation in the neighborhood after all the local mothers were invited to share a Christmas meal in the church. She enjoyed the event and became a regular churchgoer for the next two years. "I went for the fun of it," she explained, "but then I became more accustomed and got to know some of the other sisters. I also like to listen to the pastor, they play beautiful music, and the brothers don't drink. They also offer little lunches to people in this area."

Despite the manifest benefits, eventually Ticona grew disillusioned with the church and withdrew. Evangelicals were really hypocrites, she explained, citing a particular case to prove her point. "My landlady is a sister, for example, but she is really bad. She gets mad at everything and constantly complains that I don't pay the rent. But what does she want? Sometimes there is no money. They [the evangelicals] say that every brother [and sister] should help a poor person, but no, nothing. They just complain. This is why I no longer believe in them." Ticona currently describes herself as a Catholic, but her understanding of God is not bound by Catholic dogma. "Everyone talks about God," she says, "but I don't give any of them much importance now. But in my imagination I believe in God. When people say that he is our Father, I believe that it is true. I don't go to the churches, though. I just pray in my home."

Margarita Ticona's story illustrates how hard-pressed members of the lower class change their religious affiliations as a result of their struggles to survive. Her changing loyalties reflect her search for practical solutions to her problems. Ticona found neither solutions nor support, only a few free meals and many hypocrites. Her experiment with evangelical Protestantism has ended in disillusionment, at least for now.

Conclusion: God Bless the Child
Who's Got His Own?

Religious identity unfolds over the course of an entire lifetime, as men and women strive to re-create enduring bonds of support, infuse them with new significance, and improve their economic position. As the ties that bind poor Bolivians to each other are fractured by economic chaos and the growing commodification of social life, they face the world as individuals, which forces them to create personal solutions to their problems. Changing religious associations, or the maintenance of allegiances to more than one organization, is part of the ongoing drama.

Yet joining new religious groups has not provided Bolivians with lasting solutions to the current crisis of capitalism in their country. Although religious fundamentalism draws its strength from a claim to universal truth and provides individuals with a concrete program for change, its suitability for Bolivians is not so obvious to many disillusioned converts. Moreover, even as co-religionists temporarily create unity out of an ever more tenuous situation, they also distance themselves from their class peers and even, at times, from the economically less fortunate. The outcome of this process of distancing and association is never determined once and for all. It is, rather, part of the ongoing encounters of daily life, where contending groups—men and women, rich and poor, Aymara and non-Aymara—confront the dislocations of social life in an impoverished city.

In the course of these very personal struggles, there is a constant traffic in meanings that are appropriated and transported across the boundaries of hostile religious groups, in each of which they are reinterpreted. This is a process that is shaped by the competing interests of rival religious organizations and the Bolivian state but not entirely structured by them. Indeed, as Aymara men and women use religious affiliations to build networks of emotional and economic support, and to provide new explanations for the confusing circumstances of their lives, they are devising a popular religiosity that does not exactly fit into any of the conceptual frameworks that are so vigorously marketed in La Paz today.

NOTES

1. Talal Assad, "Anthropological Conceptions of Religion: Reflections on Geertz," *Man* 18, no. 2 (1990): 237–59.

2. I have borrowed the term "religious mobility" from M. W. Murphee, *Christianity and the Shona*, London School of Economics Monographs on Social Anthropology, no. 36 (London: Athlone Press, 1969), to describe the process of shifting religious affiliation.

3. I use the term "popular religion" for those beliefs and activities practiced outside of or in opposition to dominant institutionalized religions. This includes religious activities that take place within the framework of institutionalized religion but consciously criticize or alter it. See Lynn Stephen and James Dow, "Introduction: Popular Religion in Mexico and Central America," in Lynn Stephen and James Dow, eds., *Class, Politics, and Popular Religion in Mexico and Central America* (Washington, D.C.: Society for Latin American Anthropology, 1990), p. 8.

4. The research for this article was carried out from June 1987 to May 1988. It is based on participant observation in several churches and interviews with former and present believers. The fieldwork grew out of a larger project supported by a Fulbright research grant that focused on women and domestic service.

5. Protestantism's association with emerging individualism has been noted by several authors. Max Weber's thesis on the relationship between Protestantism and the entrepreneurial, individualistic spirit of capitalism is well known. See Max Weber, *The Protestant Ethic and the Spirit of Capitalism* (London: Allen and Unwin [1930], 1982). See also David Knowlton, "Social and Political Issues of Protestantism in Bolivia," paper presented at the Annual Meeting of the American Anthropological Association, Chicago, 1991; and L. R. Goldin and B. Metz, "An Expression of Cultural Change: Invisible Converts to Protestantism among Highland Guatemala Mayas," *Ethnology* 30, no. 4 (1991): 325–38.

6. Lesley Gill, "Like a Veil to Cover Them: Women and the Pentecostal Movement in La Paz," *American Ethnologist* 17, no. 4 (1990): 708–21.

7. Maria Lagos, "We Have to Learn to Ask: Cultural Hegemony, Diverse Experiences and Contested Meanings," *American Ethnologist* 20, no. 1 (1993).

8. Archivo de La Paz, Distrito Judicial La Paz, 1902, Caja 844. Calderón, who managed to escape, claimed in his suit against Sardón that "se [ha] conspirado contra mi persona . . . que yo al mayordomo . . . lo hubiera querido hechizar por haber encontrado en la asequia que entra a la huerta a un saco de limones dulces, un vidrio . . . y un poco de estiércol, todo lo que el tal mayordomo ha querido decir son de él. Los tormentos que han querido darme han sido bastante atroces, que la sentencia ha sido de azotes hasta victimarme y quemarme en leña verde mi cuerpo." ("He conspired against me . . . [saying that] I want to hex him after he found a sack of lemons, a piece of glass, and a little bit of excrement in the irrigation ditch that goes into the garden, all of which the *mayordomo* claims are his. The torments that I have suffered have been atrocious, the sentence being whiplashes that burned my entire body.")

9. David Barrett, ed., *World Christian Encyclopedia* (Nairobi: Oxford University Press, 1982), pp. 181–82.

10. Lesley Gill, "Painted Faces: Conflict and Ambiguity in Domestic Servant-Employer Relations in La Paz (1930–1988)," *Latin American Research Review* 25, no. 1 (1990): 119–36.

11. David Preston, *Farmers and Towns: Rural-Urban Relations in Highland Bolivia* (Norwich, U.K.: Geo Abstracts, 1978).

12. Godofredo Sandoval and M. Fernanda Sostres, *La ciudad prometida: Pobladores y organizaciones sociales en El Alto* (La Paz: Sistema/ILDIS, 1989).

13. This figure is almost certainly an underestimate. It represents only groups that are officially registered with the Bolivian government. Many others operate without official permission. They may be new groups that break off from a parent organization or others that enter the country from abroad without receiving official recognition.

14. The term "evangelical Protestant" refers to a theological conservative who stresses personal salvation, evangelism, and a literal interpretation of the Bible. Although in the United States, Mormons and Jehovah's Witnesses are not included in this definition, Bolivians tend to lump all non-Catholic Christians under the term *evangélico*.

15. About 30 percent of the population in Guatemala now considers itself evangelical (Stoll, personal communication), and the number of Brazilian Catholics has declined from 90 percent to 75 percent of the

total population because of the inroads made by evangelical Protestantism. See "Pope Urges Brazilians to Resist Mirage of Evangelists," *New York Times*, October 14, 1991, p. A3.

16. See Barrett, *World Christian Encyclopedia*. Tomás Bamet, *Salvación o dominación: Las sectas religiosas en el Ecuador* (Quito: Editorial El Conejo, 1986), describes similar processes in Ecuador.

17. See Barrett, *World Christian Encyclopedia*.

18. Nearly 80 percent (716) of all priests were foreigners in the 1970s (see Ibid.). Although this figure dropped somewhat during the years of most repressive military rule under General Banzer (1971–1978) and General García Meza (1980–1982), it remained high.

19. Penny Lernoux, *The Cry of the People* (New York: Doubleday, 1980), p. 143.

20. David Stoll, *Is Latin America Turning Protestant?* (Berkeley: University of California Press, 1990).

21. Lernoux, *Cry of the People*.

22. In the pastor's words, "lo han sacado muchos fetos de donde las monjas."

23. The non-Trinitarian beliefs of Pastor Luis represent a minority position within Protestant fundamentalism. Most evangelicals consider such beliefs unorthodox.

24. Unknown to the pope, *sirwiñacu* is rarely practiced anymore, even though men and women continue to live together outside of wedlock.

25. Her exact words were "A él no le gusta. 'Cuando llegue Dios, yo voy a ser él que va al infierno,' dice él. 'Yo quiero ir bailando,' dice." ("He didn't like it. 'When God arrives, I'm going to be the one who goes to Hell,' he said. 'I want to go dancing.' ")

26. See Gilles Rivière, "Cambios sociales y pentecostalismo en una comunidad aymara," *Fe y pueblo* 3, no. 14 (1986): 24–31. Similar processes have been described elsewhere. See Blanca Muratorio, "Protestantism and Capitalism Revisited in the Rural Highlands of Ecuador," *Journal of Peasant Studies* 8, no. 1 (1980): 37–60, for Ecuador; and Sheldon Annis, *God and Production in a Guatemalan Town* (Austin: University of Texas Press, 1987), for Guatemala.

27. See Elizabeth Brusco, "The Household Basis of Evangelical Religion and the Reformation of Machismo in Colombia" (Ph.D. diss., City University of New York, 1986); and Lesley Gill, "Like a Veil to Cover Them."

CONCLUSION
Is This Latin America's Reformation?

Virginia Garrard-Burnett

*F*OR MOST observers of Latin America, the sight of a small, concrete-block Protestant church filled with rapt believers and equipped with blaring loudspeakers provokes a visceral response. To many, the proliferation of Protestantism in Latin America is proof of the complete U.S. cultural conquest of the region, a conquest bought—not won—by money, political influence, and consumer goods. To others, Protestantism represents the last great hope for a continent where problems run so deep that they defy the solutions offered by a panoply of ideologies and "isms": capitalism, liberalism, Marxism, authoritarianism, and Roman Catholicism. Does evangelical Protestantism, the latest and among the most foreign of these imported ideologies, offer any real hope for reform? Or is it a divisive force that threatens to shred the already tattered fabric of Latin American society?

One of the most popular assumptions about the growth of Protestantism in Latin America is that it is a by-product of U.S. foreign policy. Supposedly, Protestantism is spreading in Latin America because politically conservative Christian groups in the United States have saturated the region with a relentless flood of money and manpower. Once lured into the fold, the critics say, converts obediently adopt the political cant of their missionary mentors.

There is obviously some truth to this argument. Since the

1960s, Protestant religion has been seen by some North American evangelical leaders as a "spiritual alternative" to Latin America's modern ills: poverty, inequality, and the looming shadow of communism cast by the Cuban revolution. The result was two waves of highly politicized missionary activity from the United States. The first movement, spearheaded by a nondenominational parachurch organization called Latin American Mission, lasted from 1959 until about 1970 and was a low-intensity, lower-tech version of what came later. It emphasized growth over denominationalism, and both electronic and personal one-on-one evangelism, and advocated moderate political reform while warning of the dangers of communism. By 1970, the evangelical movement had become increasingly sectarian and divided over issues of theology and politics, but it nonetheless set the precedent for the second wave of anticommunist missionary activity that washed over Latin America following the Sandinista victory in July 1979 and the election of Ronald Reagan to the U.S. presidency in November 1980.[1]

As a number of writers have noted, this "Great Commission" of politically conservative Protestant missionaries into Latin America reflected the influence of the religious right in the United States in the late 1970s, and the insertion of their religious, political, and social agenda into the North American national—and international—political discourse. What is less commonly noted is that the "sacramentalization" of U.S. politics in the early 1980s mirrored the sort of praxis called for by liberation theology, which had reestablished the ancient bond between Christian injunction and political action in Latin America twenty years earlier—a bond that had been greatly weakened in most of Latin America during the late nineteenth century. While the idea of sacramentalized politics is suspect to most North Americans, who are steeped in the rhetoric of the separation of church and state, it is familiar and resonant to most Latin Americans. What is not familiar to North Americans is the multiplicity of religious and political options.

Refracted in the looking glass of religious and political pluralism, Latin American Protestantism does not always resemble its

North American counterpart, even in the political sphere. David Stoll and others have pointed out that we must stop assuming that Protestantism in Latin America has "easily predictable political implications," and several of the preceding chapters underscore this point.[2] As Kenneth Coleman and his colleagues demonstrate, conservative U.S. fundamentalists poured considerable money and manpower into El Salvador during the 1980s as the superpowers played out the last act of the Cold War drama. Yet when surveyed in the late 1980s, local evangelicals were virtually indistinguishable from their secular and lapsed Catholic peers on nearly every political question. In El Salvador, at least, the "invasion of the sects" did not generate a pan-evangelical bloc of political conservatives, let alone local believers in complete lockstep with right-wing fundamentalists in the United States. This suggests that we might be able to take at face value Latin American evangelicals' claims of political neutrality, despite the dire warnings of those who see conspiracy in church growth.[3]

There is no single Protestant political paradigm in Latin America, nor is there yet a focused, articulated movement of evangelical political activism equivalent to that of the Christian right in the United States. This is not to suggest that a given church or denomination may not openly rally behind a specific political actor or cause but, rather, to underline the fact that there is no overreaching Protestant political praxis in Latin America or, for that matter, in the United States. Protestant churches in Latin America have never developed a cohesive political agenda, nor do they seem likely to in the near future. According to Coleman and colleagues and John Burdick, one reason is that many people seek out evangelical churches precisely because they offer a certain refuge from political involvement. This includes the dangers of church-based opposition to power structures exemplified by liberation theology.

However, as Paul Freston and Rowan Ireland show, evangelicals can and do involve themselves directly in the political arena. And when Pentecostals become political, they do so because of their religious beliefs, not in spite of them. Although Latin American Pentecostals place a strong emphasis on the Kingdom of God, thereby offering believers the ultimate in deferred gratification, they also believe that the last battle between God and the Devil must be played out before the final Kingdom comes. It takes only the slightest spin on this traditional Pentecostal message, as Burdick points out, for believers to start defining the struggle between good and evil in this world in class or political terms. But what differentiates Pentecostals from their secular fellow travelers is that Pentecostals see the struggle in this world as a metaphor for the final metaphysical battle, not the final battle itself.

When evangelicals do involve themselves in the political milieu, they conceptualize the nature and purpose of politics rather differently than do their Catholic counterparts. Whether of the left or the right, politicized Protestants define the political arena in fundamental terms of sin, grace, and individual salvation. Paradoxically, Latin American Protestants seek the "common good" through personal redemption: even when they act collectively, they do so as individuals. By acting as individual "children of God" to improve this world, Latin American Protestants believe that they anticipate the coming of the next.

But what about basic survival in a world defined by violence and poverty, the context that liberation theologians refer to as "structural sin"? In many ways, this is perhaps the easiest and most quantifiable dimension of Latin American Protestantism to grasp. In general, many observers (and often *evangélicos* themselves) describe Latin American Protestants as otherworldly and escapist, fatalistic about conditions in this world as they await the coming of the next. But this overlooks the complexity of evangelical detachment. In his book on Pentecostalism in Latin America, *Tongues of Fire*, David Martin argues that evangelical churches construct around believers a spiritual cocoon, a congregation of like-thinkers who are bound together by a common and particular corpus of rules, moral codes, and theological beliefs.[4] This cocoon nurtures believers and insulates them from the hostile postmodern world. As the preceding chapters indicate, the believer is empowered on many levels and is thus able to thrive not only in the next world but also in the here and now. When seen in this light, Protestantism, and especially Pentecostalism, looks less like a means of escape from the temporal world than a pragmatic strategy of survival.

The most extensive studies of the pragmatics of Protestantism have to do with personal economy.[5] Since the time of Max Weber, it has been customary to equate Protestantism with "the spirit of capitalism" and the accumulation of personal wealth and private capital. Most of the early studies of Protestantism in Latin America, such as Christian Lalive d'Epinay's study of Protestants in Chile and Emilio Willems's work on Brazil in the late 1960s, made similar arguments.[6] Willems, who studied farmers in rural Brazil, noted that most Protestant converts came from the ranks of people who were incrementally more wealthy than their neighbors. Lalive, in his study of migrants to urban Chile, found that converts were most likely to be poor, recent immigrants with few familial ties or business connections in the city. Both suggested that whether Protestants came from the ranks of the very poor or from the lower middle classes, the "work ethic" and strict moral codes of their religion enabled them to advance quickly and decisively to a higher economic stratum.

The economic crisis that has gripped Latin America since the late 1970s has altered this model somewhat. In El Salvador, where civil war and capital flight left a once-booming economy in ruins, Coleman and colleagues find that Protestants are poor when they convert and remain that way; there is no discernible pattern of economic differentiation that distinguishes poor Salvadoran evangelicals from anyone else. The Bolivian case is a bit different. There, an illegal "informal sector"—narcotrafficking—fuels a national economy that is otherwise paralyzed by a staggering foreign debt. In this land of plural economic realities, Lesley Gill sees a marginal material improvement among evangelicals, at least among Aymara Indians who migrate to the city. But in her study, religious mobility is both a product and a cause of economic change. She finds that poor urban migrants use religious affiliation to "build networks of emotional and economic support and to provide new explanations for the confusing circumstances of their lives." While Lalive d'Epinay found this same sort of networking in the 1960s, what is new here is that Bolivians change their religious affiliation—from one Protestant denomination to another, and through various Catholic identities—as they move from one economic or social class to another. This is not because any one faith is associated with prosperity, but because each economic shift requires that a support structure be created. For urban Bolivian Indians, then, Protestantism is but one element in a fluid strategy for economic survival.

One aspect of the economic advancement argument that looms large in this volume—evangelical religion's moral prohibitions against dancing, participation in religious brotherhoods, fornication, and, most important, drinking alcohol—usually (although, as Burdick indicates, not always) can greatly improve the household economies of converts, who no longer spend their meager savings on "vices." Our authors argue that to focus solely on the economic implications of what, for lack of a better term, might be called "ethical behavior" obscures its greater sociological importance: the revalorization of the material, psychological, and spiritual currency of the family and the individuals within it.

As early as 1967 Bryan Roberts, one of the first scholars to notice the growing popularity of Protestant churches among the urban poor in Guatemala City, suggested that when men give up drinking and spend more time with, and money on, their families, society's most basic unit is strengthened.[7] However, when Sheldon Annis looked at a larger "basic unit," a traditional indigenous community in Guatemala in the early 1980s, he was less sanguine. While he found that Protestant Indians were measurably wealthier than their Catholic counterparts (because they no longer paid a "Catholic cultural tax" through participation in religious brotherhoods or in expensive local fiestas), they also no longer considered themselves to be part of the community at large. Thus, while Protestantism can enhance social structures at one level, it can dramatically redefine or even destroy basic social units at another.[8]

Even when the redefinition of basic social structures is profound, as Elizabeth Brusco points out, it need not always be detrimental, and nowhere is this clearer than in terms of gender relations. It is important to note that in Latin America and in the West in general, women are often the "most religious" members of families: they are the most likely to attend Mass regularly if they are Catholic, most likely to see that the family's religious obligations (such as marriage and baptism) are met, and most likely to be the first member of a family to join a Protestant church. Although women's religiosity is often dealt with dismissively or peripherally in the scholarly literature, the work of Brusco, Linda Green, and Gill attests to the fact that Protestantism offers a quantifiable comparative advantage specifically to women. In Colombia, as Brusco notes, this advantage is part financial, part emotional, and part physical: Colombian women find that Protestant men make better husbands, fathers, and providers. When machismo is brought under control, power relations between husbands and wives become less asymmetrical. Conversion, then, restructures and reforms family dynamics, strengthening the family as a unit and the individuals within it.

This idea of "circling the wagons" around church and family in the face of social and economic decay is hardly exclusive to Latin American evangelicals; it echoes the return-to-church movement and rise of Christian fundamentalism in the United States today. However, as Green's chapter on Guatemalan widows illustrates, Latin American evangelical churches do seem to place a much greater emphasis on the notion of "community" and "belonging" than do their North American or European counterparts. Green found that one of the evangelical churches' most central tasks was to create micro communities that "preserve[d] the essentials" for their members, whose lives had been shattered by war, dislocation, and the death of loved ones. This integral concern with the identity of the "community of believers" may be a reference to the corporate Catholic past or, perhaps, to use historian Nancy Farriss's phrase, one of the mechanisms of "strategic acculturation."[9]

But it may also be a manifestation of Protestantism's new face in Latin America: corporate, nucleated, flexible, and responsive to local conditions and circumstances. Jean-Pierre Bastian and Carlos Garma Navarro, who have examined Protestantism in

Mexico in some detail, have concluded that Latin American Protestantism is bifurcating into two types. One is urban Protestantism, which is bureaucratic, technologically sophisticated, conservative in political and theological matters, and culturally wedded
to the United States. The other is rural and local, and takes its
imperative when the most marginalized sectors of society—such
as women, displaced people, or landless peasants—are denied
access to local power.[10]

In the new religious configuration, members believe that they
insulate themselves from the assaults taken against the larger
community even as their own actions abdicate the community
status quo. Believers trade their primary allegiance to community, class, or ethnic group for discipleship in the Kingdom of
God. Not surprisingly, the cost of this religious refuge is often
quite high when measured in terms of community fragmentalization and dissonance with traditional belief systems. Yet believers
assume that such is the price of power and salvation—in this
world and the next. To paraphrase David Martin, "Pentecostalism
is their very *own* fiesta," and the party is exclusive.[11]

In any event, many of the early predictions of the impact
that evangelical religion would make on Latin American life and
politics were off the mark. Perhaps this is because the few early
writers on the topic (not to mention missionaries and political
visionaries) assumed that Protestantism would transform Latin
America and its people in the same ways that it had altered other
societies—Britain, the United States, Germany—through history. Protestantism, the argument went, precipitated the dawn
of the modern age in Europe and North America. Why should it
not do so in Latin America?

The answer, of course, is that the Latin American Reformation
is taking place more than four hundred years after the original
event—in the dusk, not the dawn, of the modern age. It should
not be surprising that when set against a backdrop of dependency, malignant urbanization, chronic civil strife, and polar ex-
tremes of poverty and wealth, the family resemblance that Latin
American Protestantism bears to its North American progenitor
is growing less distinct over time.

However, there is one critical way in which the Latin American Protestant movement does fit the model of the European Reformation: it is, in fact, a genuine movement of protest. This is not to say that protest is always a conscious motive for converts, but it is, if only subconsciously, always a rejection of the status quo. As Martin has written, "The evangelical believer is one who has symbolically repudiated what previously held him in place, vertically and horizontally." [12] Latin America is still overwhelmingly Catholic in creed and culture. The decision to leave the Church is in itself a radical act, and often no one is more aware of that fact than those who choose to do so. Yet for social scientists trained to identify well-articulated, organized forms of resistance like labor organizing or guerrilla *focos* (centers), the passive resistance of evangelicalism is all to easy to overlook.

Political scientist James Scott has called passive resistance the "weapon of the weak": through subterfuge, evasion, and noncompliance, society's most marginal members can defend and even advance their interests without engaging in the confrontational behavior that invites reprisals.[13] Within this context Latin American Protestantism can be seen as a type of rebellion, the personal protest of the voiceless and powerless. Protestants by definition do not buy into the traditional Catholic-centered status quo, even when they obediently acquiesce to the political or economic "authorities in power." *Evangélicos* may be "model citizens," but their religious identity carries with it a subtext of noncompliance. This suggests that in its own way, evangelical Protestantism could potentially be both more revolutionary and more subversive than conventional forms of political mobilization.

At the most fundamental level, as a "weapon of the weak," evangelical religion enables believers to challenge ancient archetypes head-on if they dare. At its best, Protestantism creates the social space for believers to redefine their most integral social identities and relationships. When people convert, they become members of what Benedict Anderson calls an "imagined community": a philosophical homeland where all initiates have a deep, horizontal comradeship with one another.[14] For Pentecostals, the new community is even defined by a shared common language—glossolalia, the speaking in tongues that historian Stanley Johannesen has provocatively called "a language of no-place and no-one."[15] In this new community, the most basic social identities—relations between women and men, powerful and powerless—are altered and recast in Protestant terms.

At least in the case of gender relations, as Brusco and Green have shown, this change is plainly for the better. If this is so, then one could speculate that Protestantism has the potential to redefine other types of problems by changing how people understand themselves, that is, their social identity. The possibilities are intriguing. Might the same also be true, say, of class or ethnic conflict? Could conversion change the terms in which social classes and ethnic groups define their differences, making them more amenable to nonviolent resolution through the definition of new "imagined communities"?

This volume must end on a cautionary note. One problem inherent in Latin American Protestantism is that it is centrifugal and divisive. Believers not only separate themselves from the larger communities that they once imagined themselves to be a part of but also isolate themselves from other Protestants. But, as Gill's study of shifting religious affiliations suggests, the new communities cannot always hold onto the imagination or loyalty of their members, who drift from one church to the next, presumably seeking to counteract what must surely be a growing sense of isolation and alienation.[16] Moreover, the continued proliferation of tiny denominations, constantly dividing and subdividing, hints at a future where evangelical micro congregations could easily degenerate into little more than breeding grounds for further conflict and social fragmentation. In short, Protestantism in Latin America may ultimately be, as the Pentecostals like to say, a "consuming fire" that forges and purifies—or that burns and destroys. In either case, it is clear that this Protestant movement is a reformation in the most literal sense of the word: a re-forming of the religious, social, and political contours of contemporary Latin America.

NOTES

1. See David Stoll, *Is Latin America Turning Protestant? The Politics of Evangelical Growth* (Berkeley: University of California Press, 1990), ch. 5; Enrique Domínguez and Deborah Huntington, "The Salvation Brokers: Conservative Evangelicals in Central America," *NACLA Report on the Americas* 18, no. 1 (1984): 2–36.

2. Stoll, *Is Latin America Turning Protestant?*

3. For a polemic study of the relationship between evangelical church growth in Latin America and conservative politics in the United States, see Sara Diamond, *Spiritual Warfare: The Politics of the Christian Right* (Boston: South End Press, 1989), as well as Domínguez and Huntington, "The Salvation Brokers."

4. David Martin, *Tongues of Fire: The Explosion of Protestantism in Latin America* (London: Basil Blackwell, 1990).

5. The preeminent writer on this topic is, of course, the German sociologist Max Weber, whose early work, *The Protestant Ethic and the Spirit of Capitalism* (London: Allen and Unwin, 1930), established the theoretical framework for this discourse.

6. Christian Lalive d'Epinay, *The Haven of the Masses* (London: Lutterworth Press, 1969); and Emilio Willems, *Followers of the New Faith* (Nashville, Tenn.: Vanderbilt University Press, 1967).

7. Bryan R. Roberts, "Protestant Groups and Coping with Urban Life in Guatemala City," *American Journal of Sociology* 73 (1968): 753–67.

8. Sheldon Annis, *God and Production in a Guatemalan Town* (Austin: University of Texas Press, 1987).

9. Nancy Farriss, *Maya Society Under Colonial Rule: The Collective Enterprise of Survival* (Princeton: Princeton University Press, 1984).

10. Jean-Pierre Bastian, "Protestantismo y política en México," *Taller de teología* no. 5 (1979): 7–23; "Protestantismos latinamericanos entre la resistencia y la sumisión: 1961–1983," *Cristianismo y sociedad* no. 82 (1984): 49–68; *Breve historia del protestantismo en América Latina* (Mexico City: Casa Unida de Publicaciones, 1986); Carlos Garma Navarro, "Poder, conflicto y reelaboración simbólica: Protestantismo en una comunidad totonac" (*licenciado* thesis, Escuela Nacional de Antropología, Mexico City, 1984).

11. Martin, *Tongues of Fire*, p. 285.

12. Ibid.

13. James C. Scott, *Weapons of the Weak: Everyday Forms of Peasant Resistance* (New Haven: Yale University Press, 1985).

14. Benedict Anderson, *Imagined Communities: Reflections on the Origin and Spread of Nationalism* (London: Verso, 1983).

15. Stanley Johannesen, "The Holy Ghost in Sunset Park," *Historical Reflections* 15, no. 3 (1988): 558.

16. Timothy Edward Evans, "Religious Conversion in Quetzaltenango, Guatemala" (Ph.D. diss., University of Pittsburgh, 1990), examines shifting religious affiliations and backsliding in Guatemala. For more on community fragmentalization and Protestant affiliation, see Duncan Earle, "Maya Religion, Ethnicity, Recognition and Power in Guatemala" (unpublished paper in author's possession, 1992).

BIBLIOGRAPHY

Albán Estrada, María, and Juan Pablo Muñoz. *Con Dios todo se puede: La invasión de las sectas al Ecuador*. Quito: Editorial Planeta, 1987.

Alves, Rubem. *Protestantismo e repressão*. São Paulo: Ática, 1980.

Americas Watch. *Civil Patrols in Guatemala*. New York: Americas Watch, 1986.

————. *Guatemala: Massive Extrajudicial Executions in Rural Areas Under the Government of General Efraín Ríos-Montt*. Special briefing. New York: Americas Watch, July 1982.

Anderson, Benedict. *Imagined Communities: Reflections on the Origin and Spread of Nationalism*. London: Verso, 1983.

Annis, Sheldon. *God and Production in a Guatemalan Town*. Austin: University of Texas Press, 1987.

Ardener, Edwin. "Belief and the Problem of Women." In *Perceiving Women*, Shirley Ardener, ed. New York: John Wiley and Sons, 1975.

Arias, Arturo. "Changing Indian Identity: Guatemala's Violent Transition to Modernity." In Carol Smith, ed., *Guatemalan Indians and the State, 1540–1988*. Austin: University of Texas Press, 1990.

Asad, Talal. "Anthropological Conceptions of Religion: Reflections on Geertz." *Man* 18, no. 2 (1983).

Bamat, Tomás. *Salvación o dominación: Las sectas religiosas en el Ecuador*. Quito: Editorial El Conejo, 1986.

Barrett, David, ed. *World Christian Encyclopedia*. Nairobi: Oxford University Press, 1982.

Bastian, Jean-Pierre. *Breve historia del protestantismo en América Latina*. Mexico City: Casa Unida de Publicaciones, 1986.

211

————. "Les protestantismes latino-américains: Un objet à interroger et à construire." *Social Compass* 39, no. 3 (1992): 327–56.

————. "Protestantismos latinoamericanos entre la resistencia y la sumisión, 1961–1983." *Cristianismo y sociedad* no. 82 (n.d.): 49–68.

Benería, Lourdes, and Marta Roldán. *The Crossroads of Class and Gender: Industrial Homework, Subcontracting, and Household Dynamics in Mexico City.* Chicago: University of Chicago Press, 1987.

Berryman, Phillip. "Churches in Conflict." Book manuscript, 1991. Forthcoming with the New Press.

————. *Liberation Theology.* Philadelphia: Temple University Press, 1987.

Bieske, Sigifredo. *El explosivo crecimiento de la iglesia evangélica en Costa Rica.* San José, Costa Rica: EDUCA, n.d. (ca. 1990).

Blanchard, Kendall. "Changing Sex Roles and Protestantism Among the Navajo Women in Ramah." *Journal for the Scientific Study of Religion* 14 (1975): 43–50.

Bobsin, Oneide. "Produção religiosa e significado social do pentecostalismo a partir de sua prática e representação." Ph.D. dissertation, Pontíficia Universidade Católica de São Paulo, 1984.

Bogenschild, Thomas E. "The Roots of Fundamentalism in Western Guatemala 1890–1944." Paper delivered at Congress of the Latin American Studies Association, Crystal City, Va., April 4–6, 1991.

Brandão, Carlos Rodrigues. *Os deuses do povo.* São Paulo: Brasiliense, 1980.

————. "A partilha da vida." In *Caderno de condições de vida e situação de trabalho do povo de Goiás: As pessoas e as famílias.* Goiás: n.p., 1988.

Brintnall, Douglas E. *Revolt Against the Dead: The Modernization of a Mayan Community in the Highlands of Guatemala.* New York: Gordon and Breach, 1979.

Brown, Diana. *Umbanda: Religion and Politics in Brazil.* Ann Arbor, Mich.: UMI Research Press, 1986.

Bruce, Steve. *The Rise and Fall of the New Christian Right.* Oxford: Clarendon Press, 1988.

Brusco, Elizabeth. "Colombian Evangelicalism as a Strategic Form of Women's Collective Action." *Feminist Issues* 6, no. 2 (1986).

————. "The Household Basis of Evangelical Religion and the Reformation of Machismo in Colombia." Ph.D. dissertation, City University of New York, 1986.

————. "The Reformation of Machismo: Asceticism and Masculinity Among Colombian Evangelicals." Paper delivered at Congress of the Latin American Studies Association, Crystal City, Va., April 4–6, 1991.

Burdick, John. *Looking for God in Brazil: The Progressive Catholic Church in Brazil's Religious Arena*. Berkeley: University of California Press, 1993.

———. "Rethinking the Study of Social Movements: The Case of Christian Base Communities in Urban Brazil." In Sônia Alvarez and Arturo Escobar, eds., *New Social Movements in Latin America*. Forthcoming, Westview Press.

Cáceres Prendes, Jorge. "The Churches in El Salvador: From Prophetism to Mediation." Paper presented at Congress of the Latin American Studies Association, Crystal City, Va., April 4–6, 1991.

Caldeira, Teresa Píres do Rio. *A política dos outros*. São Paulo: Brasiliense, 1984.

Cambranes, Julio Castellanos. *Coffee and Peasants in Guatemala*. Guatemala City: University of San Carlos of Guatemala, 1985.

Carmack, Robert. "The State and Community in Nineteenth Century Guatemala: The Momostenango Case." In Carol Smith, ed., *Guatemalan Indians and the State, 1540–1988*. Austin: University of Texas Press, 1990.

Carvalho Soares, Mariza de. "É permitido distrubuir 'santinho' na porta de igreja?" *Comunicações de ISER* no. 4 (1983).

Chordas, T. J. "Catholic Pentecostalism." In Stephen Glazier, ed., *Perspectives on Pentecostalism: Case Studies from the Caribbean and Latin America*. Washington, D.C.: University Press of America, 1980.

Christianity Today Institute. "Why Is Latin America Turning Protestant? *Christianity Today*, April 6, 1992.

Clark, Elmer T. *The Small Sects in America*. New York: Abingdon Press, 1937.

Clawson, David Leslie. "Religion and Change in a Mexican Village." Ph.D. dissertation, University of Florida, 1979.

Cleary, Edward L., and Hannah Stewart-Gambino, eds. *Conflict and Competition: The Latin American Church in a Changing Environment*. Boulder, Colo.: Lynne Rienner, 1992.

Comblin, José. "Os leigos." *Comunições de ISER* 25 (1987): 26–37.

Conceição, Manuel da. *Essa terra é nossa: Depoimento sobre a vida e as lutas de camponeses no estado do Maranhão*. Petrópolis: Vozes, 1980.

Conniff, Michael L. *Urban Politics in Brazil: The Rise of Populism, 1925–1945*. Pittsburgh: University of Pittsburgh Press, 1981.

Cook, Guillermo. *The Expectation of the Poor: Latin American Base Ecclesial Communities in Protestant Perspective*. Maryknoll, N.Y.: Orbis Books, 1985.

Cornelius, Wayne A. "Urbanization and Political Demand-Making:

Political Participation Among the Migrant Poor in Latin American Cities." *American Political Science Review* 68, no. 3 (1974): 1125–46.

Curry, Donald Edward. "Lusiada: An Anthropological Study of the Growth of Protestantism in Brazil." Ph.D. dissertation, Columbia University, 1968.

———. *Unidade e prática da fé.* Rio de Janiero: CEDI, 1987.

Dabul, Lygia, et al. "Missão de conscientização: Agentes e camponeses em experiências comunitárias." In Nidia Esterci, ed., *Cooperativismo.* Rio de Janeiro: Marco Zero, 1984.

Daly, Mary. *Beyond God the Father: Toward a Philosophy of Women's Liberation.* Boston: Beacon Press, 1973.

Davis, Sheldon. "Guatemala: The Evangelical Holy War in El Quiche." *Global Reporter* 1, no. 1 (1983): 9–10.

Dayton, Donald W. "Algunas reflexiones sobre el pentecostalismo latinoamericano y sus implicaciones ecuménicas." *Cuadernos de teología* 11, no. 2 (1991): 5–20.

———. "The Holy Spirit and Christian Expansion in the Twentieth Century." *Missiology* 16, no. 4 (1988): 397–407.

———. "Pentecostal/Charismatic Renewal and Social Change: A Western Perspective." *Transformation* 5, no. 4 (1988): 7–13.

Departmento Intersindical de Assessoria Parlamentar (DIAP). *Quem foi quem no Constituinte: Nas questíes de interesse dos trabalhadores.* São Paulo: Cortes/Oboré, 1988.

———. "Religião, espiritualidade, y sociedade." *Cadernos de ISER* 6 (1977): 5–10.

Diamond, Sara. *Spiritual Warfare: The Politics of the Christian Right.* Boston: South End Press, 1989.

Dixon, David E. "Popular Culture, Popular Identity and the Rise of Latin American Protestantism: Voices from Santiago Poblacional." Unpublished paper at University of Notre Dame, 1992.

Domínguez, Enrique, and Deborah Huntington. "The Salvation Brokers: Evangelicals in Central America." *NACLA Report on the Americas* 18, no. 1 (1984): 2–36.

Earle, Duncan. "Authority, Social Conflict, and the Rise of Protestant Religious Conversion in a Mayan Village." *Social Compass* 39, no. 3 (1992): 379–89.

———. "Maya Religion, Ethnicity, Recognition and Power in Guatemala." Unpublished paper, University of Texas, Benson Collection, 1992.

Ehrenreich, Barbara. *The Hearts of Men*. Garden City, N.Y.: Anchor Books, 1983.

Eldridge, Joseph T. "Pentecostalism and Social Change in Central America." *Towson State Journal of International Affairs* 25, no. 2 (1991): 10–12.

————. Informal presentation at Chapel of the Cross, Chapel Hill, N.C., February 14, 1991.

Endruveit, Wilson H. "Pentecostalism in Brazil." Ph.D. dissertation, Northwestern University, 1975.

Epstein, Barbara. *The Politics of Domesticity: Women, Evangelicalism and Temperance in Nineteenth Century America*. Middletown, Conn.: Wesleyan University Press, 1981.

Esterci, Nidia, ed. *Cooperativismo e coletivização no campo: Questões sobre a prática de igreja popular*. Rio de Janeiro: Marco Zero, 1984.

"Evangelicals and Politics in Latin America." *Transformation* 9, no. 3 (1992).

Evans, Timothy E. "Percentage of Non-Catholics in a Representative Sample of the Guatemalan Population." Paper delivered at the Congress of the Latin American Studies Association, Crystal City, Va., April 4–6, 1991.

————. "Religious Conversion in Quetzaltenango, Guatemala." Ph.D. dissertation, University of Pittsburgh, 1990.

Falla, Ricardo. *Quiché rebelde*. Guatemala City: Editorial Universitaria de Guatemala, 1980.

Fals-Borda, Orlando. *Peasant Society in the Colombian Andes: A Sociological Study of Saucio*. Gainesville: University of Florida Press, 1962.

Farriss, Nancy M. *Maya Society Under Colonial Rule*. Princeton: Princeton University Press, 1984.

Federico, Celso. *Consciência operária no Brasil*. São Paulo: Ática, 1979.

Fernandes, Rúbem César. "'Religiões populares': Uma visão parcial da literatura recente." *Boletim informativo e biblográfico de ciências sociais* 18 (1984): 3–26.

Flora, Cornelia Butler. *Pentecostalism in Colombia: Baptism by Fire and Spirit*. Cranbury, N.J.: Associated University Presses, 1976.

Follman, José Ivo. "O 'ser católico': Diferentes identidades religiosas." *Comunições de ISER* 26 (1987): 17–25.

Frase, Ronald Glen. "A Sociological Analysis of the Development of Brazilian Protestantism." Ph.D. dissertation, Princeton Theological Seminary, 1975.

Garma Navarro, Carlos. "Los estudios antropológicos sobre el protestantismo en Mexico." *Iztapalapa* (Universidad Autónoma de México-Iztapalapa) 15 (1988): 53–66.

———. "Liderazgo protestante en una lucha campesina en Mexico." *América indígena* 44, no. 1 (1984): 127–41.

———. *Protestantismo en una comunidad totonaca de Puebla*. Mexico City: Instituto Nacional Indigenista, 1987.

Garrard-Burnett, Virginia. "A History of Protestantism in Guatemala." Ph.D. dissertation, Tulane University, 1986.

———. "Positivismo, liberalismo e impulso misionero: Misiones protestantes en Guatemala, 1880–1920." *Mesoamérica* no. 19 (1990).

———. "Protestantism in Rural Guatemala, 1872–1954." *Latin American Research Review* 24, no. 2 (1989): 127–42.

Garrison, Vivian. "Sectarianism and Psychosocial Adjustment: A Controlled Comparison of Puerto Rican Pentecostals and Catholics." In Irving T. Zaretsky and Mark P. Leone, eds., *Religious Movements in Contemporary America*. Princeton: Princeton University Press, 1974.

Geertz, Clifford. *The Social History of an Indonesian Town*. Cambridge, Mass.: MIT Press, 1965.

Gellner, Bernhard John. "Colta Entrepreneurship in Ecuador." Ph.D. dissertation, University of Wisconsin, 1982.

Gill, Lesley. "Like a Veil to Cover Them: Women and the Pentecostal Movement in La Paz." *American Ethnologist* 17, no. 4 (1990): 708–21.

———. "Painted Faces: Conflict and Ambiguity in Domestic Servant-Employer Relations in La Paz (1930–1988)." *Latin American Research Review* 25, no. 1 (1990).

Glazier, Stephen D., ed. *Perspectives on Pentecostalism: Case Studies from the Caribbean and Latin America*. Washington, D.C.: University Press of America, 1980.

Godwin, David E. *Church Planting Methods*. DeSoto, Tex.: Lifeshare Communications, 1984.

Goldin, L. R., and B. Metz. "An Expression of Cultural Change: Invisible Converts to Protestantism among Highland Guatemala Mayas." *Ethnology* 30, no. 4 (1991): 325–38.

Gomes, José Francisco. "Religião e política: Os pentecostais no Recife." Master's thesis, Universidade Federal de Pernambuco, Brazil, 1985.

Goodman, Felicitas. *Speaking in Tongues: A Cross-Cultural Study of Glossolalia*. Chicago: University of Chicago Press, 1972.

Green, Linda. "Social Chaos, Moral Order and Protestant Evangelicals." Paper delivered at the Annual Meeting of the American Anthropological Association, Chicago, 1991.

Gregory, Affonso. *CEBs: Utopia ou realidade?* Petrópolis: Vozes, 1973.

Grover, Mark L. "Mormonism in Brazil: Religion and Dependency in Latin America." Ph.D. dissertation, Indiana University, 1985.

Handy, Jim. "The Corporate Community, Campesino Organizations, and Agrarian Reform: 1950–1954." In Carol Smith, ed., *Guatemalan Indians and the State, 1540–1988*. Austin: University of Texas Press, 1990.

Hardesty, Nancy, Lucille Sider Dayton, and Donald W. Dayton. "Women in the Holiness Movement: Feminism in the Evangelical Tradition." In Rosemary Ruether and Eleanor McLaughlin, eds., *Women of the Spirit*. New York: Simon and Schuster, 1979.

Herman, Edward S., and Frank Brodhead. *Demonstration Elections: U.S. Staged Elections in the Dominican Republic, Vietnam and El Salvador*. Boston: South End Press, 1984.

Hewitt, W. E. "Myths and Realities of Liberation Theology: The Case of Basic Christian Communities in Brazil." In Richard L. Rubenstein and John K. Roth, eds., *The Politics of Latin American Liberation Theology*. Washington, D.C.: Washington Institute Press, 1988.

Hill, Robert M., and John Monaghan. *Continuities in Highland Maya Social Organization: Ethnohistory in Sacapulas, Guatemala*. Philadelphia: University of Pennsylvania Press, 1987.

Hoffnagel, Judith Chambliss. "The Believers: Pentecostalism in a Brazilian City." Ph.D. dissertation, Indiana University, 1978.

Hoornaert, Eduardo. "Os três fatores da nova hegemonia dentro de igreja católica no Brasil." *Revista eclesiástica brasileira* 26 (1986): 371–84.

Howe, Gary N. "Representações religiosas e capitalismo: Uma 'leitura' estruturalista do pentecostalismo no Brasil." *Cadernos de ISER* 6 (1977): 39–48.

Ireland, Rowan. "The Prophecy That Failed." *Listening: Journal of Religion and Culture* 16 (1981): 253–64.

———. *Kingdoms Come: Religion and Politics in Brazil*. Pittsburgh: University of Pittsburgh Press, 1991.

Johannesen, Stanley. "The Holy Ghost in Sunset Park." *Historical Reflections* 15, no. 3 (1988): 558.

Johnstone, Patrick. *Operation World: A Day-to-Day Guide to Praying for the World*, 4th ed. Bromley, U.K.: Send the Light Books, 1986.

Jorgensen, Dan. "Telefolmin Follow-up." *Newsletter, Cultural Survival Inc.* 4, no. 2 (1980).

Kamm, Thomas. "Evangelicals Stressing 'Cures' for Masses' Misery Make Inroads in Roman Catholic Latin America." *Wall Street Journal*, October 16, 1991, p. A12.

Kaplan, Temma. "Female Consciousness and Collective Action: The Case of Barcelona 1910–1918." *Signs* 7, no. 3 (1982): 545–66.

Kessler, Jean B. A. "A Summary of the Costa Rican Evangelical Crisis: August, 1989." Pasadena, Calif.: IDEAS/Church Growth Studies Program, 1989. Mimeograph.

Kliewer, G. U. "Assembléia de Deus e eleições num município do interior de Mato Grosso." *Comunicações de ISER* 3 (1982).

Knowlton, David. "Searching Minds and Questing Hearts: Protestantism and Social Context in Bolivia." Ph.D. dissertation, University of Texas, Austin, 1988.

————. "Social and Political Issues of Protestantism in Bolivia." Paper delivered at the Annual Meeting of the American Anthropological Association, Chicago, 1991.

Lagos, Maria. "We Have to Learn to Ask: Cultural Hegemony, Diverse Experiences and Contested Meanings." *American Ethnologist* 20, no. 1 (1993).

Lalive d'Epinay, Christian. *The Haven of the Masses.* London: Lutterworth Press, 1969.

Lancaster, Roger. *Thanks to God and the Revolution.* New York: Columbia University Press, 1988.

LaRuffa, Anthony. *San Cipriano: Life in a Puerto Rican Community.* New York: Gordon and Breach, 1971.

Lernoux, Penny. *Cry of the People.* New York: Doubleday, 1980.

————. *People of God: The Struggle for World Catholicism.* New York: Viking, 1989.

Levine, Daniel H. "Popular Groups, Popular Culture and Popular Religion." *Comparative Studies in Society and History* 32, no. 4 (1990): 718–64.

————. "Protestants and Catholics in Latin America: A Family Portrait." Paper prepared for the Fundamentalism Project, University of Chicago, 1991.

Lewis, I. M. *Ecstatic Religion.* Harmondsworth, U.K.: Penguin Books, 1971.

Lovell, W. George. "Surviving Conquest: The Maya of Guatemala in Historical Perspective." *Latin American Research Review* 23, no. 2 (1988): 25–57.

Mainwaring, Scott. *The Catholic Church and Politics in Brazil, 1916–1985*. Stanford, Calif.: Stanford University Press, 1986.

Marcom, John, Jr. "The Fire Down South." *Forbes Magazine*, October 15, 1990.

Mariz, Cecilia Loreto. "Religion and Coping with Poverty in Brazil." Ph.D. dissertation, Boston University, 1989.

Martin, David. *A General Theory of Secularization*. London: Basil Blackwell, 1978.

————. *Tongues of Fire: The Explosion of Protestantism in Latin America*. London: Basil Blackwell, 1990.

Martin, David, and David Lee. "After Catholicism: The New Protestants and the Rise of Capitalism in Latin America." *National Review*, September 29, 1989, pp. 30–35.

Martin, Emily. *The Woman in the Body: A Cultural Analysis of Reproduction*. Boston: Beacon Press, 1987.

Martínez, Abelino. *Las sectas en Nicaragua: Oferta y demanda de salvación*. San José, Costa Rica: Departmento Ecuménico de Investigaciones, 1989.

Maynard, Kent. "Christianity and Religion: Evangelical Identity and Sociocultural Organization in Urban Ecuador." Ph.D. dissertation, Indiana University, 1977.

McCreery, David. "State Power, Indigenous Communities, and Land in Nineteenth Century Guatemala, 1820–1920." In Carol Smith, ed., *Guatemalan Indians and the State, 1540–1988*. Austin: University of Texas Press, 1990.

Meyer, Jean. *Historia de los cristianos en América Latina, siglos XIX y XX*. Mexico City: Vuelta, 1989.

Mintz, Sidney. *Worker in the Cane: A Puerto Rican Life History*. New Haven: Yale University Press, 1960.

Molnar, Augusta. "Women and Politics: The Case of the Kham Magar of Western Nepal." *American Ethnologist* 9, no. 3 (1982): 485–502.

Molyneaux, Maxine. "Female Collective Action in Socialist Revolutions: Some Reflections." Unpublished MS, n.d., Pacific Lutheran University, Tacoma, Wash.

————. "Mobilization without Emancipation? Women's Interests, State, and Revolution," in Richard Fagen et al., eds., *Transition and Development*. New York: Monthly Review Press, 1986.

Mondragón, Rafael. *De indios y cristianos en Guatemala.* Mexico City: COPEC/CECOPE, 1983.

Monteiro de Lima, Délcio. *Os demônios descem do norte.* Rio de Janeiro: Francisco Alves, 1986.

Montejo, Victor. *Testimony: Death of a Guatemalan Village.* Willamantic, Conn.: Curbstone Press, 1987.

Morchio, Giovanna. "Trends in NES Response Rates." Memo to Board of Overseers, National Elections Study. Ann Arbor: University of Michigan, 1987.

Muratorio, B. "Protestantism and Capitalism Revisited in the Rural Highlands of Ecuador." *Journal of Peasant Studies* 8, no. 1 (1980): 37–60.

Murphee, M. W. *Christianity and the Shona.* London School of Economics Monographs on Social Anthropology, no. 36. London: Athlone Press, 1969.

Nash, June. "Protestantism in an Indian Village in the Western Highlands of Guatemala." *Alpha Kappa Deltan,* Winter 1960.

National Opinion Research Center. *General Social Surveys, 1972–1991: Cumulative Codebook.* Chicago: National Opinion Research Center, 1991.

Novaes, Regina C. "Os crentes e as eleições: Uma experiência de campo." *Comunicações do ISER* 3 (1982).

———. *Os escolhidos de Deus.* Rio de Janeiro: Marco Zero, 1985.

———. "Os escolhidos: Doutrina religiosas e prática social." Rio de Janeiro, Museu Nacional, 1979. Mimeograph.

Opazo Bernales, Andrés. "El movimiento protestante centroamericana: Una aproximación cuantitativa." In Luis E. Sawande, ed., *Protestantismos y procesos sociales en Centroamérica.* San José, Costa Rica: EDUCA, 1990.

Ortiz, Renato. *A moderna tradição brasileira.* São Paulo: Brasiliense, 1988.

Page, John Anthony. "Brasil para Cristo: The Cultural Construction of Pentecostal Networks in Brazil." Ph.D. dissertation, New York University, 1984.

Paul, Benjamin D. "Fifty Years of Religious Change in San Pedro La Laguna, a Mayan Community in Highland Guatemala." Paper delivered at the American Anthropological Association, Chicago, November, 1987.

Paul, Benjamin D., and William Demarest. "The Operation of a Death Squad in San Pedro La Laguna." In Robert Carmack, ed., *Harvest of Violence.* Norman: University of Oklahoma Press, 1988.

Perani, Claudio. "Pastoral popular: Serviço ou poder?" *Cadernos no Centro de estudos e ação social* 82 (Nov./Dec. 1982): 7–19.

Pierucci, Antônio Flávio. "As bases da nova direita." *Novos estudos CEBRAP*, 19 (December 1987): 26–45.

"Pope Urges Brazilians to Resist Mirage of Evangelists." *New York Times*, October 14, 1991, p. A3.

Preston, David. *Farmers and Towns: Rural-Urban Relations in Highland Bolivia*. Norwich, U.K.: Geo Abstracts, 1978.

Rappaport, Joanne. "Las misiones protestantes y la resistencia indígena en el sur de Colombia." *América indígena* 44, no. 1 (1984): 111–26.

Read, William. *Fermento religioso nas massas do Brasil*. Campinas: Livraria Cristã Unida, 1967.

Ribeiro de Oliveira, Isabel. *Trabalho y política: As origens de partido dos trabalhadores*. Petrópolis: Vozes, 1988.

Ribeiro de Oliveira, Pedro. "Comunidades e massa: Desafio de pastoral popular." *Revista eclesiástica brasileira* 44 (1984).

"The Rise of the Religious Right in Central America." *Resource Center Bulletin* (Albuquerque, N.M.) no. 10 (Summer/Fall 1987).

Rivière, Gilles. "Cambios sociales y pentecostalismo en una comunidad aymara." *Fe y pueblo* 3, no. 14 (1986): 24–31.

Roberts, Bryan. "Protestant Groups and Coping with Urban Life in Guatemala City." *American Journal of Sociology* 73 (1968): 753–67.

Robertson, Roland. "Liberation Theology, Latin America, and Third World Underdevelopment." In Richard L. Rubenstein and John Roth, eds., *The Politics of Latin American Liberation Theology*. Washington, D.C.: Washington Institute Press, 1988.

Rodrigues, Leincio Martins. *Quem é quem na Constituinte*. São Paulo: OESP/Maltese, 1987.

Rolim, Francisco C. "Afinal, o que estaia levando as pessoas ao pentecostalismo?" Paper delivered at ISER seminar on religious diversity, ANPOCS, 1987.

———. "Igrejas pentecostais." *Revista eclesiástica brasileira* 42 (1982): 29–59.

———. *Pentecostais no Brasil*. Petrópolis: Vozes, 1985.

Rosset, Peter. "Non-traditional Export Agriculture in Central America: Impact on Peasant Farmers." Working paper no. 20. University of California, Santa Cruz, 1991.

Rubbo, Anna. "The Spread of Capitalism in Rural Colombia: Effects on Poor Women." In Rayna Reiter, ed., *Toward an Anthropology of Women*. New York: Monthly Review Press, 1975.

Ruether, Rosemary. "Introduction." In Rosemary Ruether and Eleanor McLaughlin, eds., *Women of Spirit*. New York: Simon and Schuster, 1979.

Samarin, William J. *Tongues of Men and Angels: The Religious Language of Pentecostalism*. New York: Macmillan, 1972.

Sandoval, G., and M. Fernanda Sostres. *La ciudad prometida. Pobladores y organizaciones sociales en El Alto*. La Paz: Sistema/ILDIS, 1989.

Schneider, Jane, and Shirley Lindenbaum, eds. "Frontiers of Christian Evangelicals." *American Ethnologist* 14, no. 1 (1987).

Scotchmer, David G. "Symbols of Salvation: Interpreting Highland Maya Protestantism in Context." Ph.D. dissertation, State University of New York at Albany, 1991.

Scott, David C. "Salvador Election Results Prompt Rebel Cease-fire Plan." *Christian Science Monitor*, March 25, 1991.

Scott, James C. *Weapons of the Weak: Everyday Forms of Peasant Resistance*. New Haven: Yale University Press, 1985.

Sexton, James D. "Protestantism and Modernization in Two Guatemalan Towns." *American Ethnologist* 5, no. 2 (1978): 280–302.

Silletta, Alfredo. *Las sectas invaden la Argentina*. Buenos Aires: Editorial Contrapunto, 1987.

Simon, Jean-Marie. *Guatemala: Eternal Spring—Eternal Tyranny*. New York: W. W. Norton, 1987.

Smith, Carol A. "The Militarization of Civil Society in Guatemala: Economic Reorganization as a Continuation of War." *Latin American Perspectives* 17, no. 4 (1990): 8–67.

Souza, Beatriz de. *A experiencia da salvação*. São Paulo: Duas Cidades, 1969.

———. "Protestantismo no Brasil." In Candido Camargo, ed., *Católicos, protestantes, espíritas*. Petrópolis: Vozes, 1973.

"Spreading the Faith: The Protestant Explosion in Latin America." *Insight* (supp., *Washington Times*), July 16, 1990, pp. 8–17.

Stafford, Tim. "The Hidden Fire." *Christianity Today*, May 14, 1990, pp. 23–26.

Steeh, Charlotte. "Trends in Nonresponse Rates, 1952–1979." *Public Opinion Quarterly* 45, no. 1 (1981): 40–57.

Steigenga, Timothy J. "The Protestant Role in State-Society Relations in Guatemala, 1871–1989." M.A. thesis, University of North Carolina at Chapel Hill, 1991.

Stephen, Lynn, and James Dow. "Introduction: Popular Religion in Mexico and Central America." In Lynn Steven and James Dow, eds., *Class, Politics and Popular Religion in Mexico and Central America*. Washington, D.C.: American Anthropological Association, 1990.

Stoll, David. "Between Two Fires: Dual Violence and the Reassertion of Civil Society in Nebaj, Guatemala." Ph.D. dissertation, Stanford University, 1992.

————. *Fishers of Men or Founders of Empire? The Wycliffe Bible Translators in Latin America*. Cambridge, Mass.: Cultural Survival Quarterly/ Zed Press, 1983.

————. *Is Latin America Turning Protestant?* Berkeley: University of California Press, 1990.

————. " 'Jesus Is Lord of Guatemala': The Prospects for Evangelical Reform in a Death Squad State." In Emmanuel Sivan and Gabriel Almond, eds., *Accounting for Fundamentalism*. Chicago: University of Chicago Press, forthcoming 1994.

Stoll, Sandra. "Embu, eleições de 1982: A mobilização política de CEBs e pentecostais." *Comunicações de ISER* 3 (1982).

————. "Púlpito e palanque: Religião e política nas eleições de 1982 num município de grande São Paulo." Ph.D. dissertation, Universidade Estadual de Campinas, 1986.

Sylvestre, Josuç. *Os evangélicos, a Constituinte e as eleições municipais*. Brasília: Papiro, 1988.

————. *Irmão vota em irmão*. Brasília: Pergaminho, 1986.

Taussig, Michael. *The Devil and Commodity Fetishism in South America*. Chapel Hill: University of North Carolina Press, 1980.

Urdang, Stephanie. "Women in National Liberation Movements." In M. Hays and Sharon Stichter, eds., *African Women South of the Sahara*. London: Longman, 1984.

Warren, Kay B. *The Symbolism of Subordination: Indian Identity in a Guatemalan Town*. Austin: University of Texas Press, 1978.

Weber, Max. *The Protestant Ethic and the Spirit of Capitalism*. London: Allen and Unwin, 1982 [1930].

————. *The Sociology of Religion*. Boston: Beacon Press, 1963.

Westropp, Mary. "Christian Counterinsurgency." *Cultural Survival Quarterly* 7, no. 3 (1983): 28–31.

Whitten, Norman. "Strategies of Adaptive Mobility in the Colombian-Ecuadorian Littoral." *American Anthropologist* 71, no. 2 (1969).

Willems, Emilio. *Followers of the New Faith*. Nashville, Tenn.: Vanderbilt University Press, 1967.

Wilson, Everett A. "Sanguine Saints: Pentecostalism in El Salvador." *Church History* 52, no. 2 (1983): 186–98.

Wolf, Eric R. "Closed Corporate Peasant Communities in Mesoamerica and Central Java." *Southwestern Journal of Anthropology* 17, no. 1 (1957): 1–18.

Zaluar, Alba. *A máquina e a revolta*. São Paulo: Brasiliense, 1985.

ABOUT THE
CONTRIBUTORS

EDWIN ELOY AGUILAR is a graduate of the University of Texas–Pan American and a Ph.D. candidate in political science at the University of North Carolina at Chapel Hill.

ELIZABETH BRUSCO is assistant professor of anthropology and chair of the women's studies department at Pacific Lutheran University. She is the author of *The Reformation of Machismo* (University of Texas Press, forthcoming 1994).

JOHN BURDICK is assistant professor of anthropology at Syracuse University. His book *Looking for God in Brazil: The Progressive Catholic Church in Brazil's Religious Arena* was published by the University of California Press in 1993. He is currently at work on a study of the black consciousness movement in Brazil.

KENNETH COLEMAN is professor of political science and associate director of the Institute of Latin American Studies at the University of North Carolina–Chapel Hill. He is currently studying the informal economies, as well as politics and religion, of Central America.

PAUL FRESTON, a graduate of Cambridge University, is completing a Ph.D. in sociology at the University of Campinas in Brazil. He contributed a chapter on Gilberto Freyre to the *História das ciências sociais no Brasil*, published by the São Paulo Institute for Economic, Social and Political Studies (1989). A seventeen-year resident of Brazil, he is a practicing Protestant and a member of the Latin American Theological Fraternity.

VIRGINIA GARRARD-BURNETT, who has written extensively on Protestantism in Guatemala, is on the faculty of the Institute of Latin American Studies and a member of the department of history at the University of Texas–Austin.

LESLEY GILL is the author of *Peasants, Entrepreneurs and Social Change: Frontier Development in Lowland Bolivia* (Westview Press, 1987). She is currently on the faculty of the department of anthropology at American University in Washington, D.C.

LINDA GREEN is a Fulbright scholar finishing a dissertation on war widows in Guatemala for the department of anthropology at the University of California–Berkeley.

ROWAN IRELAND, a sociologist, directs the Institute of Latin American Studies at La Trobe University in Australia. He is author of *Kingdoms Come: Religion and Politics in Brazil*, which was published in 1991 by the University of Pittsburgh Press. Currently he is studying urban social movements in São Paulo and Recife.

JOSÉ MIGUEL SANDOVAL, a graduate of the Universidad de Chile, holds M.S. and M. Phil. degrees from the University of Sussex. He is a data analyst, archivist, consultant, and instructor at the Institute for Research in Social Science, University of North Carolina at Chapel Hill.

TIMOTHY J. STEIGENGA is a graduate of Calvin College and a Ph.D. candidate in political science at the University of North Carolina at Chapel Hill.

DAVID STOLL is the author of *Is Latin America Turning Protestant?* (University of California Press, 1990) and *Fishers of Men or Founders of Empire? The Wycliffe Bible Translators in Latin America* (Cultural Survival Quarterly/ Zed Press, 1983). His latest book is *Between Two Armies in the Ixil Towns of Guatemala* (Columbia University Press, 1993).

INDEX